An Introduction To PROLOG

Ramachandran Bharath, Ph.D

TAB BOOKS Inc.
Blue Ridge Summit, PA 17214

FIRST EDITION
FIRST PRINTING

Library of Congress Cataloging in Publication Data

Bharath, Ramachandran.
An introduction to Prolog.

Bibliography: p.
Includes index.
1. Prolog (Computer program language) I. Title.
QA76.73.P76B47 1986 005.13'3 85-30382
ISBN 0-8306-0582-7
ISBN 0-8306-2682-4 (pbk.)

श्रीरामरामरामेति रमे रामे मनोरमे ।
सहस्रनाम तत्तुल्यं रामनाम वरानने ॥

(An ancient prayer from India, circa the first millenium B.C., invoking divine blessings)

Contents

Introduction

The programming language Prolog has steadily increased in importance and general availability since the announcement in 1981 at the First International Conference on Fifth Generation Systems in Tokyo that Prolog would have a key role in Japan's plans for computer systems for the 1990s. During the last year or so, a number of microcomputer versions of Prolog, especially for IBM PCs, have become available.

This book is an easy-paced introduction to Prolog. It is aimed at home computer enthusiasts who wish to experiment with Prolog through self-study. Appendix A reviews the major Prolog interpreters available.

Conventional programming is based on the concept of giving specific commands to the computer about how to solve a particular problem. Prolog is an example of attempts to make the process of human-computer communication significantly different in style. In brief, it tries to achieve the goal of requiring the user to describe the problem in a logically coherent and correct manner, leaving it to the computer to work out and execute the necessary steps for solving the problem. Though Prolog does not fully realize this aim, it is a significant step towards this new style of *declarative* or *descriptive* programming.

Because of this characteristic of Prolog, it might be of interest also to those with little or no experience using computers, but who are interested in the question of the role of computers in human affairs, and therefore in improving means of communication between humans and computers. It has been suggested that readers not familiar with programming immediately find Prolog a natural and pleasing method of communication, whereas those who have already learned conventional programming need time to reorient their view that programming consists of giving specific commands geared to the characteristics of each machine, and to begin thinking in terms of merely describing problems to be programmed. Furthermore, because Prolog tries to achieve the declarative, that you can get a good understanding of the language and appreciate the nature of declarative programming even without using software, by reading about Prolog and studying examples of its use. It adds to your enjoyment to actually try Prolog.

Because of Prolog's relationship to the nature of human-computer communication, a natural next step would be for readers to study the field of artificial intelligence—i.e., of how to make computers do things that would make them more "intelligent" assistants. I have briefly discussed this in Appendix B and have given a Bibliography of suggested readings. I have also discussed in Appendix B one particular aspect of artificial intelligence, which is the design and analysis of problems using so-called expert systems or programs that can emulate the abilities of human experts.

The book starts with four chapters that lead you through the basics of Prolog. Chapter 5 contains a discussion of what is special about declarative programming and Prolog. The examples previously discussed can be used as vehicles for illustrating the difference between conventional and declarative styles of programming. After this pause for perspective, Chapters 6 through 9 discuss various aspects of programming in Prolog. Chapter 10 indicates further directions you may wish to pursue.

Problems for you to work on are provided at the ends of chapters 1, 2, 3, 4, and 6. The suggested solutions are discussed in full detail as an aid to self-study. Chapter 9 consists of an assortment of problems. At various places in the text I have set sections between two rules. These alert you to pause and formulate a solution to the question posed before reading further. Appendix D was written by my colleague Professor Margaret Sklar, and it gives many examples of the use of Prolog and some problems with solutions.

The whole book has been written in a question-and-answer format, which I hope is in the spirit of what Ezra Pound wrote in his *Cantos*: "It was all done by conversation, possibly because one repeats the point when conversing."

Chapter 1

First Steps: Facts, Questions, and Variables

How does one write programs in Prolog?

Programs are written in Prolog by providing the system with information about the *objects* with which we are dealing. The Prolog system will use this information to draw logical conclusions.

An extremely appealing characteristic of Prolog, which adds to its increasing popularity, is that the emphasis in writing a Prolog program is on *specifying* or describing the nature of the problem, rather than on spelling out the steps the computer should take to solve the problem, as one is required to do in conventional languages like BASIC or COBOL or Pascal. This difference, that makes Prolog markedly different, is often described by saying that Prolog is a *declarative* or *assertional* language, as contrasted with conventional languages, which are usually called *imperative.* These languages require the user to give a series of commands to the computer about the procedure or steps it should take to solve the problem.

To appreciate this difference properly, it would be useful if we first look at how a program is written in Prolog.

In the first few chapters I shall discuss the basic principles of writing a program in Prolog and give several examples of Prolog programs. We shall cover enough of Prolog to write useful programs, and provide the necessary background for detailed consideration of what is meant by declarative programming versus imperative programming. In chapter 5 we will also gain some historical background on Prolog. In subsequent chapters we will further consider aspects of programming in Prolog.

The examples and exercises are such that even if you do not have access to Prolog software you should gain a working knowledge of Prolog by studying the examples and doing the exercises with pencil and paper.

What is a simple example of providing information and asking the system to draw conclusions or inferences?

Let's say we give the system information about the chief executives of the governments of various countries. We tell it that the president of the United States of America is Ronald Reagan, the president of France is Francois Mitterand, the prime minister of Canada is Brian Mulroney, the prime minister of Great Britain is Margaret Thatcher, and so on. We could enter all this information and then later ask the system to state who is the president of France, or who is the prime minister of Canada, etc. Using the information it has, the system will give us its conclusions or inferences.

Can we type in the information just the way we could tell someone the facts, or the way we would write them?

Unfortunately, no. Prolog goes much further than most other languages in making it easy to communicate with computers, and one of its major aims is to make the process more natural for human beings. However, in its current state of development we must follow some formalities about the way the information is expressed.

Let me describe a typical Prolog system. The Prolog disk comes with instructions explaining that you should first boot your computer's operating system (DOS), then insert the Prolog disk and type in the command for handing over control of the computer to the Prolog system. The exact command varies from manufacturer to manufacturer. (Appendix A contains details abut the different software available.) If you are familiar with any software package you will recognize that this initial procedure is exactly the same—first booting the operating system, then "invoking" the package you want to use. A more detailed explanation for those who have never used a microcomputer is given in Appendix A.

When you enter the word prolog (or the equivalent command for the particular Prolog disk you are using), the screen displays a prompt sign which varies from system to system. Let's assume the sign that appears is a ?- . The question mark followed by a hyphen indicates that the system is waiting for you to give further instructions.

When you first want to enter some information into the system, you want the system to store the information we give it. For our first example, concerning heads of different countries, in response to the prompt we would type in:

```
?- assertz( chief_exec(usa,president,reagan) ).
?- assertz( chief_exec(france,president, mitterand) ).
?- assertz( chief_exec(canada,prime_minister,mulroney) ).
?- assertz( chief_exec(uk,prime_minister,thatcher) ).
```

What does assertz mean, and what is important about the way we put the information into the system?

The command assertz is a standard Prolog feature which tells the system that whatever follows, enclosed in parentheses, should be stored by the system as information for future use. So, the system will store the information:

```
( chief_exec)(usa,president,reagan) ).
( chief_exec)france,president, mitterand) ).
```

etc,

Since these are contained in parentheses following **assertz**. There are two things to note when you actually do this on a computer:

a) The period at the end of each line is vital. It tells the system you have finished that particular instruction. The system will come back again with the prompt (?-) for the next instruction.

b) In Prolog, information is viewed as information about relationships between objects. The information we have added to the system above can be thought of as saying that a relationship which we call chief_exec connects three objects: the country **(usa)**, the title given in that country to the chief_exec **(president)**, and the person who currently occupies the post with that title **(reagan)**. The other information we have given gives other instances of the same relationship.

Is there anything else of note about the information we have put into the system?

Yes, some technical terms are used to describe the various parts of the information. The name of the relationship (in the above example, **chief_exec**) is called the *predicate*. The various objects connected by the predicate are called the *arguments*. In the above example, **chief_exec** has three arguments. Each example or instance of the predicate is called a *clause*. We have given four clauses for the predicate **chief_exec**. There are two different types of clauses, called *facts* and *rules*. The four clauses we have given are all of the type called facts.

We should note also that:

- ☐ The names we give the predicate normally begin with lowercase letters. A sequence of letters, beginning with a lowercase letter, is called an *atom*. The name of the predicate would generally be an atom.

  We will see later that an atom can sometimes be expressed in a different way than by a sequence of characters beginning with a lowercase letter, However, most often we would express an atom as we have here.
- ☐ In the examples above, the names of the arguments or objects also begin with lowercase letters. They could begin with uppercase letters, but that has a special meaning attached to it which we will discuss shortly. We may say that in these examples we have used atoms as arguments of the predicate. Arguments are separated by commas.
- ☐ To use a name which usually would be two or more words, we should use an underline symbol to connect the words. Because we wanted to say "chief executive" of the country, instead of entering it as two words we have used an underline to connect the two words.

When we put in information into the system, it is described as adding information to the Prolog database.

Do the arguments of a fact always have to be atoms?

They can be atoms, as in the examples above, or they can be numbers. For example, you could enter a fact:

```
income(john,20)
```

to represent the relationship between John and his income (expressed in thousands of dollars).

Arguments can also have more complicated forms, which we will look at when we come to the chapter on structures. Until then, we will consider facts with atoms or numbers as arguments.

To summarize all this, we can say that a fact is a clause containing information which is given to a Prolog system. It has a predicate which is an atom, followed by a number of arguments in parentheses.

What is the major difference between a fact and the second type of clause, which is called a rule?

A fact has a predicate followed by a number of arguments enclosed in parentheses. A rule will also have a predicate, and arguments in parentheses following the predicate; but it will also have information following the arguments. We will look in detail at rules in chapter 3.

How many arguments can a fact have?

One or more. The predicate **chief_exec** has three arguments. We can have a predicate which expresses a relationship between two objects, so we could have a fact with two arguments. For example, we could say:

```
first_name(thatcher,margaret)
first_name(mitterand,francois)
first_name(reagan,ronald)
first-name(mulroney,brian)
```

etc.

Are these clauses called facts or rules?

They are facts, because they have a predicate and arguments in parentheses, and nothing else. If there was something further, they would be rules.

What is an example of a fact with one argument?

We might put information into a Prolog database listing all the people who have some qualification, say a Ph.D:

```
ph_d(mary)
ph_d(john)
ph_d(anne)
```

etc.

We could say the predicate **ph_d** has one argument, the name of any person who has a Ph.D. Usually when a predicate has only one argument we say it describes a property of the object, which is the single argument, whereas when a predicate has a number of arguments, it is more natural to say that the predicate describes a relationship between the various objects.

How do we discern all the clauses in the database?

The usual method of seeing the contents of the Prolog database is to type in:

```
?- listall.
```

and the system will display all the clauses on the screen. Some systems let you look only at the clauses which have the same predicate. For instance, by using

```
?- listing (income).
```

you get a display of all clauses which have the predicate *income*. In such cases, the systems may or may not also have an instruction that will display all the clauses.

How do we remove clauses in the database?

The usual method is to say:

```
?- retract(  ph_d(mary)  ).
```

to remove or delete the clause in parentheses following **retract** from the database. Again, there are slight differences from system to system; some use **retractall** to delete all clauses.

When we have entered all the information above (the facts for the predicate* chief_exec *as well as the facts for the predicate* first_name*), how can be get the system to use the information?

The simplest use of the information is to ask the system to verify whether it has the information stored. This is known as *querying the Prolog database.* In response to the prompt from the system, type in the fact for which you want it to search:

```
?- first_name(reagan,ronald).
```

The system will search its stored information to see if it has the information. Since we have put it in, it will respond affirmatively.

Another useful way of looking at this is to say that we have asked Prolog to satisfy the goal:

```
first_name(reagan,ronald)
```

When the goal is found in the database, it responds "yes," otherwise it fails to satisfy the goal and responds "no."

How will the system respond to this query?

```
?-first_name(enstein, albert).
```

It will respond with a "no," since we have not put this information in the database. Prolog is said to operate on a *closed-world assumption.* When it says "no," it means "Not as far as I know," or "No, as far as the closed world consisting of the information in the database is concerned," or "This goal is not found in the database."

Checking to see if some information is in the Prolog database we have created seems to be a very simple task. How else can Prolog use the information in the database?

Verifying whether something is in the database is only the first step. Prolog can also pull the information we want out of the database and display it. This is done by asking it questions in a particular form.

Suppose we want to find out who is the **chief_exec** of **usa**. We would ask this question, following the Prolog prompt, in the following manner:

```
?-chief-exec(usa,Title,Who).
```

What will be Prolog's response to this?

Prolog will display the following on the screen:

```
Title = president, Who   = reagan.
```

How does this work?

The important thing to keep in mind is that Prolog works essentially by a process of *pattern matching.* This is also the basis of the earlier example we considered, of asking Prolog to verify if a certain fact is in the database. The system tries to match the pattern of our query:

```
?- first_name(reagan,ronald).
```

with anything it can find in the database. If it finds a successful match it replies "yes."

Since it cannot find a match for the pattern

```
?-first_name(einstein,albert).
```

it says "no."

When we ask the question

```
?-chief_exec(usa,Title,Who).
```

the difference is that now our query has some arguments which start with an uppercase letter—the two arguments Title and Who. The convention in most versions of Prolog is that if an argument starts with a lowercase letter, or is a number, it should be treated as having a constant and fixed value. If it starts with an uppercase letter it should be treated as a *variable.*

Is the idea or concept of a variable in Prolog the same as we use in algebra or in other programming languages?

Absolutely. It is a symbol to which any value can be assigned; in other words, a kind of place-holder to which a specific meaning will be assigned, just as in algebra we might say, "Let X represent the number of hours each person works . . . etc. When Prolog tries to match a query with variables in the arguments, it has flexibility in trying to match the pattern, for it can allot a suitable value to the variable and thus make a successful match.

In the above example, Prolog can make a successful match between our query

```
?- chief_exec(usa,Title,Who).
```

and the clause/fact it has in its database:

```
chief_exec(usa,president,reagan).
```

To make the match, it has to allot the value **president** to the variable Title, and the value **reagan** to the variable Who. Having done this, it displays the results by telling us:

```
Title = president
```

and

```
Who = reagan.
```

We should keep in mind that the first argument in our query is a constant, **usa**. Prolog has to find an exact match for this, and for the predicate name **chief_exec**.

Suppose we put in one more clause in the database, giving the name of someone who was president of the United States at a different time:

chief_exec(usa,president,roosevelt).

How will Prolog decide with which of thse clauses it should match our query?

This brings us to a second important principle about Prolog. It always searches the database for all the clauses with a particular predicate *in the order in which they were entered.* So if we enter the **chief_exec** clause for **roosevelt** after the clause for **reagan**, Prolog will first find the solution:

Title = president

and

Who = reagan.

When you say Prolog will first find the above solution, you mean it will find the second solution as well?

Yes, in most versions of Prolog, having found the first solution the system will ask the user if it should search for alternative solutions, if any. If the user responds with a "yes" the system will search again, starting from the point it found the previous solution. If it finds another answer it will display this answer, and again ask the user if it should search further for alternative answers. This process will go on until the user says "no" or the system finds after going through all the clauses that no more answers are possible. In this case it will inform the user there are "no more answers."

In some systems, instead of specifically asking whether it should search for more solutions the system will just wait. If the user types a semicolon (;) it will search for the next solution, and if the user hits the return key Prolog will take this to mean that it should not search for alternative solutions.

Does "order in which the clauses were entred in the database" mean the order in which we typed them?

Yes, if we entered the clauses using the command **assertz** which we saw earlier. The **assertz** command means more specifically, "Add to the database at the end of the existing clauses." Prolog also provides for adding clauses at the beginning instead of the end of the existing clauses. To do this one would say asserta instead of assertz. As you can see, "a" and "z" at the end of **assert** are meant to remind us that one goes at the beginning and the other at the end.

What if we want to add a clause somewhere between the existing clauses, instead of the beginning of the end?

Some versions of Prolog allow clauses with a particular predicate to be added at whatever position we want between the clauses already in the database for that predicate (see the description of **assert** in Prolog-1 in Appendix A).

When you want to create a Prolog database with a large number of clauses, it is much more convenient to create it using any suitable editor or word processor and then transfer the whole file of information for use by the Prolog system. We will look at this later. But for getting a good grip on the principles of Prolog, let us first look at it in terms of the simplest way of adding clauses to the database, by using **asserta** or **assertz.**

How does Prolog keep track of the order in which clauses for a particular predicate are found in the database?

A helpful way of visualizing this is to think of Prolog placing some sort of marker opposite a clause in the database when it makes a successful match with a question. So, if we ask for an alternative solution to the same question, Prolog knows it has to restart the search at the next clause beyond the marker.

Can we use any number of variables in a query?

Yes. In the example above, we used two variables. Title and Who. A free translation of our question:

```
?- chief__exec(usa,Title,Who).
```

would be: "Who is the **chief__exec** of the United States, and what is his or her title?" We might ask the question in the form:

```
?- chief__exec(usa,president,Who).
```

This would amount to asking: "What is the name of the president of the United States? Prolog will respond with **Who = reagan**. The point to note is that the response tells us the values allotted to the variables in our question, in the process of making a successful match. In this case we gave the fixed or constant value president to the second argument, so Prolog tells us only the value for the variable Who.

What would be a free translation of this question?

```
?- chief__exec(Where,president,Who).
```

How will Prolog respond to this question? How many possible solutions can be found, and in what order will they be found? (Write out your answer before reading further.)

The above question was meant to emphasize three key aspects of programming in Prolog:

a) The fundamental operation is that Prolog tries to match the pattern of the question with a clause in the database.

b) If any of the arguments starts with an uppercase letter, it is treated as a variable which can be flexibly allotted any value.
c) Prolog starts the search at the "top" of the database, i.e., it searches the clauses with the required predicate in the order in which they appear in the database.

Applying these principles, we can see that the first match the system will make gives the results:

Where = usa, Who = reagan.

If we ask the alternative solutions, the system will produce:

Where = france, Who = mitterand.

These are the only two possible solutions on the basis of the sample database given above.

A free translation of the question would be: "Which countries have chief executives who have the title 'president,' and what are the names of those persons?"

What will be the response if we ask this question?

?- chief_exec(Where,Title,Who).

(Write your answer before reading further.)

Here we have variables for all three arguments. Prolog will be able to match the question with all four clauses for the **chief_exec** predicate, and would be able to produce four answers, starting with: **Where -usa, Title =president, Who=** reagan.

A second set of clauses was given above having the predicate first-name *and two arguments. How would you ask a Prolog system to use these clauses to answer the following questions?*

1) *What is the first name of Reagan?*
2) *What is the last name of the person whose first name is Margaret?*
3) *Give one by one the first names of all persons about whom the relevant information is contained in the database.*

(Write your answers before reading further.)

Here is some practice in using variables:

1) ?- first_name(reagan,What).

The response would be **What = ronald.**

2) **?- first-Name(Who,margaret).**

The response would be **Who = thatcher.**

3) **?-first_name(Who,What).**

By asking for all possible answers, the system would in turn produce the responses:

```
Who = reagan, What = ronald
Who = mitterand, What = francois
Who = thatcher, What = margaret
Who = mulroney, What = brian.
```

What is meant by resatisyfing a goal?

As mentioned earlier, the process of asking a question is often referred to as "setting a goal for Prolog to satisfy." This description applies whether we are asking it to verify whether a clause is in the database (by using a question with no variable) or are asking it to flexibly match a question containing variables. When we ask for alternative solutions, this is referred to as asking Prolog to *resatisfy the goal*; it has satisfied the goal with its first response. From now on, I shall use the expressions "setting a goal," "satisfying a goal," and "resatisfying a goal," when appropriate.

What is an anonymous variable?

Sometimes we may not want to know the particular value Prolog has assigned to a variable when it makes a successful match. For example, we may want to know what the name of the **chief_exec** of the government of Canada is, but may not be interested in knowing what the exact title is. Based on the principles we have seen so far, if we ask the question in the form:

```
?- chief_exec(canada,Title,Who).
```

we would get the response:

```
Title = prime_minister, Who = mulroney.
```

If we do not want to know the title, we would ask the question in the form:

```
?- chief_exec(canada,_ , Who).
```

and the response would be:

```
Who = mulroney.
```

The underline character which we have used as one of the arguments in our question is called the *anonymous variable.* It is a variable that Prolog can flexibly match with any value when it pattern-matches. But Prolog does not display the value it assigned to this variable, so information we may not require is suppressed. Because our database has clauses for **chief__exec** with three arguments, the goal we set has to have three arguments, as well. It is therefore essential to use the anonymous variable even if we do not want the information about its value.

What is meant by instantiation?

We have seen that when we set a goal in which some of the arguments are variables, Prolog flexibly allots some specific value to the variables when it makes a successful match. A variable to which a value is given is said to be *instantiated to that value.* When we ask the question:

```
?-firstname(mulroney,What)
```

What is an uninstantiated variable. But when a successful match with the:

```
first__name(mulroney,brian)
```

has been found by the system, the variable What has been instantiated to the value **brian.**

When we have found one solution and ask the system to search for an alternative solution, the variables which were previously instantiated become uninstantiated and Prolog starts the search for a second solution after the uninstrantiation. Also remember, when the variables in the question have been instantiated and the goal has been satisfied and we ask for resatisfaction of the goal, the search using uninstantiated variables starts from the point the previous instantiation was made. As mentioned earlier, a useful way to visualize this is by thinking of Prolog as placing a marker in the database whenever it makes a successful match.

When we ask a question, does it have to be based on just one predicate, or can we use more than one? If we can use more than one, how do we express the question?

We have considered in this chapter the fundamental principle of how Prolog satisfies a single goal by trying to match a question with a fact in the database. The natural extension of this is to consider *multiple goals*, which we look at in chapter 2

Before you go on to that, I urge you to try the exercises at the end of this chapter. They are meant to reinforce the basic principles we have considered in this chapter. Even if you have access to software, please write out your solutions to the problems with pencil and paper first, and compare them with the solutions given at the end of the book. Some of the solutions give additional information which supplements the contents of the chapter.

(If you are using software: remember the period at the end of your statement, whether you are using **assert** or **retract** or asking a question.)

Exercises:

Please write out your solutions to these exercises, and then compare your answers with those at the back of the book.

1) Suppose we enter the following fact into a Prolog database to record the information that John's income, expressed in thousands of dollars, is 30:

```
income (john,30).
```

a) What is the predicate?
b) What are the arguments ?
c) Classify the arguments into the following categories (an item could fall into more than one category): atoms, constants, variables, numbers.
d) Is the predicate an atom?

2) What are **asserta, assertz** and **retract** used for?

3) How would you express the information that the Declaration of Independence was signed in 1776, using a suitable predicate and two arguments? How would you enter this into a database?

4) Suppose we have created a database with the following facts entered into it:

```
capital_of(michigan,lansing).
capital_of(california,sacramento).
capital_of(montana,helena).
capital_of(new_york,albany).
```

a) How would you ask a Prolog question to find out what city is the capital of Montana?
b) How would you ask a Prolog question to find out which state has Albany as its capital?
c) How would you ask a question to find out the first fact in the database which gives information about capitals of states?

5) Give an example of a Prolog fact with three arguments.

6) We have a database with two clauses with two predicates, **income** and **age**. The income clauses have the name of a person as the first argument, and a classification of his or her income as high, middle, or low as the second argument. The age clauses have a name as the first argument, and a classification of the person's age as **young, middle_aged,** or **old:**

```
income(john,high).
```

```
income(mary,middle).
income(bill,low).
income(anne,high).
```

etc.

```
age(bill,middle_aged).
age(john,young).
age(mary,middle_aged).
age(anne,young).
```

etc.

a) How would you ask Prolog to find out what income group John is in?
b) What will be the response of Prolog to the question:

```
?- age(anne,whatgroup).
```

c) How will Prolog respond to the question:

```
?- income(Who,WhichGroup).
```

7) We have a Prolog database which contains facts with the predicate **book**, and three arguments: the title of the book, the first name of the author, and the last name of the author:

```
book(grapes_of_wrath,john,steinbeck).
book(tom_sawyer,mark,twain).
```

etc.
How would you use an anonymous variable to ask a question so that when you give the title of the book in your question, the response will display only the last name of the author, and not the first name as well?

8) What is meant by instantiation and resatisfaction? Explain, considering what Prolog's responses will be if we use the database in problem 6, and ask for all possible solutions one by one to the question:

```
?- income(Who,WhichGroup).
```

Chapter 2

Multiple Goals and Backtracking

We saw in the last chapter that programming in Prolog involves creating a database of facts and asking questions to extract information from the database. Variables play a key role in this process of information extraction.

The next step in understanding Prolog is to see how to extract information which requires the use of more than one predicate in the database. To illustrated this, let us consider the following problem, using the same database we had before:

```
first__name(thatcher,margaret).
first__name(mitterand,francois).
first__name(reagan,ronald).
first__name(mulroney,brian).
first__name(gandhi,rajiv).
chief__exec(usa,president,reagan).
chief__exec(france,president,mitterand).
chief__exec(canada,prime__minister,mulroney).
chief__exec(uk,prime__minister,thatcher).
chief__exec(india,prime__minister,gandhi).
```

Using the database above, which contains clauses for chief__exec *as well as* first__name*, suppose we want to find out the first name of the chief executive of the government of France. How do we frame a Prolog question for this?*

This really involves satisfying two goals. First, we have to find out the last name of the **chief__exec** of France, and use this information to find out that person's first name. The question would be expressed in the following form:

```
?- chief__exec(france,__,Who), first__name(Who,What).
```

When we ask a question which consists of two (or more) goals, separated by commas, Prolog does the following:

1) It tries to satisfy the first or left most of the goals.
2) It starts the search at the "top" of the list of clauses which have the required predicate, in this case, **chief__exec**.
3) It is able to satisfy the first goal by instantiating the anonymous variable to the value **president**, and the variable **Who** to the value **mitterand.**
4) Now it tries to satisfy the next goal to the right, in this case, the goal: **first__name(Who,What).**
5) Now, a very important point to be noted carefully: The second goal *looks as if it has two variables, but really doesn't.* One of them, Who, has already been instantiated by the first goal. So Prolog treats the second goal as if it is:

   ```
   first__name(mitterand,What).
   ```

6) This goal is satisfied for the first time, so the general principle applies; it searches from the "top" of the list of clauses with the predicate **first__name**. It finds a match with the clause:

   ```
   first__name(mitterand,francois)
   ```

   and instantiates the variable What to the value **francois.**
7) Both the goals have been satisfied, so it prints out the solution **Who = mitterand, What = francois.**

In this example, we know from the database that there is only one solution for the combination of two goals which we have included in our question. What happens if we have more than one solution possible for the combination of goals?

Let us consider a question which we know has more than one solution. We want to find out the first and last names of all persons who bear the title of prime minister. We can formulate this as a two-goal question. The first goal is to find out the last name of someone who bears the title of prime minister, for which we have to use the set of clauses for **chief__exec**. Using this, the second goal will find out the first name of the person, using the clauses for **first__name.** On the basis of the principles and examples we have seen, we could formulate this question as:

```
?-chief__exec(Where,prime__minister,Who),
first__name(Who,What).
```

Let us look step-by-step at how Prolog will try to satisfy this combination of two goals.

First, it will search the list of **chief__exec** clauses to try to satisfy the first, or left-most, goal. Given the order in which we have listed the clauses, the first match will be using the clause:

```
chief__exec(canada,prime__minister,mulroney).
```

Which variables in the question have been instantiated at this stage? What is the next goal to the right, which Prolog will now try to satisfy? (Write your answer before reading further.)

The instantiations made when the first goal is satisfied are: **Where = canada**, and **Who = mulroney**. The important point that this question reminds you about is this: Because the variable Who has been instantiated, the second goal is no longer:

```
first__name(Who,What)
```

Instead, it is:

```
first__name(mulroney,What).
```

Where will Prolog start in the database to search for a solution to the second goal? (Write down your answer before reading further.)

Because it is trying to satisfy the goal for the first time, it will start at the top of the list of clauses for **first__name**. It will be able to find a match using the last of these clauses, and so will print the first solution after succeeding on both goals:

```
Where = canada, Who = mulroney, What = brian.
```

What will be the various steps taken by Prolog if we now ask for an alternative solution to the question?

What follows is one of the most important things in understanding how Prolog works. When there is a combination of goals Prolog tries to solve them one by one, moving from *left to right.* We also saw that when any variable is instantiated the value allotted to that variable is "passed on" to the goal on the right. In this example, we have only one goal to the right of the first goal. If there were two or more goals to the right of the first goal, then any instantiation made by the first goal would be passed on to *all the goals on its right.* When any goal makes an instantiation the values are passed on to all the goals on the right of that goal.

Now when we ask for an alternative solution, two things happen. First, the variables which were instantiated by the last goal which was satisfied are uninstantiated. In this case, it would be those instantiated by the second goal.

Then Prolog now tries to find an alternative solution to this goal. Since the goal is now being resatisfied after succeeding once, the search starts from the clause next to the clause where the previous success was achieved.

What is the second goal that Prolog tries to solve now, and which clause does it try in an attempt to resatisfy the goal? (Write your answer before reading further.)

This question emphasizes the point that only the variables instantiated by the second goal are uninstantiated. The variables instantiated by the first goal remain as they are. The goal is:

```
first_name(mulroney,What).
```

This goal succeeded with the clause:

```
first_name(mulroney,brian).
```

The search will therefore start with the next **first_name** clause in the database. But there are no more **first_name** clauses, so the attempt to resatisfy the second goal fails.

What happens next is known as the mechanism of *backtracking*. Prolog now tries to resatisfy the goal to the left of the goal which failed. In this case, that means it tries to resatisfy the first goal. This implies two things. First, the variables instantiated in the first success are uninstantiated. In the present example, this means that the variables Where and Who which were instantiated to **canada** and **mulroney** in the first success are uninstantiated. So, the goal is now:

```
chief_exec(Where,prime_minister,Who).
```

Second, since this is an attempt to resatisfy, the search starts from the clause next to where it succeeded previously. Prolog will go down the database clauses for **chief_exec**, starting with the clause:

```
chief_exec(uk,prime_minister,thatcher).
```

We can see that it will succeed, and will now instantiate the variables Where and Who again, and once again proceed to the second goal.

What is the second goal, and where will Prolog start its search to satisfy this goal? (Write your answer before reading further.)

The second goal is now:

```
first_name(thatcher,What).
```

But the important point this question emphasizes is that the search for the second goal will now start at the top of the set of clauses for **first_name** and *not* from where it succeeded previously. Why? Because this is not an attempt to resatisfy a goal which has succeeded, but a fresh start on this goal. The first attempt to satisfy a goal always starts at the "top." Incidentally, if you wondered earlier why I changed the order in which the persons were listed in the two predicates, now you know—it was to illustrate this point.

Clearly this will succeed with the top-most **first_name** clause, and since both goals have again succeeded, Prolog will display the second solution:

```
Where = uk, Who = thatcher, What = margaret.
```

If we ask for one more solution, you can see what will happen. Prolog will try to resatisfy the goal:

```
first_name(thatcher,What).
```

Since this is a resatisfaction attempt, it will go down the list of **first_name** clauses, beyond the one where it previously found a match. This goal will fail, and Prolog will backtrack to the first goal, which after uninstantiation of variables, will once again be:

```
chief_exec(Where,prime_minister,Who).
```

The next solution be found as **Where = india, Who = gandhi, What = rajiv.** If we ask again, our database does not allow resatisfaction of this goal, and there are no goals to the left of this goal to which Prolog can backtrack. The system will tell us that there are no more answers.

This example has only two goals, so backtracking was from the right-most goal to the only goal on the left. The principle is the same when there are three or more goals. When we ask for alternative solutions, Prolog first tries to resatisfy the right-most goal, uninstantiating any variables instantiated in the previous success. But any values passed on by instantiation of goals to the left of this goal retain their values.

After all possible resatisfactions of the right-most goal fails, Prolog backtracks to the next goal on the left. It uninstantiates the variables previously instantiated by this goal, and tries to resatisfy the goal. If it can do so, it again goes to the goal on the right. But this is a *new* attempt, *not* a resatisfaction of the goal on the right. Finally there will be a backtracking to the left-most goal, and when that fails no more answers are possible.

This mechanism is sometimes explained by saying that "success" is transmitted from each goal to the goal to the right of it, and "failure" is transmitted from each goal to the goal to the left of it.

Now let us look at an example involving three goals to see how the backtracking mechanism works. Suppose our database has clauses involving three predicates. The first predicate, **owns**, tells us the brand of home computer owned by various persons. Of course one person may own more than one home computer:

```
owns(john,apple).
owns(mary,apple).
owns(anne,atari).
owns(zach,apple).
owns(george,commodore).
owns(john,ibm).
owns(mary,ibm).
owns(rajneesh,ibm).
owns(zach,sinclair__QL).
```

The second predicate, **home**, gives information about the state in which the various persons live:

```
home(mary,california).
home(zach,michigan).
home(anne,ohio).
home(george,michigan).
home(rajneesh,oregon).
```

The third predicate classifies the states as belonging to a particular region of the country:

```
region(california,west).
region(michigan,midwest).
region(ohio,midwest).
region(oregon,west).
```

Based on the foregoing information, how would you formulate a three-goal question which will give us the information about what brands of home computer are owned by persons in our database who live in a particular region, such as the Midwest? Also, analyze step-by-step how Prolog will set about finding all possible solutions to the question. (Write down your answers before reading on.)

Based on the principles we have seen, we can first analyze the problem to see what the goals should be. We could start by locating a state in the Midwest and then locate a person living there, and then check what brand of computer the person owns. So, our question might be:

```
?- region(State,midwest),home(Who,State),owns(Who,Brand).
```

We can see that as the goals are tried left to right, the following things will happen:

- ☐ The first goal will succeed by instantiating State to the value **michigan**.
- ☐ This will be passed on to the second goal, making it: **home(Who,michigan)**.

- ☐ This will succeed by instantiating Who to the value **zach**.
- ☐ This will be passed on to the third goal, making it **owns(zach,Brand)**.
- ☐ This will succeed first by instantiating **Brand = apple**, giving the first solution. If we ask for an alternative solution, it will be resatisfied with **Brand = sinclair_QL**. Any further attempt to resatisfy this goal will fail. So, if we ask for one more solution, Prolog will backtrack to the next goal on the left, uninstantiating the variable Who.
- ☐ There will now be an attempt to resatisfy the second goal, **home(Who,michigan)**. This can be resatisfied by instantiating Who to the value **george**.
- ☐ Now the third goal, **owns(george,Brand)**, will be tried. This can be satisfied—note that it is being *satisfied*, not *resatisfied*—by instantiating Brand to the value **commodore**. There is no possibility of resatisfying this.
- ☐ There will be another backtrack to the second goal, and an attempt to resatisfy the goal **home(Who,michigan)**. Since our database has no possibility of resatisfying this, it will backtrack to the first goal.
- ☐ The variable State will also be uninstantiated, and there will be an attempt to resatisfy the goal **region(State,midwest)**. This can be resatisfied by instantiating State to **ohio** and so on.

It is very important to keep in mind the distinction between satisfying a goal and resatisfying it. It is also important to be clear on which variables are uninstantiated at each stage of backtracking.

Could we get the answers we wanted—information about the brands of home computers owned by people in the Midwest—by forming the question in a different way? (Write your answer before reading further.)

We could have changed the order of the goals. We could have put the question as:

?-owns(Who,Brand),home(Who,State), region(State,midwest).

We can see intuitively that this should lead to the same results. We are asking the system to find a person, check where the person lives, and check whether the person lives in the Midwest. But why will this lead to the results in a different order? (Even if you can show this through a "general" argument, it would be good practice to follow the flow of success from left to right and the flow of failure from right to left, to strengthen your feel for the backtracking mechanism.)

Do you think it makes any difference in which order we give the goals? (Write your answer before reading further.)

I will not give the detailed backtracking analysis, but I hope you have carried it out and found that the results will be in this order: Anne owns an ATARI, Zach owns an Apple, George owns a Commodore, and Zach owns a Sinclair QL. This is different from the previous order, which was: Zach owns an Apple, Zach owns a Sinclair QL, George owns a Commodore, and Anne owns an ATARI. We can see in a commonsense way why this is so. In the earlier ordering, when a state in the Midwest was picked on the first goal (Michigan), it checked all people living there (Zach and George) and then went to another state. In the second ordering, it first picks a person; the first person it picks who lives in the Midwest is Anne, so it displays this result first.

The more important point here is that in the second ordering, it checks every person to see whether they live in the Midwest. In the first ordering, it checks only persons it has found to be in a state in the Midwest. Prolog does less work in the way the goals were first ordered.

One goal of declarative or assertional programming is that the user should not have to think about procedural details. To some extent Prolog does not quite achieve this ideal; as this example illustrates, when programming in Prolog it is useful to take into account the procedural details of how Prolog works to decide the order of goals. If you have had some experience in any of the standard imperative/procedural languages like BASIC, COBOL, Pascal etc., you will see that this same kind of search would have required much effort spelling out the strategy for searching, whereas the Prolog program has been essentially a description of the problem: find a state in the Midwest and then check what brand of computer is owned by any person who lives in that state.

When we say "database" in Prolog, is it the same as the database in database programs?

There is a strong similarity. Any database really consists of ordered information. When we put in a fact with various arguments, we can say it is similar to the way information is entered in standard databases. If we enter a Prolog fact such as **owns(anne,atari).**, we could say this is a *record*, which has two *fields*, one field showing the name of the person, and the second field the brand of computer owned by that person. However, not only does Prolog make it convenient to enter information very flexibly, without any restriction on the number of different items (arguments) we enter, it also makes it very convenient to draw conclusions combining different clauses. Sometimes Prolog is referred to as being partly a *deductive database*, combining the advantages of holding information in the database and drawing conclusions by setting suitable goals. I say "partly" because in subsequent chapters we will see some more powerful uses of Prolog.

As indicated earlier, information in a Prolog database is held in the form of clauses, and there are two types of clauses, facts and rules. We have looked in detail at facts, and in the next chapter we will look at rules, which are really an extension of the "multiple-goal questions" we have seen in this chapter.

There are some exercises below which should help you review the principles of backtracking, etc. Even if you have no software, I urge you to try them and compare your solutions with those given at the back of the book.

Exercises

1) Consider the database we had in one of the exercises in the previous chapter:

```
income(john,high).
income(mary,middle).
income(bill,low).
income(anne,high).
income(jim,high).

age(anne,young).
age(jim,middle_aged).
age(bill,middle_aged).
age(john,young).
age(mary,middle_aged).
```

a) How would you ask a question involving two goals, which will find out, one by one, the names of all individuals in the high income group *and* also in the young age group? Describe the various backtrackings, resatisfactions, instantiations, and uninstantiations that occur in the process of finding all possible solutions.

b) Suppose you switch the order of the two goals in your question. What difference will that make, if any?

2) We have a database with clauses involving three different predicates:

```
lives_in(michigan,john).
lives_in(new_york,mary).
lives_in(ohio,anne).
lives_in(michigan,zach).
```

etc.

```
knows(zach,latin).
knows(anne,french).
knows(mary,spanish).
knows(john,russian).
knows(zach,french).
knows(john,chinese).
```

etc.

```
used_in(spain,spanish).
used_in(france,french).
used_in(argentina,spanish).
used_in(canada,french).
used_in('The Vatican',latin).
```

etc.

a) How would you ask a question with two goals, which uses three variables and will instantiate these variables to show all possible solutions for three bits of information: name of a person, state the person lives in, and language known by that person? (The variables need not necessarily be in this particular order).

b) Will it make any difference if you switch the order of the two goals you have chosen in your previous answer?
c) If our aim is to find out the names of those who know a particular language, such as French, along with information on where they live, then does the order in which we give the goals in our question make a difference?
d) If our aim is to find out the names and the languages known by those who live in a particular state (say, Michigan), will the order in which we give the goals make a difference?
e) How would you ask a question with two goals to find out from the database what countries use each of the languages known to each person in our database?
f) Would the order in which the goals are given make a difference in the preceding question?
g) What would be the solution we get if we ask for only the first solution to the question:

```
?- knows(Who,_), used_in(Where,_).
```

3) A database contains two predicates, one connecting the names of cities with the states they are in, and the other indicating which time zone the state is in:

```
state(spokane,washington).
state(san_francisco,california).
state(boston,mass).
state(new_york,n_y).
state(casper,wyoming).
etc.
```

and

```
time_zone(n_y,eastern).
time_zone(wyoming,mountain).
time_zone(mass,eastern).
time_zone(ca,western).
time_zone(washington,western).
etc.
```

a) How would we ask a multiple-goal question to find out which particular time zone a given city is in?
b) Would the order in which the goals are given make a difference in this case?

Chapter 3

Rules in Prolog

In chapter 2 we saw that a fundamental part of programming in Prolog is to create a database of clauses which contain relevant information about the objects with which we are dealing. Clauses are of two types: *facts,* which we considered in the last chapter, and another type called *rules*.

We will start by reviewing some of the key concepts you have already learned as a basis for going on to learn about rules.

Suppose we have a database in which one of the facts is:

```
address(reagan,1600_pennsylvania_ave,washington,d_c)
```

What is the predicate, and how many arguments does this fact have?

This question is to remind you of the key concept that a fact has a predicate followed by a number of arguments separated by commas, with the arguments enclosed in parentheses. In this case the predicate is **address** and there are four arguments. (Remember also that an underline character is used to connect names of arguments which would be two words in English.)

How would you extract from the database the name of the person who lives in 1600 Pennsylvania Avenue, Washington, D.C.?

This question is to remind you about the concept of *variables*, which in standard versions of Prolog should start with a capital letter. Frame a question thus:

```
?-address(Who,1600_pennsylvania_ave,washington,d_c).
```

The system will match the pattern of the question to the pattern of a clause in the database, if possible, and instantiate any variables in the question. In the present case, it will instantiate Who to the value **reagan** and print out **Who = reagan**.

There is a graphical way of looking at the way Prolog matches patterns. We saw that a fact like **income(john,20)** represents the information that the objects **john** and **20** are connected by the relationship **income**. A graphical way of showing this connection is by using a tree, as shown in Fig. 3-1A. (In computer science, trees grow downwards, with the root at the top.)

When we ask a question like **?- income(john,Howmuch).**, we can think of this also as a tree (Fig. 3-1B) and we can think of Prolog as trying to find an answer to questions by trying to "unify" the trees, by putting one tree over the other to match them, with of course the understanding that when a tree contains a variable beginning with an uppercase letter, Prolog is free to unify it with any other object, including another variable. This way of looking at Prolog will be especially helpful when we look at rules. The concept of "unification" has some deeper theoretical significance, which we discuss later when we look in more detail at some of the theory underlying Prolog.

How are rules different from the facts we have seen so far?

To answer this, let us go back and look at the concept of asking questions involving "multiple goals."

Suppose we have a database with a number of facts which use two different predicates: **address** and **owns_car**. The predicate **address**, as in the example above, has four arguments showing the name of the person, the street address, the city and the state. The predicate **owns_car** has two arguments, showing the name of the person and the make of car the person owns. The database may look something like this:

```
address(mary,100_east_street,marquette,michigan)
address(john,200_west_street,marquette,michigan)
address(frank,000_middle_street,san_francisco,ca)
address(jim,300_north_street,boston,mass)
address(anne,400_south_street,new_york,ny)

    owns_car(john,honda)
    owns_car(reagan,presidential_limousine1)
    owns_car(mary,ford)
    owns_car(anne,chevrolet)
    owns_car(jim,toyota)
    owns_car(elizabeth,mercedes)
    owns_car(frank,ford)
    owns_car(reagan,presidential_limousine2)
```

and so on.

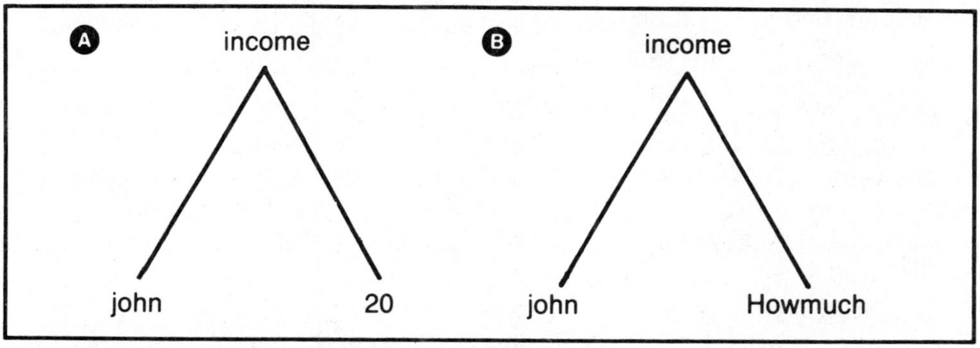

Fig. 3-1. Tree representations of a relationship and a question.

We know we can extract information from any particular clause by asking a suitable question. For instance, to find out what make of car Elizabeth owns, we would ask:

```
?- owns_car(elizabeth,Make).
```

Or, to find out where Jim lives, we would ask:

```
?- address(jim,Street,City,State).
```

We know that we can extract information which depends on more than one predicate. For instance, suppose we want the names of people who live in a particular city, (Marquette, say) and own a particular make of car, such as Fords. We would need to ask a question which has two goals, the first making use of the **address** predicate, and the second making use of the **owns_car** predicate:

```
?- address(Who,Street,marquette,State),owns_car(Who,ford).
```

Instead of asking questions like this by giving all the goals one by one, you can use a rule which has the same effect.

In the above example, in exactly the same way we would enter a fact into the database, we could enter the following piece of text, which is an example of a rule:

```
owns_this_make(Person,City,Make) :-
    address(Person,Street,City,State),
    owns_car(Person,Make).
```

Let us first look at how this is like and unlike to the facts we have looked at so far.

Just like the facts we have seen, a rule has a predicate followed by a number of arguments in parentheses. In this case, the predicate is **owns_this_make**, and the arguments are **Person**, **City**, and **Make**. This part of a rule, the first predicate and the arguments which go with it, are called the *head* of the rule, or the *parent goal* of the rule.

A rule also has a symbol :- following the head. After the head there are, in this example, two pieces of text which have the same structure as a fact or the head of a rule: each of them has a predicate followed by arguments in parentheses:

```
address(Person,Street,City,State)
owns__car(Person,Make)
```

These together are known as the *body* of the rule. In general, a rule can have one or more structures in the body.

The important things to remember about how Prolog handles a rule are these:

1) First, it matches the question with the head of the rule, just as it does when dealing with facts.
2) Next, a rule says in effect that to succeed in the goal given by the head of the rule, replace it by the goals given in the body of the rule. Or we can say that the symbol :- can be read to mean *if*. That is, the goal in the head can succeed if the goals in the body succeed.

Let us see how this would work, by considering what would happen if we asked Prolog the question:

```
?- owns__this__make(Who,marquette,ford).
```

We have seen that the general principle underlying the process by which Prolog answers questions is *pattern matching*. Prolog will try to match the pattern of the question to some clause in the database. In the previous examples the question could be matched to a fact by instantiating variables in the question to values found as arguments in the facts. Now the question can be matched with the first part of the rule, the part before the :- symbol, the head of the rule. Let us look at it in terms of tree diagrams (Fig. 3-2). Looking at parts A and B, we see that the two trees can be matched:

owns__this__make	with	owns__this__make
Who	with	Person
marquette	with	City
ford	with	Make.

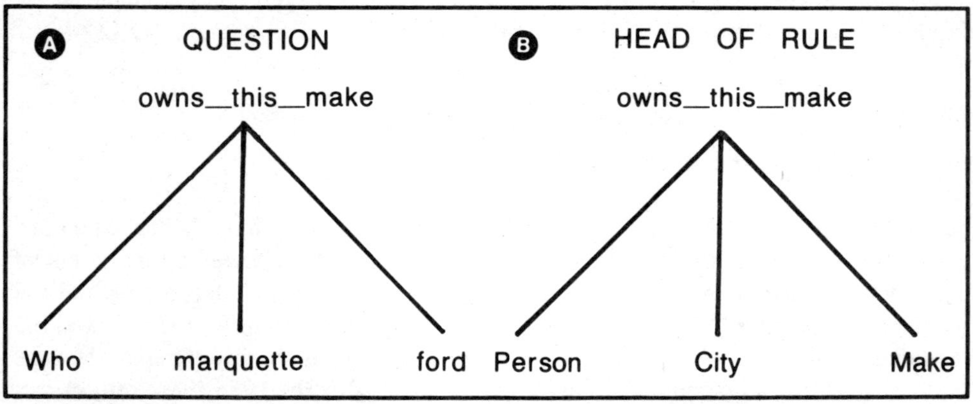

Fig. 3-2. Prolog answers questions by means of pattern matching, which can be visualized as comparing tree diagrams.

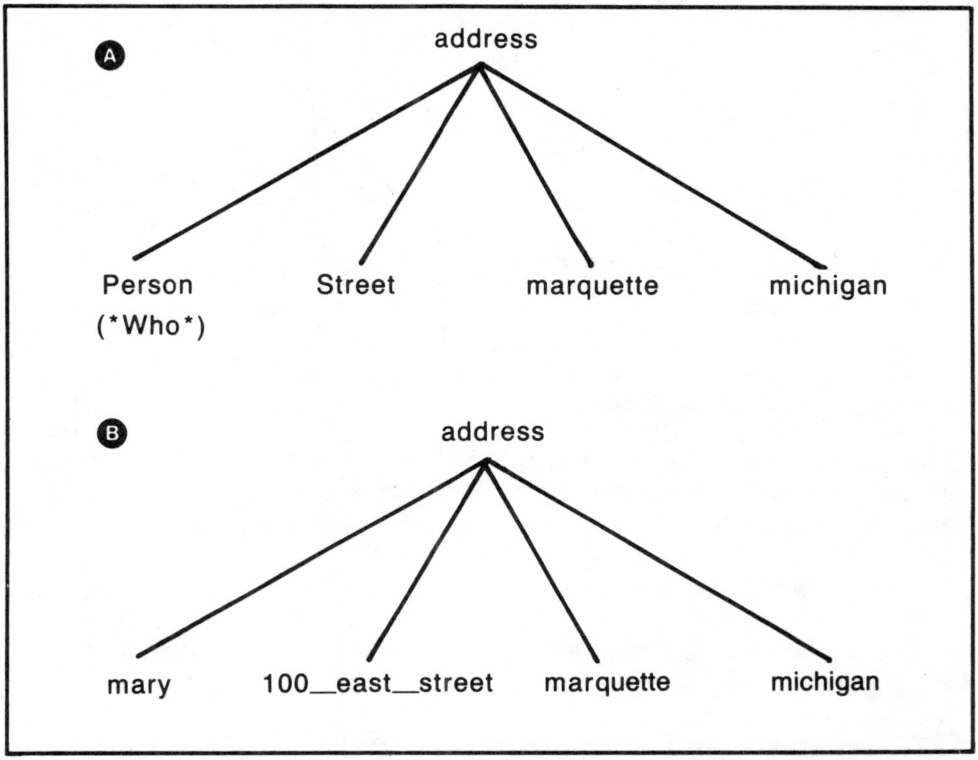

Fig. 3-3. Tree diagrams showing A) the result of matching a question and the head of a rule, and B) a match found within the database.

The variable City in the head of the rule is instantiated to the value **marquette**, and the variable Make in the head of the rule is instantiated to **ford**. But neither Who nor Person, which are matched, has a value, though they *share*, or are *bound to each other*. What this means is that if either of them acquires a value by instantiation, the other will also share and acquire the same value.

The next step is that the goal in the head is replaced by the goal or goals in the body of the rule. In this example we have two goals, separated by a comma, which means a combination or conjunction of goals. So in terms of tree diagrams, Prolog now has two trees to deal with. Remember, it deals with a conjunction of goals from left to right. Also remember that when any variables are instantiated by a particular goal, the values are passed on to all the goals to the right of that goal.

So, the first tree Prolog has to solve looks like Fig. 3-3A, after the instantiations made when the question and the head were matched. (I have put in the variable Who along with Person to indicate that they are variables which share.) From our database, searching from the top of the list of address clauses, you can see that a match can be found, first with the fact shown in Fig. 3-3B.

At this stage the variable **Person(*Who*)** in the first goal in the body of the rule is instantiated to **mary**, the variable Street is instantiated to **100_east_street**, and the variable State is allotted the value **michigan**.

Since there is one more goal to the right of this, the values allotted by first goal

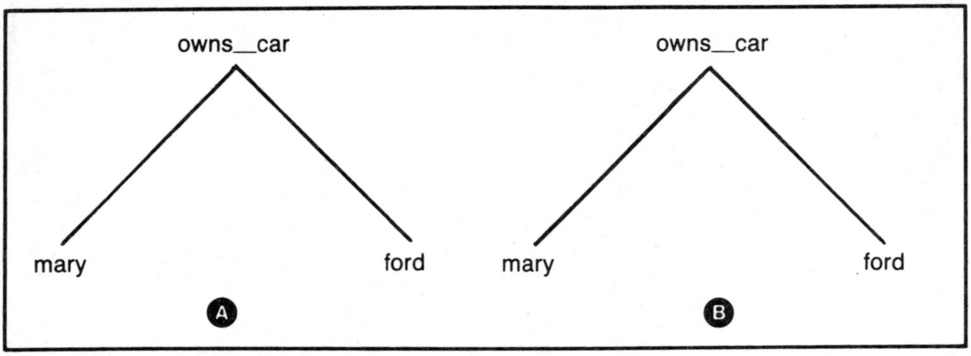

Fig. 3-4. When a goal (A) and database fact (B) are the same,the search succeeds and Prolog prints values for the variables in the question.

are passed on to the next goal. In tree form, it is shown in Fig. 3-4A. This will be matched with the fact in the database shown in Fig. 3-4B. Since all the goals have succeeded, Prolog will print out the values for all the variables in the question:

```
Who = mary, City = marquette.
```

How does Prolog deal with a rule if there is more than one solution possible for a question which matches with a rule?

The important things to remember about how Prolog deals with a rule are that first it matches the question with the head, and next it treats the head goal as represented by the combination of goals in the body of the rule. So, everything we discussed in the last chapter about backtracking, success being transmitted to the right and failure to the left, etc., applies. The only thing to remember is that when the head and the question are matched, some variables may be instantiated, and some variables may share.

Since backtracking is one of the key concepts in Prolog, it would be useful to write an analysis of the various steps by which Prolog will find a first solution and then backtrack to find further solutions, when we ask the question:

```
?- owns_this_make(Who,Where,What_car).
```

Notice that this time we have three variables in the question.

Draw tree diagrams to show how Prolog processes the question above, and identify all the variables which share. (Write your answer before reading further.)

We can represent the question by the tree diagram shown in Fig. 3-5A. There is no fact in the database which has the predicate owns_this_make, but there is a rule whose head is shown in Fig. 3-5B. We see that when Prolog matches these, three things happen:

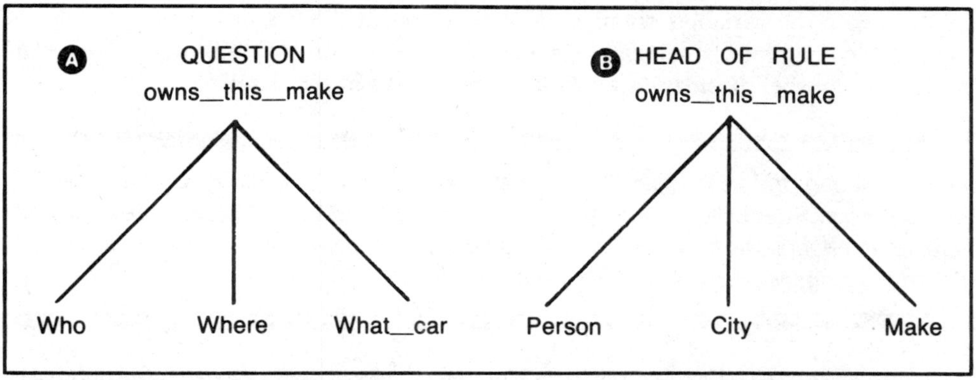

Fig. 3-5. Tree comparison for the question: ?__owns__this__make(Who,Where,What__car).

1) The variables Who and Person share with each other.
2) The variables Where and City share with each other.
3) The variables What__car and Make share with each other.

We know that by using these sharings Prolog will replace the head goal by the goals in the body, and try to achieve these goals, one by one, from left to right. The first goal it will try to solve is shown in Fig. 3-6A. Note the indication of sharing variables in the tree.

From our database we can see it will be able to succeed by matching this with:

address(reagan,1600__pennsylvania__ave,washington,d__c).

Prolog will now instantiate Person, Street, City, and State, and will proceed to the next goal on the right, as shown in Fig. 3-6B. It will succeed on this, and will instantiate Make to the value presidential__limousine1. It will then print out the first solution as: Who = reagan, Where = washington__d__c, What__car = presidential__limousine1.

Applying the principle of backtracking, only the variables instantiated by the right-most (second) goal will be uninstantiated, so it will try for an alternate solution for the goal owns__car(reagan,Make). Having found this solution, it will backtrack and will

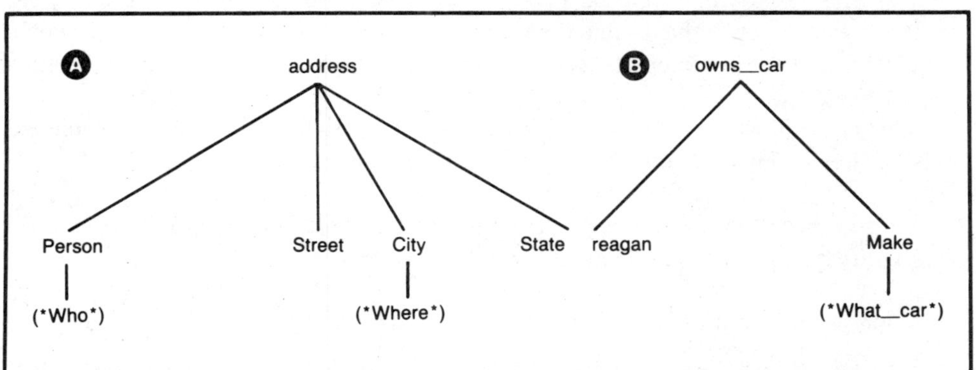

Fig. 3-6. Prolog will attempt to solve goal A and then proceed to goal B.

uninstantiate the variables obtained on the success of the first goal, going down the database looking for further solutions for **address(Who,Street,City,State)**. It will eventually display the information for all the car owners in the database.

In formulating the rule above, we had two goals in the body of the rule **address(Person,Street,City,State)**, *and* **owns__car(Person,Make)**. *Would it make any difference to change the order of these goals? If so, what difference will it make and why? (Write your answer before reading further.)*

We can see that the rule says to pick up the address of a person from the database, and find out one by one what cars they own, then backtrack and pick up the address of another person, list all the cars owned by that person, and so on.

If we use the goals in the reverse order, it will pick up the first item in the **owns-car** database, find the address of that person, then try to find if that person has another address. This would normally not be so, so an attempt to find an alternative solution for the second goal will fail. There will then be a backtrack to the first goal, to find the next item in the **owns__car** set of clauses. Either way we would get the list of all car owners, but the listing will be different if the owners are listed in a different order in the **address** set of clauses and the **owns__car** set of clauses.

When we ask the question in the form:

```
?- owns__this__make(Who,Where,Make).
```

our question asks that all the car owners be listed. But if we ask the question in the form:

```
?- owns__this__make(Who,Where,ford).
```

we would be asking only for owners of Fords to be listed. In that case, it is more efficient to check first in the list of owners to find out if the person owns a Ford and then search for his or her address, rather than first pick up a person from the list of addresses and check for car ownership. If our database is extensive, the proportion of persons who own Fords would be small, so it makes no sense to satisfy the address goal for every person in the list and then check whether he or she owns a Ford. It would be quicker to scan the owners list and go to the address goal when we know the person owns a Ford.

This again illustrates that although Prolog is essentially declarative, to some extent it helps to think of how Prolog goes about its task.

Let's go back to the example we had in the last chapter, of a database which had facts with two different predicates:

```
chief__exec(usa,president,reagan)
etc.
```

and

```
first__name(reagan,ronald)
etc.
```

We saw how to ask a two-goal question which would display the first names of the chief executives of governments who had the title of prime minister.

Based on the information given above, design a rule which will serve the same purpose. (Write out your answer before proceeding.)

We saw in the last chapter that we could ask the question:

```
?- chief__exec(Where,prime__minister,Who), first__name(Who,What).
```

We could convert this in a straightforward way into a rule, with a predicate **find__pm**:

```
find__pm(Where,Who,What) :-
    chief__exec(Where,prime__minister,Who),
    first__name(Who,What)
```

This rule will enable us to search only for those who have the title prime minister.

We want to make our rules as flexible as possible so we can use them for many related purposes. If we want to search for all the persons with the title of president, we don't want to put in another rule called **find__president**. The point of this question is to emphasize that one should design rules to be as flexible as possible by using variables. A better version of the rule would be:

```
find__by__title(Where,Title,Who,Name) :-
    chief__exec(Where,Title,Who),
    first__name(Who,Name)
```

We can use this rule to search for prime ministers by asking a question in the form:

```
?-find__by__title(Country,prime__minister,Lastname,Firstname),
```

and we can use it to search for presidents by asking:

```
?- find__by__title(Country,president,Lastname,Firstname).
```

Can we think of a Prolog fact as really a special kind of Prolog rule, where the number of goals in the body of the rule is zero?

Yes, indeed. Now that we have considered rules, we can see that facts are really a special case.

We saw that a convenient way of looking at a rule is to say that after matching the question with the head of the rule, the goals in the body of the rule are substituted for the head goal. Another way of describing this would be to say that the head goal is *dependent* on the goals in the body, since it succeeds only if the goals in the body succeed. A fact is therefore a rule for drawing conclusions in which the goal is not dependent on any other goals.

There is yet another way of looking at the similarity between facts and rules. We could say that every fact is a rule in which there is a goal in the body of the rule, but the rule is *implicit*. That is, when we have a fact like **first-name(reagan,ronald)**, what we actually have is a rule:

```
first__name(reagan,ronald) :- true.
```

What is this "true" in the body of the rule?

The **true** above is an example of what are called *built-in predicates* in Prolog, or goals whose definition is part of the system and already defined. This makes built-in predicates different from the predicates or goals the user defines. We will see more examples of built-in predicates, but at this stage, we should note that the predicate **true** is defined as something that always succeeds. So, if we ask **?- true.**, we would get the response **yes**. We can say that a fact in the database behaves like a rule which has a single goal, **true**, in the body.

When we write a rule, can we use other rules as goals in the body of the rule?

Yes. We saw that when Prolog deals with a rule it replaces the tree for the head goal by the trees for the goals in the body of the rule. If some or all of these are rules, we can visualize the process of solving these goals as in-turn replacement of a tree by a further set of trees, until ultimately we end up with a tree which has a predicate that can be matched with a fact in the database.

What are the various stages of backtracking that the system goes through when we have the database discussed in the clauses for* find__by__title *above, and we ask the question:

```
?- find__by__title(Where,prime__minister,Who,Firstname).
```

and after getting the first question, ask for more solutions? (Write your answer before reading further.)

By now you are familiar with the principles of backtracking, and see that the question will try to satisfy the first goal:

```
head(Country,prime__minister,Lastname),
```

and will find the first match by instantiating **Country = canada, Lastname = mulroney**.

It will now move to the next goal on the right, passing on the value of instantiated variables, so the second goal is:

first_name(mulroney,Firstname).

This can be matched by instantiating **Firstname = mulroney**, and so we get the first solution for the head goal of the rule.

Let us consider what happens when we ask for a second solution. We know that the next step the system will take is to try to resatisfy the second goal:

first_name(mulroney,What).

We know this cannot be resatisfied, so after searching to the end of the set of **first_name** clauses, Prolog will backtrack to the **first_goal**, and try to resatisfy:

chief_exec(Where,prime-minister, Who).

We can see from this small database that the system can find two more solutions to the question.

There is another point involved here, which is the reason for this question. The point is delineated in the following question.

We know the second goal* first_name(mulroney,Firstname) *cannot be resatisfied. But the backtracking mechanism of Prolog makes it try, anyway, before it fails and backtracks to the goal on the left. Would it not be more efficient to ask Prolog not to backtrack in situations where we know that resatisfaction is not possible?

Yes. Prolog does provide a mechanism for *cutting out* backtracking when we do not want it to do so. This is provided in the form of another built-in predicate or goal, called the *cut*, and is represented by the exclamation mark symbol (!). This built-in goal is often useful, but it can also be misleading. First let us see how it is useful in regard to the problem we saw above.

The definition of the cut goal is that: 1) it automatically succeeds, and 2) if it is located as one of a combination or conjunction of multiple goals, Prolog will never backtrack to any goals the system satisfied in the process of reaching the cut goal.

Now, let's put in the facts about first names in a new order:

first_name(mulroney,brian) :- !.

In the program above, for **find_by_title** we saw that the system tried to satisfy the subgoal **first_name(mulroney,Firstname)**. As before, it will succeed by matching the new clause **first_name(mulroney,brian)**. But in satisfying this clause it has also satisfied the cut goal. The definition of the cut goal is that none of the goals which lead to trying to satisfy the cut goal will be retried by backtracking. The system will not try again to satisfy the goal **first_name(mulroney,Firstname)**; the unnecessary backtracking to try to satisfy a goal which has only one possible solution is avoided by using the cut goal.

Rather than put a cut into every fact, a better way to do it might be as follows. We change the rule to read:

```
find__by__title(Where,Title,Who,Name) :-
      chief__exec(Where,Title,Who),
      find__first__name(Who,Name).
find__first__name(Who,Name) :-
      first__name(Who,Name),!.
```

Introducing the second predicate **find__first__name** and putting the cut there is simpler than putting a cut in each fact in the database.

This example is the simplest possible situation in which one would want the system not to backtrack.

There is another situation in which the cut is useful—where we want to tell the system that though it is possible more than one clause with the same predicate may match a particular question, other clauses should not be tried if one succeeds. The following example illustrates why sometimes we do not want the system to try further clauses.

In public universities, students are classified as residents of the state or as nonresidents. The fees per credit hour payable by the students is higher for nonresidents. At Northern Michigan University, for example, the fees per credit hour are $46 and $106 for residents and nonresidents, respectively. Suppose the database containing information about the classification of various students is as follows:

```
non__resident(john).
non__resident(mary).
non__resident(anne).
```

What would be the flaw if we put in the following clause for fees payable?

```
fees(Person,106) :- non__resident(Person).
fees(Person,46).
```

On the face of it, it seems to express the idea that for nonresidents the fees would be 106, otherwise it would be 46.

If we consider what happens if we ask a question like **fees(john,Howmuch)**, we can see that Prolog will try to match the first clause, will be able to satisfy the clause in the body, **non__resident(john)**, and will give us the correct solution: **Howmuch = 106**. But suppose we ask for an alternative solution. The system will backtrack and use the second **fees** clause, and will tell us **Howmuch = 46**. Obviously this should not happen. We want to tell the system that if the first **fees** clause succeeds there should be no backtracking. We can do this by modifying the first clause as follows:

```
fees(Person,106) :- non__resident(Person), ! .
```

By definition once the cut goal succeeds none of the goals which it satisfied in the process of reaching the cut should be backtracked to and tried again. With this modification, if we ask for a second solution the system will tell us there are no more answers possible, since it will not try to resatisfy the **fees** goal which led it to the cut goal.

Is it possible in such situations to use some alternative form which has the same effect, instead of using the cut goal?

Yes. In situations of this type, the cut can often be replaced by another built-in predicate called *not*, which takes one argument which is itself a goal. As the name suggests, the **not** goal will succeed if the goal which it has as an argument fails. In the example above, instead of putting a cut in:

```
fees(Person,106) :- non_resident(Person).
```

we could have modified the second **fees** clause to the following form:

```
fees(Person,46) :- not( non_resident(Person) ).
```

We can see that now, even if we ask for a second solution to the question **?-fees(john,Howmuch)**, we would get no success on the second clause. By making our definitions slightly longer by using not, we could get around using the cut when we want to tell the system not to try alternative clauses.

We will look at more examples of the cut operator in some of the later chapters. It can be used in a variety of ways other than the two main ones we have illustrated. The key fact to remember is that it is a method of saying, "Do not backtrack to any of the goals which led to trying this cut goal."

The cut operator is a matter of some controversy, since it seems to "interfere" with the fundamental basis of Prolog, the principle of backtracking. However, it does seem to be useful in some situations. Perhaps the rule to adopt in the beginning stages of learning Prolog is to avoid using the cut, and try to program as if the cut were not available. Later, when you get to complicated programs where it feels as if a cut could reduce and streamline your programs, use it judiciously.

Now try the exercises that follow and then go on to the next chapter.

Exercises

Note: Even if you have access to Prolog software, first try to figure out the answers to all the questions below using the general principles we have looked at in this chapter, and only then try them on the computer. If you think one or all of these questions would produce multiple solutions, explain all the possible solutions.

1) Convert the multiple-goal question in Problem 1 of the previous chapter into a suitable rule.

2) Convert the multiple-goal questions in parts (a) and (e) of Problem 2 of the previous chapter into rules.

3) Convert the multiple-goal question in Problem 3 of the previous chapter into a rule.

Chapter 4

Arithmetic and Comparisons

The examples we have seen so far deal with extracting information from the database, operating with words or names, etc. What about the usual calculations with numbers? How do we do arithmetic in Prolog?

Prolog, like LISP, was designed to be especially convenient for nonnumeric information processing, or symbolic processing. The examples we have seen were meant to indicate this aspect of Prolog.

However, Prolog is not incapable of handling arithmetic operations. In situations where a lot of number-crunching is required, Prolog has no distinct advantage over other languages, in the way it has for symbolic processing.

What would be a Prolog program for adding or subtracting numbers?

The most important Prolog operator to be familiar with for arithmetic operation is *"is."* This works as follows: if we set Prolog the goal:

```
?- Answer is 2.
```

It would come back with the response:

```
Answer = 2.
```

The goal we set for Prolog does not seem to have the usual structure of predicate and

arguments we saw as characteristic of Prolog.

That is true. The structure we have seen so far is sometimes referred to as a *prefix form*. The predicate which describes the relationship comes before the objects or arguments. On the other hand, "is" has an *infix* form, that is, it comes in between the objects it connects.

The "is" operator is also called one of the built-in operators in Prolog. Its definition and how it works are part of the software. This is in contrast to the predicates or programs the user defines.

When we say* Answer is 2, *can we think of Prolog as assigning a value to the variable Answer?

Yes. But in most programming languages we think of *assignment* as involving designating some particular place in memory by the name of the variable, and storing the value in that place in memory, so that we can, if necessary, recover the value. In Prolog, the value given to the variable is a "meaning," for the variable which is valid only within the clause where it occurs. It may be better to think of Answer as instantiated to the value 2.

The "is" operator also has another role. If we set the goal **3 is 3**, we are asking Prolog to check if the two are equal. Similarly, if at some stage a variable, say Result, has already been instantiated to some value, let us say 5, then

```
?- Result is 5.
```

would produce the response "yes," and

```
?- Result is 4.
```

would produce the response "no." When the variable is uninstantiated, the value on the right is alloted to the variable.

What other roles does "is" have?

It is used in Prolog for all the standard arithmetic operations. For example:

```
?- X is 2 + 3.
```

produces the response X = 5, provided X is an uninstantiated variable. For subtraction one can use a goal like:

```
?- Y is 10 - 3.
```

We have to remember that if X or Y in these examples are already instantiated, Prolog compares them with the arithmetic expression on the left to see if they are the same number.

I suppose one can multiply or divide numbers in the same way?

Yes. The operator for multiplication is *, as in:

```
?- P is 3* 4.
```

The symbol for division is /. For arithmetic, some versions of Prolog allow only whole numbers or integers to be used. The result of division would give only the whole number part of division. For example:

```
?- R is 32 / 3.
```

gives the response R = 10.

Some versions of Prolog, which restrict arithmetic to whole numbers, also have an additional operator for obtaining the remainder when whole numbers are divided. This is called the *mod operator.* For example:

```
?- L is 32 mod 3
```

gives the response L = 2.

The reason this is called "mod" is that another name for integer division is "modulo arithmetic." A convenient way to think of modulo arithmetic is to think of it as "clock arithmetic." If we consider at noon what the time will be eight hours from now, we would say 8 o'clock. If we consider any number of hours greater than 12 (15 hours or 30 hours, for example) we would take away as many multiples of 12 as possible, giving the results as 3 o'clock and 6 o'clock respectively. We could say that 15 mod 12 is 3, and 30 mod 12 is 6.

Using what we have seen above about how "is" works, how can we write a Prolog program with a predicate sum *and with three arguments, so that when we give the first two arguments to be added, the third argument will give the result of the addition? (Write your answer before reading further.)*

How about this?

```
sum(First,Second,Result) :-
Result is First + Second.
```

In terms of the principles of pattern matching, we can see that if we ask a question like:

```
?- sum(10,20,What).
```

we should be able to get the response What = 30.

Consider in detail the process of pattern matching and instantiation of variables which the system will go through if we ask a question like:

```
?- sum(10,What,40).
```

(Write your answer before reading further.)

This question emphasizes the fact that there are some restrictions on how a built-in operator like "is" works. On applying the normal principles of pattern matching, you would expect that What would get instantiated to 30. However, the "is" operator works *only* if both the variables between which an arithmetic operator like + or – is applied are instantiated. In this case, when it applies the body of the rule the variable First has been instantiated to 10, but Second merely shares with the variable What in our question. so, the body of the rule looks like:

```
40 is 10 + Second(*What*).
```

We would get an error message saying that "arithmetic variables must be bound," meaning they must have been instantiated.

It would be nice if we could modify the rule so that when we use the **sum** predicate we can carry out subtraction by asking:

```
?- sum(10, What, 40),
```

as well as addition, by asking:

```
?- sum(10,30,Total).
```

To do this, we will have to introduce more clauses for **sum**, which will also involve a new Prolog expression we have not seen before.

We want to determine which of the arguments we are giving in the question is uninstantiated. In case Result is not instantiated, we know the user is looking for the sum of the other two variables, which have been instantiated. But if Result is instantiated, we know that this is a situation where only one of the other arguments is instantiated, and we have to subtract it from the value of Result.

The clauses we want to use for this would be:

```
sum(First,Second,Result) :- var(Result),
    Result is First + Second.
sum(First,Second,Result) :- var(First),
    First is Result – Second.
sum(First,Second,Result) :-
    Second is Result – First.
```

The new word used in the program is the predicate **var**. As you have probably guessed, it is a predicate which checks whether the single argument passed to it is an uninstantiated variable. If so, the goal will succeed, otherwise it will fail.

We can see that if we ask a question like:

```
?- sum(10,20,What).
```

What shares with Result in the rule and the goal **var(Result)** succeeds, so Prolog will use the first sum clause to evaluate **Result is 10 + 20**, which is what we want.

On the other hand, if we ask a question like:

```
?- sum(What,10,40).
```

we can see that the first clause will fail since Result is instantiated to 40, so **var(40)** is not true. The next rule will be tried. First and What are variables which share, but are not instantiated, so the goal **var(First)** will succeed, and Prolog will evaluate: **First is 40 - 10.**, which is what we want.

When we want Prolog to subtract First from Result, should we not have a goal* var(Second) *in the third clause, just as we had* var(First) *in the second clause? (Write your answer before reading further.)

It is true that if we look at the third clause by itself it looks incomplete. But we have to remember the basic characteristic of Prolog—that it tries the different clauses for a particular predicate in the order in which they appear in the database. So, this clause is tried only when the first two have failed, showing that Result is instantiated and so is First. We know we have the case where First is to be subtracted from Result to give us the value of Second.

What are comparison operators?

The power of a computer, whether for arithmetic or for nonnumeric processing, depends very much on its ability to compare two numbers to see if they are equal, and, if not, which is larger. Similarly, a very necessary task is that of comparing two characters, or two sequences of characters, to decide if they are the same, and, if not, which would come first in terms of some order we usually use to arrange the characters. We may think of this in general terms as alphabetic order, with the understanding that the set of characters or the alphabet we use would include, in addition to the upper- and lowercase letters A-Z and a-z, other symbols such as &, %, @, etc. We need some working rule about where these rank in our "alphabet."

Let us first look at the comparison operators for numbers. The = operator tests to see if two numbers are equal. The goal **?- 3 = 3.** produces a "yes" response, and **?- 4 = 5.** produces a "no" response.

If we use variables, and have somewhere in a program an expression like X = Y, we will similarly get a yes or no depending on whether the variables are instantiated to the same value.

What if one or both are not instantiated?

In that case, the = operator makes them variables which share. So, if one is instantiated the other acquires the same value. If both are uninstantiated, they are just linked together; then when one becomes instantiated, the other will get the same value.

What are the other important comparison operators?

As we saw, we usually want to check if two numbers are equal, and, if not, which is smaller. Prolog, like most programming languages, provides the less-than operator <, (the goal **?- 2 < 3**) will succeed, and the goal **?- 4 < 3.** will fail) and the greater-than operator >. Most implementations also provide:

< > or \ =	not equal to
> =	greater than or equal to
= <	equal to or less than

Sometimes the last operator is in the form < =.

Let us consider a simple program which uses one of these operators. Let us suppose we have a database which contains facts about the age of various people in the form:

```
age(reagan,74).
age(smith,22).
age(jones,31).
age(franklin,66).
age(johnson, 16).
age(robinson,14).
```

and so on.

How can we design a program or define a predicate under30 *which will examine this database and print out the names of all the persons whose age is less than 30 years? (Write your answer before reading further.)*

You can define such a predicate as shown below:

```
under30(Person) :- age(Person,Age), Age < 30.
```

Notice that the facts in the database have the predicate age with "a" in lowercase. We can therefore use a variable Age (with uppercase A) without causing any problems.

Suppose we want to modify the under30 *program so that it will print out not only the name of the person, but his or her age as well. What change is necessary? (Write your answer before reading further.)*

Change the head of the rule to **under30(Person,Age)**. With this change, instead of just giving an output such as **Person = smith**, etc., the output will be of the form: **Person = smith, Age = 22**, etc.

What about comparing symbols other than numbers?

The comparison operators we have seen above work with single characters or with sequences of characters. The goal **?- a = a**, would succeed, and the goal **?- a = b** will fail. Similarly, if we use an uninstantiated variable X, the effect of **?- X = a.** will be to instantiate X to have the value **a** (character).

When we use the > or < operators with characters, Prolog takes it to mean that < is earlier in alphabetic order, and > later in alphabetic order. So, the question **?- p < q.** will produce a "yes" response, and **?- c > d.** will produce a "no" response.

Remember, any sequence of characters starting with a lowercase letter is called an *atom*. The comparison operators will operate with atoms, too. The goal **?- apple<apricot.** will produce a "yes" response, and **?-apple>orange.** will produce a "no" response.

How can we design a Prolog predicate* bigger *which has three arguments and, given some numbers for the first two, will instantiate the third argument, a variable, to a value which is the larger of the two numbers? (Write down your answer before reading on.)

Let us start by asking ourselves: What would be the question I would ask? This is generally a good way to begin designing a Prolog program. As you can see in this example, it immediately suggests that we might want to ask something like

```
?-bigger(6,4, What).
```

We will have to think in terms of a head for the rule which has three arguments, and this gives us a place to start, when we try expressing the specification in Prolog. Also, we can express the logic of what we want as follows: The bigger of the first and second numbers if the first *if* the first is greater than the second. If this fails, the bigger of the two is the second number.

Once put this way it is straightforward to code it in Prolog as:

```
a) bigger(First,Second,First) :- First > Second.
b) bigger(First,Second, Second).
```

We see that what rule (a) tells us is that if First is greater than Second, the third argument should be made the same as the first. Rule (b) tells us that if rule (a) fails, the second argument is what should be displayed as the result.

If we ask a question like:

```
?- bigger(6,4,What).
```

the pattern-matching principles we have considered tell us that having instantiated First to 6 and Second to 4, the system will be able to satisfy the goal **First> Second**. The rule will succeed, and What will be instantiated to the same value as First; the response will be **What = 6.**

Think about rule (b) given above. Does there seem to be something wrong with it? (Write your answer before reading further.)

This question is intended to remind you of the key principle that Prolog always searches the clauses in the database in the order in which they appear in the database. By itself, rule (b) seems to say that Second is always the bigger of First and Second. But remember, Prolog will try this rule *only* if it has failed on rule (a).

Could we put rule (b) as:

```
bigger(First,Second,Second) :- First < Second.
```

or would this cause some problem? (Write your answer before reading further.)

Provided First and Second are different, it should work. but if we ask a question

```
?- bigger(4,4,What).
```

it will fail on both rules.

If we ask the question:

```
?- bigger(4,4,What).
```

which is the rule which gives us the answer, (a) or (b)? (Write your answer before reading further.)

This question is intended to give you practice in following Prolog's actions as it starts at the top of the database. When Prolog tries to match **bigger(4,4,What)** with rule (a), it identifies the first 4 with First in the head of the rule, and the second 4 with Second in the head of the rule. The body of the rule says **First > Second**, and so this rule will fail since both First and Second have been instantiated to the value 4. Prolog will go down the database and try the next rule which has **bigger** as the predicate, i.e., rule (b). This rule has no body, just a head which says

```
bigger(First,Second,Second).
```

This is the rule which succeeds and gives the result, **What = 4**. When we use the **bigger** program with two equal numbers, it is the second which is picked up by the program.

Are there any other operators which are useful for comparisons?

The comparison operators we have considered for greater-than, less-than, equal-to, not-equal-to, etc., can often be conveniently used in combination with another built-in operator, the word "not." The effect of **not** is that it reverses the condition which follows it. For instance, if we ask

```
?-not(3>4).
```

we would get a "yes" response, since it is true that 3 is not greater than 4.

Can "not" be used in other situations as well?

Yes. We could say **not ( )** and put any goal within the parentheses when the condition we want is that the goal should fail rather than succeed.

We will see some more applications of the arithmetic operator after we have studied the use of lists of data items in chapter 6. Try the following exercises to familiarize yourself with the arithmetic and comparison operators. If you are using a version of Prolog, you may find that the built-in comparison operators in your version may be slightly different from what I have given above.

Exercises

1) We saw how to design a predicate **sum** with three arguments so that when we supply any two of the arguments we can get the third, and both addition and subtraction can be handled.
   Design a similar predicate, **product**, for handling multiplication and division.

2) We have a database of facts containing information about the average income of persons living in various countries of the world, given below:

```
average_income(australia,11490).
average_income(canada,12310).
average_income(denmark,11570).
average_income(finland,10740).
average_income(france,10500).
average_income(japan,10120).
average_income(kuwait,17880).
average_income(norway,14020).
average_income(spain,4780).
average_income(saudi_arabia,12230).
average_income(sweden,12470).
average_income(switzerland,16290).
average_income(u_a_e,22870).
```

```
average_income(u_s_a,14100).
average_income(west_germany,11430).
```

a) How can we ask a question to find out the average income in a particular country, say Switzerland?
b) How would you ask a two-goal question which will find out the names of countries in which the average income is higher than in the United States?
c) How would you ask a two-goal question to find out the names of countries in which the average income is lower than it is in the United States?
d) Design a rule, with two arguments for the head goal, so it can be used for both (b) and (c) above, and also in general for comparing the average income of any two countries.

3) Suppose we have a database giving details about the winners of the Wimbledon tennis championships as well as the U.S. Open tennis championships, listing the year, name and nationality of the winner. This is done separately for the men's and women's championship, as follows:

```
wimbledon(men,1985,becker,west_germany).
wimbledon(men,1984,mcenroe,u_s_a).
wimbledon(men,1983,mcenroe,u_s_a).
wimbledon(men,1982,connors,u_s_a).
wimbledon(men,1981,mcenroe,u_s_a).
wimbledon(men,1980,borg,sweden).
wimbledon(men,1979,borg,sweden).
wimbledon(men,1978,borg,sweden).
wimbledon(men,1977,borg,sweden).
wimbledon(men,1976,borg,sweden).
wimbledon(women,1985,navratilova,u_s_a).
wimbledon(women,1984,navratilova,u_s_a).
wimbledon(women,1983,navratilova,u_s_a).
wimbledon(women,1982,navratilova,u_s_a).
wimbledon(women,1981,lloyd,u_s_a).
wimbledon(women,1980,goolagong,australia).
wimbledon(women,1979,navratilova,u_s_a).
wimbledon(women,1978,navratilova,u_s_a).
wimbledon(women,1977,navratilova,u_s_a).

u_s_open(men,1985,lendl,czechoslovakia).
u_s_open(men,1984,mcenroe,u_s_a).
u_s_open(men,1983,connors,u_s_a).
u_s_open(men,1982,connors,u_s_a).
u_s_open(men,1981,mcenroe,u_s_a).
u_s_open(men,1980,mcenroe,u_s_a).
u_s_open(men,1979,mcenroe,u_s_a).
u_s_open(men,1978,connors,u_s_a).
u_s_open(men,1977,vilas,argentina).
```

```
u_s_open(women,1985,mandalikova,czechoslovakia).
u_s_open(women,1984,navratilova,u_s_a).
u_s_open(women,1983,navratilova,u_s_a).
u_s_open(women,1982,lloyd,u_s_a).
u_s_open(women,1981,austin,u_s_a).
u_s_open(women,1980,lloyd,u_s_a).
u_s_open(women,1979,austin,u_s_a).
u_s_open(women,1978,lloyd,u_s_a).
```

a) How would we ask a question to find out who won Wimbledon in a particular year?
b) How would we ask a question to find out if a particular player won the U.S. Open at any time, and, if so, in which year?
c) How would we ask a multiple goal question to find out the names of any players who won both the U.S. Open and Wimbledon in the same year? How could we design a suitable rule for finding this information?
d) How would you design a rule which will give us the names of players *other than* from a particular country? For instance, if we want to find out which non-U.S. player won the U.S. Open, and when, we should be able to use the rule for this purpose.
e) Design a rule which will extract the names of players who won the U.S. Open more than once.
f) Design a rule which will find the names of persons who won in three successive years. The answer should display the name of the person and also the years in which the person won.

4) Suppose we have created a database with information about Nobel prize winners, giving details of the year they won the prize and the field in which they won it, as follows:

```
winner(1901,roentgen,physics).
winner(1901,hoff,chemistry).
winner(1918,planck,physics).
winner(1921,einstein,physics).
winner(1954,pauling,chemistry).
winner(1954,hemingway,literature).
winner(1906,roosevelt,peace).
winner(1952,schweitzer,peace).
winner(1962,pauling,peace).
winner(1980,klein,economics).
winner(1983,debreu,economics).
```

and so on.

a) How would you frame a question to find out who won prizes in a particular year?
b) How would you frame a question to find out the year and subject for which a particular person (Roosevelt, for example) won the prize?

c) How would you frame a question to find the names of persons who won the Nobel prize in two different fields?
d) Design a rule for part c above.

5) Suppose we have created a database with the following information about some of the presidents of the United States, giving their names and the years in which they began and ended their terms as President:

```
president(washington,george,1789,1797).
president(adams,john,1797,1801).
president(jefferson,thomas,1801,1809).
president(madison,james,1809,1817).
president(adams,john_quincy,1825,1829).
president(tyler,john,1841,1845).
president(buchanan,james,1857,1861).
```

a) How would you frame a question to find the last names of all the presidents with a particular first name?
b) How would you frame a multiple-goal question to get the names of two presidents with the same first name?
c) Convert the multiple-goal question in (b) into a suitable rule.

Chapter 5

Prolog in Perspective

In this chapter we will look at the origins and background of Prolog. The details of programming in Prolog which we have already seen will be used to illustrate what is distinctive about Prolog and makes it different from conventional programming languages, and why it holds promise for better communication between human beings and computers, as well as for designing programs for solving problems which at present are at the limits of what computers can do for us.

Why has Prolog started receiving more and more publicity in the last few years?

The major reason for Prolog's rise in prominence is connected with the fact that Japan announced a few years ago that Prolog would play a key role in the new types of hardware and software they are developing for the 1990s.

In October 1981, Japan's Ministry of International Trade and Industry organized an International Conference on Fifth Generation Systems, which was attended by leading computer scientists from all over the world. At this conference Japan announced the details of their plans for the next decade.

The principal aim of their Fifth Generation Computer Systems Project is to develop systems which are "handy" for the user. It was also announced that Prolog would play a key role in the development of the Knowledge Information Processing Systems (KIPS), which are the major goal of the project.

Until the conference, Prolog was a language used by a number of researchers in artificial intelligence, especially in Europe, and was not well-known outside these circles. It was originally designed to be a more convenient language for "natural language processing," by Professor Alain Colmerauer and his associates at the University of Marseilles in 1972; it was meant to enable people to communicate with computers in languages like English or French rather than in artificial programming languages. Prolog had subsequently been used at various universities, including the Universities of Edinburgh and London.

The Institute for New Generation Computer Technology (ICOT), set up by Japan to handle the Fifth Generation Project, organized a Second International Conference in November 1984. The report given at this conference regarding progress in the project showed that Prolog was indeed a central part.

A "kernel" language, KL0 for all software in the project has been created; KL0 is an extension of Prolog. The new hardware being developed is called the Personal Sequential Inference Machine (PSI), and its machine language is KL0. Prolog obviously will play a key role; it will not be Prolog as it is today, but languages based on Prolog, which will be the important languages of the future.

What is special about Prolog, and why is it of particular relevance to the goals of the Fifth Generation Project?

Prolog is a logic programming language. Its name is a portmanteau word derived from PROgramming in LOGic. To appreciate the difference between declarative programming, including programming in logic, and programming in other languages, it is useful to consider briefly the evolution and purpose of programming languages.

In the earliest day, instructions had to be given to the computer in the form of numbers which were codes for the different actions the computer could carry out. Suppose the task we want to carry out is an arithmetic task, adding two numbers. There might be a code number to instruct the computer to copy a particular number from a specific location in its memory into the arithmetic unit. There might be another code to tell the computer to fetch a second number from another location, yet another code to tell the arithmetic unit to add the two numbers, and one more code for storing the result in the main memory.

All of this required the programmer always to think in terms of the limited set of actions the hardware could carry out. The surprising fact is that only a very simple or limited set of actions is required for the computer to carry out any information processing task whatever: moving information to and from storage to a processing unit, simple arithmetic operations, comparisons, etc. The art of programming consisted of finding ways to express any complex task in terms of these very simple operations and giving the series of numbers which represented these actions in proper sequence.

In the next stage of programming, instead of number codes the programmer could use words like MOVE, ADD, COMPARE, and STORE (called *mnemonics*) which were translated into the appropriate number codes by a program designed for such translation, which was loaded into the computer first. This was "assembly language" programming, so called because the translator program "assembled" the mnemonics into numeric codes which would activate the hardware of the computer.

In the next step towards making programming easier for humans, "high-level languages" like Fortran, COBOL, BASIC, Pascal, and others were developed. These made communication with the computer easier because the user did not have to give instructions which matched one-to-one with the actions the computer could carry out. In assembly language the user has to give one instruction for each step, like "move the first number from the main memory to the arithmetic unit," then "move the second number,", then "add the two numbers," and so on. In a high-level language, the user could give a compound instruction like:

```
Result := First + Second ;
```

which would be translated into the step-by-step specification the computer can act upon. These translators (called *compilers* or *interpreters*) are more sophisticated and go through more steps to produce the "machine code" required for the computer to respond.

You can see that the way the user communicates with the computer has become more *declarative:* the user describes what is required to be done, rather than giving a series of explicit commands (imperative programming), the high-level languages still included a significant amount of imperative features.

The most significant feature of the logic programming approach is that it tries to make programming as declarative as possible. The user of a logic programming language has only to give a logic specification of the problem, describing the relationship between the data to be processed and the results required. The Prolog interpreter translates the description of the problem into a series of instructions which can be executed by the computer. By requiring the user to give only a description of the problem instead of a detailed procedure, logic programming takes a step further along the process of making human-computer communication easier for humans.

How do the examples of Prolog programs we have seen in the earlier chapters tie in with these ideas?

To illustrate this point, let us look at one of the Prolog programs from an earlier chapter. We had a Prolog database containing information about first names of various persons, such as: **first_name(reagan,ronald)**, **first_name(thatcher,margaret)**, etc. To find the first name of Thatcher, a number of procedural steps were involved. The database had to be searched, the first argument of the fact had to be compared to see if it was **thatcher**. If so, the second argument had to be displayed. If not, the process of checking had to be repeated (*iterated*) with the next fact in the database, and this was repeated until the search was successful or there were no unchecked facts. In a conventional programming language it would be necessary to explicity describe this series of actions, but in Prolog we have only to declare the goal to be sought.

This feature of declarative programming becomes even clearer when we look at examples which involve multiple goals or rules and depend for their operation on backtracking. Look again at the database of Nobel prize winners, with a predicate of **winner**, and arguments which gave the year, the name of the person, and the field in which the prize was awarded. To find out whether any person had won the prize in two different fields, all we had to do was to describe what we wanted, as a combination of three goals:

```
winner(Year1,Person,Field1),
    winner(Year2,Person,Field2),
        Field1 < > Field2.
```

This is not quite the same as an informal description in English, but is fairly close. In contrast, a similarly organized collection of data processed using a conventional programming language would require a long list of detailed, explicit instructions.

There are two important concepts underlying this whole process by which Prolog, or any logic programming language, works. They are generally attributed to Professor Robert Kowalski of the Imperial College of Science and Technology, London. The first of his insights can be summarized in terms of an equation:

PROGRAM = ALGORITHM + CONTROL.

What is an "algorithm" and what does this equation signify?

Algorithm is a word used in mathematics and computer science to mean a systematic description of a procedure for solving a problem. We say there is an algorithm for solving a problem if we can logically establish that the finite series of steps to be taken will either lead to a solution or will tell us the problem cannot be solved. There would be no possibility of endless searching, not knowing whether we can find a solution or not, and we are guaranteed that we have the best solution possible for the problem.

(Historically the word *algorithm* is derived from the name of an Arab mathematician of the 10th century A.D., who wrote a book setting out systematic procedures for solving various mathematical problems. He was called Al-Khwarizimi.)

The significance of Kowalski's equation is that it highlights the two important aspects of getting a computer to carry out a task. The first is the "algorithm" aspect—that is, the steps to be taken must be clearly specified, and we must have satisfied ourselves that these steps will lead to the solution (if there is one) or show that there is no solution. The second aspect is that the program needs information about coordinating or controlling the various parts of the solution procedure, referred to as the "control" aspect.

Kowalski suggested that in conventional programming languages these two different aspects are not clearly distinguished; a style of programming in which they are separated would be much more convenient because one could focus on improving the solution procedure without taking into account the problems of how the computer would implement the procedure. This is precisely the separation of the two aspects of programming which the declarative style of programming, of which logic programmming is an example, tries to capture.

What is the second major insight mentioned above that is helpful in understanding the nature of declarative programming?

The second insight is very directly connected with "programming in logic." It has to do with the way in which we represent the information to be used by the computer.

We have represented information using two key concepts: First, we can think of information as relationships between various objects. We used this as the basis of representing information in the form

<predicate>(various arguments).

This way of representing information is known as the *predicate form* and it has a long history. We also say that essentially the same predicate form can be used in rules, with the difference that we use a relationship between the predicate or goal in the head of the rule and the various goals in the body of the rule, connecting them by the symbol :-, which could be interpreted as "if." Logical conclusions which depend on other facts or rules are also essentially represented, by way of rules, in a predicate form.

Kowalski pointed out that this method of representing information using predicate logic has a built-in advantage. From the point of view of the designer of the program, it is a description or declaration of the nature of the problem to be solved. But at the same time it can be interpreted as implying a set of steps, a procedure which should be carried out. This is usually referred to as the *procedural interpretation* of the logical or declarative specification of the problem.

What would be an example the procedural interpretation of a logical description?

In fact, in discussing the various Prolog programs we have tried to understand them by using the procedural interpretation implicitly contained in any logical description of a problem. For instance, one of the examples we considered was a rule:

```
find__by__title(Country,Title,Who,Name) :-
     chief__exec(Country,Title,Who),
      first__name(Who,What).
```

and we analyzed how this rule would work in conjunction with a database of facts with predicates of the types:

```
chief__exec(usa,president,reagan).
  first__name(reagan,ronald)
```

etc.

To understand how this rule works when we ask a question, we see that the description of a head goal in terms of two body goals asks Prolog to satisfy both the body goals. We saw that this means satisfying each body goal by requiring Prolog to conduct a series of steps to match patterns in the database, pass instantiated values to the right, backtrack when necessary, etc.

The interpretation of the description as a series of steps or a procedure is an inherent feature of the Prolog system. Kowalski's assertion—that every logical description using predicate-and-objects form and rules with head and body goals can be interpreted as implying a series of steps—pointed the way to design of Prolog interpreters which would translate the procedural interpretation into a working software system.

We can say that using predicate logic to represent information has two advantages: allowing a declarative specification by the user which is at the same time capable of a procedural interpretation by the Prolog system, and separating the control aspects of programming from the solution design aspects of programming.

What would be examples of how the control aspect of programming is implicitly handled

by the Prolog system, instead of having to be explicitly specified by the programmer?

Whenever we put in two or more clauses with the same predicate, we are saying, in effect "*If* the first clause fails, *then* try the second, and if this fails too, *then* try the third, and so on." The control information is embedded in the Prolog program, though it is not explicitly set out.

There is a closely related built-in predicate for control which we have not used in any of the examples. We have looked at rules where the body of the rule has two or more goals separated by a comma, and we saw that this comma really means *and* (try to satisfy the first goal and the second goal and the third goal, and so on). In exactly the same way, if we separate the goals in the body of the rule by a semicolon it means try the first goal, and if it fails, try the second goal as an alternative, and if it fails . . . . in other words, the semicolon conveys the meaning of *or*. This is an implicit control mechanism, asking the system to try alternative ways of satisfying the head goal, so that if we have:

```
goal a   :-   goal b   ;   goal c   ;   goal d.
```

it means there are three alternative ways of satisfying the head goal.

Normally programs are more readable if we do not use the semicolon and instead put them as separate clauses, which is what we have done in the examples so far:

```
goal a :- goal b.
goal a :- goal c.
```

What is another major aspect of control in most programming languages and how is it built into Prolog?

A second major idea in the control aspect of programming is that there should be provision for repeating the same set of actions. When processing a number of sets of data, all of which have to be processed in the same way, essentially the same action is repeated on the different groups of information. In most programming languages this has to be explicitly provided for in the program. The typical instruction one would find, for instance in Pascal, would be something like:

```
FOR COUNT := 1 TO 10 DO
    BEGIN
     { various actions like read the data, process it in a particular way, display
       or print the results , etc. }
         END
```

which would be understood by the computer to mean that the whole set of actions contained between **BEGIN** and **END** should be repeated 10 times.

We have seen that such repetitive, or *looping* action in Prolog is something the programmer does not have to attend to in detail. To get multiple solutions, for instance, the system takes over the task of arranging repetition of the search, and all the user has to do is to prompt for repetitions. Whenever there is backtracking there is implicitly a repetition of the same kind of search procedure over and over again.

Since the aim of the Fifth Generation Project is to develop systems which are as handy as possible for the user, you can see why logic programming is the appropriate tool for building such systems. The natural way in which human beings think of problems is in terms of a logical specification of what the goals are in relation to the available data, and this is what a declarative description amounts to.

The difference between the new type of programming and conventional programming is not absolute. Even in conventional programs there are declarative aspects, and even in Prolog one has sometimes to give commands. The difference is really a question of emphasis.

The "fifth generation" systems, envisaged in the Japanese project, are not restricted to more handy ways of programming. In fact, they involve a significant new approach to the whole question of the *role* of a computer system. As mentioned earlier, the reports of the project refer to Knowledge Information Processing Systems (KIPS). This is meant to emphasize that the goal is something more than ordinary data processing, and is concerned with "knowledge." This brings the project into the realm of artificial intelligence.

What is the definition of artificial intelligence?

Though there is no rigid definition of artificial intelligence, broadly speaking it is the field of study concerned with trying to make computers smarter than they are today. Another way of describing this would be to say that artificial intelligence tries to make computers do more and more things which, when they are done by human beings, we describe as "intelligent." (This is essentially the definition given by Professor Marvin Minsky, one of the leaders in this field.) Among other things, it includes the field of expert systems—designing programs which emulate the working of human experts.

Logic programming represents a trend towards fuller use of the computer as an aid to problem solving. Historically, computers were designed to help in problems where the focus was on manipulation of numbers. But at the same time, work on nonnumeric applications, or symbol-processing applications, was also being carried out. Fields in which the emphasis is less on calculations than on general symbolic manipulation are: voice recognition, developing capabilities for computers to respond to natural language, playing games like chess, and so on. The approaches to programming and the programming languages which are most useful for numeric processing are not really well-suited for these other tasks. Among the different languages developed for such applications, the most famous is LISP, which was designed at MIT in the 1960s and is perhaps the language most widely used in artificial intelligence applications.

It would be helpful to keep in mind that ultimately the purpose of any programming language is to provide the user with a different type of "virtual machine," using the same physical hardware. The design of the hardware, and of the actual operations it can carry out, are of concern to the computer engineer. But the questions of interest to the user is: What does it do ? How can I make it do what I want it to do?

It is here that the concept of a *virtual machine* becomes important. When we load a word-processing software package, the hardware in conjunction with the package makes it a machine which will respond to instructions. Using the same physical devices, if we load a different piece of software (such as a spreadsheet), we would have a different virtual machine which performs different functions in a different way.

We may think of different programming languages as tools for us to combine with the hardware to produce a virtual machine appropriate for a different purpose. There are hundreds of programming languages; for illustration let us consider the most widely used languages, like Fortran, COBOL, BASIC or Pascal.

Fortran gives us a virtual machine which is most helpful when we want to carry out the kind of numeric calculations which are used in scientific calculations. COBOL gives us a virtual machine convenient for tasks involving rearranging and organizing a lot of data into reports etc, with some amount of calculations; these are the kind of tasks most often found in business data processing.

Pascal's strength is in emphasizing on the basic principles of designing programs; it is more general-purpose, is used as the primary teaching language in universities, and can be used for a wide variety of applications. BASIC gives us a virtual machine most convenient for writing short programs for quick use, and this, combined with the fact that it generally requires less hardware memory, makes it a popular choice in circumstances where its strengths come into play.

These distinctions are not clear cut; with a little exaggeration, you may say that one can carry out any information processing task using any of the major languages; particular types of applications will simply be much more convenient in some languages than in others. From this perspective, we can say that Prolog's strength is in applications where we want a virtual machine that will respond to logical descriptions of our problems, and will take over the job of converting to a suitable machine-executable procedure.

Artificial intelligence applications, and especially expert systems, are areas where Prolog has an advantage. In particular, Prolog is handy in applications where the information has some kind of inherent structure—the items are related or linked together according to some pattern. An illustration is the "natural languages" used by human beings; the natural structure of sentences is in terms of relationships between individual items, such as the subject of a sentence, the verb or predicate, the adjectives, the adverbs, and so on. The rules governing such structures make up the grammar or *syntax* of the language.

Once again, it is useful to keep in mind the general principle that for every programming language or software package, a clue to its value is given by thinking in terms of: What does it do? What kind of communications from the user does it respond to? What tasks are more convenient in this language or using this package?

Another illustration of the general usefulness of a declarative or nonprocedural approach is provided by looking at software for word processing or spreadsheet calculations. They can be fairly described as nonprocedural "languages." However, each has a narrow range of problems with which they can deal conveniently. Contrasted with them, Prolog or LISP can be thought of as more flexible in the kind of problems they can handle declaratively.

The description of the Fifth Generation Project given in this chapter has been very brief. Some references are given below which give more detail about the project. The book by Feigenbaum and McCorduck gives a lot of thought-provoking discussion of what the implications of the Japanese project are for the rest of the world.

References

1) Bramer, Max. "The Japanese Fifth Generation Project." In *New Information Technology*, edited by Alan Burns. New York: Ellis Horwood/John Wiley & Sons, 1984.
2) Feigenbaum, Edward, and McCorduck, Pamela. *The Fifth Generation.* New York: New American Library, 1984.
3) Johnstone, Bob. "Japan Unveils Its Fifth Generation." *New Scientist,* 8 November 1984, 10ff.
4) Manuel, Tom. "Cautiously Optimistic Tone Set for 5th Generation." *Electronics Week,* 3 December 1984, 57ff.

Chapter 6

Using Lists and Recursion

In this chapter we will look at some aspects of Prolog which illustrate the declarative style of programming. The two useful concepts we will focus on are the use of *lists* of data, and *recursion*.

Lists of items or lists of persons are familiar to all of us. It is often helpful to group sets of connected data into a list and deal with the list as a single entity, rather than dealing with the individual *elements* of the list.

The concept of the list is very important in programming, especially when carrying out *nonnumeric processing*—dealing with items of information to be processed in other ways than by arithmetic operations. The operations useful for dealing with such data are adding new items to a list, deleting items, extracting particular items, or rearranging the order of the items.

Prolog provides some very easy and concise ways of carrying out operations on lists, or *list processing*. List processing is particularly important in the field of artificial intelligence, designing programs for tasks like game playing, optical recognition, speech recognition, robotics, natural language communication with computers, and other tasks on the frontier of computer capabilities. The key language used in this field is LISP, a portmanteau for "List Processing Language."

How is a list defined?

One way to define a list is to say that it is an *ordered* sequence of items; each item in the list has a position relative to the others. The list of names **[mary,tom,anne]** is different from the list **[anne,mary,tom]** because the order has changed and the items are in different positions in the list. I have shown the items enclosed by square brackets and the items in the list separated by commas. This is one of the two ways we represent lists in Prolog.

A second definition of a list, which is particularly convenient for list-processing Prolog programs, leads into the idea of *recursion*.

What is the alternative definition of a list?

The other definition of a list is really a different way of looking at a list. First we say that a list can be an empty list, with no elements in it. We represent this in Prolog by a pair of empty brackets, [ ]. Second, a list which is not empty has two parts. The first part is the first element of the list, called the *head* of the list. When the head of a list is removed from a list, what is left is also a list, called the *tail* of the list. We represent this in Prolog by **[A¦B]**, where A is the head, and B is the tail.

To make the definition complete, we should also say what an element is. An *element* of a list can be an atom, a number, or even a list.

Does this definition cover all types of lists?

The simplest case is of a list containing no items at all, the empty list, which is covered by our definition.

The next simplest list contains one item. Our definition covers this case, because when we remove the first item, or head, we are left with an empty list, which qualifies as a list.

If we have two items, when we remove the head, we have one item left, which is covered by the definition and fits the definition of a list with one item.

We can extend this item indefinitely, so the definition always remains true: when we remove the head, what is left is a list. We can also check the definition in reverse.

Let us look again at the alternative way in which lists are represented in Prolog, by using a notation of the form **[A¦B]**., where A represents the head of the list, and B represents the tail of the list. Always remember that the tail is itself a list.

What is a simple Prolog program, using this notation, which checks whether a particular data item is a list?

Consider the following two clauses with a predicate **is_list**:

```
is_list([ ]).
is_list( [Head ¦ Tail] ) :- is_list(Tail).
```

Using the general pattern matching principles we have considered earlier, let us consider how Prolog will respond to a question:

```
?- is_list( [mary,john,anne]).
```

You can see that it will not be able to match the pattern of the question with the first **is_list** clause, so it will go down the database and try the second clause, which is a rule. The question and the head of the rule match by instantiating Head to **mary** and Tail to **[john,anne]**. Now the body of the rule asks for a solution of the question: **is_list([john,anne])**. To satisfy this goal, once again Prolog starts at the top of the database, and fails on the first clause. It again tries the second clause, which leads it to try the goal: **is_list([anne])**. This in turn will lead it to try the goal **is_list([ ])**. Prolog succeeds using the first **is_list** clause, and responds "yes" to our question.

Why is this second definition of a list called a recursive definition?

A *recursive definition* is a definition in which the definition includes the concept being defined. In the second part of the definition of a list, and in the second **is_list** clause which translates this into Prolog, it is said that something is a list if, after the first item is removed, what remains is a list. In other words, our definition of a list includes the concept of a list.

Doesn't this make it a circular definition?

Not quite. The difference between a recursive definition and a circular definition is that a recursive definition does not go 'round in an endless circle. For example, when we ask if something is a list, we are told that it is, if its tail is a list. To find out if the tail is a list, we have to find out if *its* tail is a list. And to verify this, we have to verify whether the tail of the tail of the original list is a list . . . and so on. What prevents this from becoming an endless process? As we saw, at some stage, the tail of the tail of the tail . . . of the original list becomes the empty list. Now, we have another definition which tells us that an empty list is a list. When this stage is reached, the recursion stops.

This is a key characteristic of recursive definitions. There are two parts: the recursive part, where something seems to be circularly defined in terms of itself, and the *boundary condition* which stops the recursion from going on forever. In the above example the boundary condition is that an empty list is defined as a list.

Any other general facts about lists which should be remembered?

If we have an empty list, it has no head or tail. But if we have a list with even one item, we can identify the head, the first item, and the tail, which is the empty list.

What would be a simple Prolog program which will extract the head of a list?

Consider this program or clause:

```
head_of([Head | Tail], Head)
```

Having put this in the database, suppose we ask the question:

```
?- head_of ([a,b,c,d],What).
```

We can see by the principles of pattern matching that Prolog will match **[a]** with head, [b,c,d] with tail, and will treat What and Head as shared variables. It will display the solution: What = a.

Using the head_of clause above as a guide, write a clause which will display the tail of a given list. (Write your answer before reading further.)

How about this?

```
tail_of([Head | Tail], Tail)
```

The response to the question:

```
?-tail_of([a,b,c,d],What).
```

is

```
What = [b,c,d].
```

Remember, the tail of a list is always a list. We could also get a response to a question:

```
?- tail_of([a],What).
```

The response would be What =[ ].

What would be Prolog's response to this question?

```
?- head_of ( [ [1,2],3,4 ] , What ).
```

(Write your answer before reading further.)

This question introduces the concept that it is possible for an item in the list to be a list. In this case we have a list of three items, in which the first item is itself a list [1,2], whereas the second and third items are not lists. The response would be: What = [1,2].

What is another list processing operation which illustrates the concept of recursion?

A standard operation with lists, very handy in many applications, is that of combining two lists by "attaching" one to the end of the other to produce a single list. This is referred to as *appending* two lists. For example, if we append the two lists [a,b,c], and [d,e], we would get the single list [a,b,c,d,e].

Is there some generally helpful rule for developing recursive definitions?

There are two approaches to developing recursive definitions, and we will look at both of them. The first approach is based on the fundamental nature of recursion. We saw that the basic idea in recursion is to try to define something in terms of itself, but in such a way that ultimately we are led to the boundary condition. The natural question to ask about recursive definitions in list processing is: Can this operation on lists be defined in terms of a similar operation on the tail of a list? If we can do this, we know that we will be led to considering what happens when we deal with the tail of the tail of the tail . . . of the original list, and we know that will ultimately lead us to an empty list.

Trying that approach here, we can say that to append a list (**Firstlist**) to another list (**Secondlist**), we can isolate the head of the first list, append the tail of the first list to the second list, and then return the head of the first list as the head of the final list. For example, appending **[a,b,c]** to **[d,e,f]** is the same as appending **[b,c]** to **[d,e,f]** and then putting back **[a]** at the head of the resulting **[b,c,d,e,f]**. Looking at the problem this way enables us to write a recursive definition in Prolog:

```
append([Head|Tail],SecondList, [Head|NewTail]) :-
    append(Tail,SecondList,NewTail).
```

Now let us think of what happens as we "recurse." We set aside the first element of the first list and try to append the tail of the first list to the second list. To do this, we set aside the first element of this tail (the second element of the first list), and append the new tail from the third element onward to the second list. As we keep doing this, ultimately the tail of the tail of the tail . . . of the first list becomes empty. At this stage, appending it to the second list has an obvious solution: appending an empty list to another list leaves the second list unchanged. This gives us our boundary condition:

```
append([ ],Anylist,Anylist).
```

Will it make any difference whether we put the boundary condition first or the recursive rule first, in our database?

If we are going to use it to append two lists, by asking, for example:

```
?- append([a,b,c],[d,e,f],What).
```

it will make no difference. But in the exercises we will look at some other uses we can make of this same rule, and you will see that it makes a difference.

What is the second approach to developing recursive definition?

We saw above that we consider defining what we want to do in terms of doing the same thing with the tail of the list, until we ultimately reach the simple case represented by the boundary condition.

The second approach is to consider the simplest case first, and then see how the next simplest case can be "reduced" to the simplest case, and so on—a kind of "bootstrapping" of more and more elaborate cases, starting with the simplest case.

Let us think of the simplest case, in which the first list has no elements. All we have to do to append the empty list to some other list is to reproduce the second list.

The next slightly less simple case, has one item in the list. If we remove the head of this list, we are left with an empty list, and we know how to deal with this case. To carry out the operation of appending when the first list has one item, all we have to do is take out the first item, append the tail to the second list, and then place the first item of the first list as the head of the combined list. We can extend this to the case where we have two elements in the first list:

- ☐ Remove the head of the first list.
- ☐ Append the tail of the first list to the second list. We can do this because the tail of the first list has one item in it, and we have solved the problem of appending when the first list has a single item in it.
- ☐ Place the head of the first list as the head of the combined list.

You can see that we can extend this to handle the operation of appending, whatever the number of items in the first list. We see that we are really doing the same thing as in the first approach, but in reverse, starting with the boundary condition and building on it.

For our purposes, keep in mind that it is useful to think in terms of "recursing" until we reach the boundary condition, and sometimes it is helpful to think of the boundary condition first and then build up or "recurse in reverse" to the general case.

Using the two clauses for* append *which we have looked at above, suppose we put them in the database with the boundary condition first and next the recursive definition. What are the various steps by which Prolog processes this question?

```
?- append( [a,b,c], [d,e], What).
```

We know that Prolog tries the clauses with the same predicate in the order in which they appear in the database. Prolog will first try to match the question:

```
append( [ ], SecondList,SecondList).
```

This will fail because **[a,b,c]** cannot be matched with the empty list.

Prolog will then try the next **append** clause, which is a rule with a head and a tail. It will be able to successfully match the question with the head of the rule:

```
append([Head |Tail],SecondList,[Head |NewTail]).
```

by instantiating Head to **a**, Tail to **[b,c]**, and SecondList to **[d,e]**, and identifying **[a|[NewTail]** with What. Note that neither NewTail nor What has been allotted any value at this stage.

We know the next step in processing a rule is to replace the goal in the head of the rule by the goal(s) in the body of the rule. Prolog will now try the goal:

```
append( [b,c],[d,e],NewTail).
```

Complete the analysis in the last answer until you reach the stage where the boundary condition applies. (Write your answer before reading further.)

Prolog will try to satisfy the goal:

```
append([b,c,],[d,e],Newtail)
```

by trying the first **append** clause, and will fail. This leads it to try the second clause. It matches the head, and the body of the second clause will lead Prolog to try the goal:

```
append([c],[d,e],Newtail).
```

It will fail again with the first **append** clause, and again be led through the second clause to try:

```
append([ ],[d,e],NewTail).
```

This time it succeeds with the first clause, since the boundary condition has been reached.

Now it will in succession add back **c**, then **b**, then **a** to the head of the list **[d,e]**, giving a final result **What = [a,b,c,d,e]**.

One of the exercises at the end of this chapter asks you to consider what happens if we put the two clauses in the reverse order in the database and ask the same question.

The same variable seems to be used to mean different things at different stages. At one stage the program deals with:

```
append([b,c],[d,e],NewTail).
```

and at a later stage the program deals with:

```
append([ ],[d,e],NewTail).
```

How are the different "meanings" of NewTail at different stages kept distinct?

We should look now at an important aspect of how Prolog handles recursion. In the analysis above, at one stage Prolog tried to solve the goal:

```
append([b,c,],[d,e],NewTail).
```

At a later stage, it tried to solve the problem:

```
append( [ ],[d,e],NewTail).
```

Though the same name, NewTail, is used to represent different entities, Prolog keeps track of these different uses by using a form of storing information called a *stack*.

As the name suggests, a stack is something to which you add information on top of previous information. When you take information off a stack, what you placed on the stack last is taken off first.

At the stage where the goal is:

```
append([b,c],[d,e],NewTail).
```

we can think of Prolog as storing somewhere in memory all the relevant information, including the fact that the result of solving the problem is to be assigned to the variable NewTail. When in the process of solving this Prolog is led to solve the goal

```
append([c],[d,e],NewTail),
```

we can imagine that all this information is stacked on top of the information stored previously. When the problem is finally solved, the value of **NewTail = [d,e]** is used to go back to the stack and look at the problem:

```
append([c],[d,e],[c¦ NewTail) :-
      append([ ],[d,e],NewTail).
```

and get the result:

```
append([c],[d,e],[c,d,e]).
```

The problem of solving

```
append([c],[d,e],[c¦NewTail).
```

itself arose from the body of the previous application of the rule at the stage:

```
append([b,c],[d,e],[b¦ NewTail]) :-
      append([c,[d,e],NewTail).
```

Now Prolog can take this problem off the stack and know that the solution for the head goal is:

```
append([b,c],[d,e], [b,c,d,e]).
```

and by similarly "unstacking" the first problem, it gets the final result: **What = [a,b,c,d,e]**.

This process is sometimes referred to as "the unwinding of the recursion." Another way of describing it is to say that the results of each stage of the recursion are "passed back" to the previous stage of the recursion. We could say that a copy of the whole clause is made for each stage of recursion and kept on the stack. There is never any mix-up between the values for NewTail (or any other variables involved) in different stages of the recursion.

What would Prolog's response be to this question?

```
?- append(First,Second,[mary,john,anne]).
```

(Let us apply the general principle of pattern matching, keeping in mind the concepts of instantiation and sharing variables.)

This question emphasizes the fact that because of the fundamentally declarative nature of Prolog, the same program definition can be used in different ways. We saw that the append program gives us a combined list if we supply it with two lists. But because it is essentially a declaration saying that the combined list is formed by attaching the two lists, if we give it the combined list as information it will break it up into two parts which make up the list.

There are many ways to break up **[mary,john,anne]** into two lists which can be appended to produce the combined list. Let us analyze step by step the first result Prolog will give us.

The first clause:

```
append([ ],SecondList,SecondList),
```

will match with:

```
append(First,Second,[mary,john,anne]).
```

If First is instantiated to the empty list, and Second to **[mary,john,anne]**, the first solution Prolog will display is:

```
First = [ ] , Second = [mary,john,anne].
```

What happens if we ask for an alternative solution? Remember that when we ask for another solution after a goal has succeeded, Prolog looks at the marker it placed to indicate where the previous success was achieved, and goes down the database to the next clause for the required predicate. It will try the next **append** clause:

```
append([Head¦Tail],SecondList,[Head¦NewTail]) :-
      append(Tail,SecondList,NewTail).
```

It will try to match with the question, which it can do by instantiating **[Head¦NewTail]** to **[mary,john,anne]**, which means instantiating Head to **mary** and NewTail to **[john,anne]**. Now Prolog has to solve the goal in the body of the rule:

```
append(Tail,SecondList,[john,anne]).
```

This is the first time it tries this goal; we know from the previous analysis that the solution would be:

```
Tail = [ ] , SecondList = [john,anne].
```

These are the values "passed back" to the head of the rule, making it:

```
append([mary  [ ] ],[john,anne],[mary| [john,anne]).
```

This head was matched with:

```
append(First,Second,[mary,john,anne])
```

in the question. The solution which will be displayed is: First = [mary], Second = [john,anne].

At this point we have established a recursive relationship; the second solution can be solved by using the first solution. We already know that the first solution is to break up the list into [ ] and [john,anne]. Using this knowledge, we are able to say that the second solution is to break up the list into [mary] and [john,anne].

It is now only a matter of pursuing this same reasoning to say that the third solution can be solved by finding the second solution to:

```
append(First,Second,[john,anne]).
```

What we already know about the second solution to the original problem tells us that this second solution is to break it up into the sublists [john] and [anne], which leads us to conclude that the third solution must be the sublists [mary,john] and [anne]. And finally, the third solution should be the sublists [john,anne] and [ ], from which we can conclude that the fourth solution to the original problem must be [mary,john,anne] and [ ]. There cannot be a fifth solution to the original problem because that would require a fourth solution to finding sublists of [john,anne], which requires a third solution to finding sublists of [anne], which involves a second solution to finding sublists of [ ]. There is only one solution to finding sublists of [ ], because it can be broken into sublists only one way: [ ] and [ ].

Another very handy Prolog program is one for determining whether a particular item we are looking for is in a given list. This is usually called a "member" program. How can we analyze this task so as to express it in terms of a recursive definition with a boundary condition for the simplest case?

Let us think of it this way. There are three possibilities:

a) The item we want is not in the list.
b) The item is the first item in the list.
c) The item is in some other position in the list.

The simplest case is (a); we do not need a clause because if the goal fails on the clauses for the other possibilities, we know the third possibility is true.

Now let us consider possibility (b). We see this fits in well with our general concept of expressing a list as consisting of a head and a tail. We can express this in Prolog as:

```
member(Wanted,[Wanted|_]).
```

We use the anonymous variable when we have a variable whose allotted value we are not interested in knowing. If the item we are looking for is the first item, we do not care what the other items in the tail of the list are, so we use the anonymous variable for the tail of the list.

Now for possibility (c), where the item we are searching for is in some position other than the head of the list: this fits in well with a recursive description. We could say that when the required member is not the head of the list, it is still a member if it is a member of the tail of the list. This is recursive; if it is not the head of the list, we check to see if it is a member of the tail; if it is not the head of this tail, we check to see if it is a member of the tail of the tail . . . and so on. This process stops when either the required item turns out to be the head of the tail of the tail of the tail . . . or the tail of the tail of the tail . . . becomes empty, in which case the program fails, because there is no further tail (of an empty list) which could be checked.

We have two boundary conditions which stop further recursion. But one of them doesn't need a specific clause, since it stops by failure of the program.

We can express the recursive part of the definition by:

```
member(Wanted,[Wanted| Tail]) :-
    member(Wanted,Tail).
```

Obviously, if we ask a question like:

```
?-member(a,[b,c,a,d]).
```

This program will work by recursion to give us a "yes" response, whereas a question like:

```
?-member(p,[a,b,c,d])
```

will recurse to where both clauses fail to match **member(p,[ ])** with the result that we would get a "no" response.

Let us look at another way of using the **member** ***program. How will Prolog respond if we ask this question?***

```
?-member(Which,[a,b,c]).
```

Intuitively, we can see that this should produce multiple answers, **Which = a**, **Which = b**, etc. But it would be good to reinforce the concepts of recursion to analyze the steps involved.

First, the match will be with the first member clause, instantiating Wanted to **a** and treating **[b,c,d]** as the value of the anonymous variable. If we ask for an alternative solution, because the marker for the previous success is at the first member clause, Prolog will now try the second clause.

When the question:

```
?-member(Which,[a,b,c,d])
```

is matched with the head of the second clause:

```
member(Wanted,[Head¦Tail])
```

what are the instantiations which occur? (Write your answer before reading further.)

This question reminds you about sharing variables. At this stage neither Which nor Wanted will be allotted a value, but they will be identified as shared variables, so that any instantiation made of one will also apply to the other. Head is instantiated to **a**, and Tail to **[b,c,d]**.

The goal in the body of the clause is tried: **member(Wanted ,[b,c,d])**. This problem is similar to the first solution to the original problem, so we know the solution is **Wanted = b**, and since Which and Wanted share, we will get the display **Which = b**.

Applying recursive reasoning, the third solution to **member(Which,[a,b,c,d])** will be the second solution to **member(Which,[b,c,d])**, which in turn is the first solution to **member(Which,[c,d])**, which we know is **c**. And finally, the fourth solution will be **d**, and there will be no fifth solution, for that requires the first solution to **member(Which,[ ])**, which will fail on both clauses.

We should keep in mind that Which at the different stages of the recursion represents different entities, and the separateness is preserved by keeping different copies of the program for different stages of the recursion on a stack.

We have seen simple items of data as arguments of a data statement, and also of lists. Are there any other types of data?

In Prolog the general concept of data is in the form of a structure of items, which may themselves have structure, and lists are only one example of such structures. We will discuss the concept of structure in the next chapter. Meanwhile, let us look at one more example of using recursion.

How can we write a recursive program to find the largest number in a given list of numbers?

You could give the declarative description of the problem as follows. To find the largest number in the list, if the first number is smaller than the second, drop the first number and find the largest number in the rest of the list; otherwise, drop the second number and then find the largest number in what remains of the list.

The definition is one you will recognize as recursive. Let us try the bootstrap approach, and looking first for the simplest case or boundary condition: if there is only one number in the list, that number is the largest in the list. We can put this as a Prolog rule:

```
1) largest([Single],Single).
```

Notice that this does not require a body to the rule. On the basis of the pattern-matching principles, a question like:

```
?-largest([4],What).
```

will lead to the response: **What = 4**.

Now we have to consider the recursive part of the rule, when the list contains more than one number. As we have seen, Prolog lets us represent any list as a head element and a tail list containing all the other elements in the list. In this case we need to look at the first and second numbers in the list, so we use a slightly different representation in the two rules which follow:

```
2) largest([First, Second¦ Tail], Result) :-
       First < Second,
     largest([Second ¦Tail], Result),
        !.

3) largest([First, Second ¦Tail], Result) :-
     largest([First  Tail], Result).
```

In these two rules, because we want to distinguish the first element from the second element, we represent the elements individually as **First,Second**, and treat the rest of the elements as the Tail, using the tail(¦) notation. We see that rule 2 handles the case where the first element is smaller than the second, by dropping the first element and recursing on the rest of the list. When rule 2 fails, we go to rule 3, which drops the second element and recurses on what is left of the list. In either case, ultimately the boundary condition rule 1 would be reached.

There are some other operations we might want to carry out with lists. For example, we might want to remove a particular element from the list, or we might remove the set of elements in one list from another list and so on. Some of these additional concepts are introduced in the exercises which follow; try writing your own programs and then comparing them with the solutions at the back of the book.

I have used the notation **[Head ¦ Tail]**, to indicate the head and tail of a list, which is provided by most Prolog systems. Some may use an alternative: **[Head,..Tail]**.

Exercises

1) We saw how to write a Prolog program which will extract the first item of a list. Use that program as a guide to write a similar recursive program which will ex-

tract the last item of a list.

2) We saw that the append program will combine two lists to produce a new list:

```
?-append([a,b],[c,d],What).
```

will give us the response What = [a,b,c,d]. What would happen if we asked the question:

```
?- append(First,[d,e],[a,b,c,d,e].?
```

Trace step by step the various matchings, instantiations, etc., which take place in the process of trying to satisfy this goal.

3) Suppose we change the order of the two clauses for **append** in our database, putting the recursive rule first and the boundary condition second. What difference would it make to the questions:

```
?-append([a,b],[c,d],What).
?-append(First,Second,[a,b,c,d,e]).
```

Analyze the various backtracking steps the program will take to answer these questions.

4) What would happen if we use the member program discussed in this chapter, and ask a question:

```
?-member(a,X).
```

5) The member program had two clauses:

a) `member(Wanted,[Wanted|_] ).`
b) `member(Wanted,[_|Rest]) :- member(Wanted,Rest).`

Would it make any difference if we put them into a database with clause (b) first and clause (a) second? (Follow through the actions the Prolog system will take if we have the two clauses in reverse order and ask the question:

```
?- member(a,[a,b,c])
```

and the question:

```
?- member(What,[a,b,c]).
```

6) Design a rule which will delete or remove a given element from a list. The head clause will have three arguments—the first, the element to be deleted, the second,

the list from which the deletion should be made, and the third, the result. For example, if we ask:

```
?- delete(c,[a,b,c,d], What). ,
```

it should respond **What = [a,b,d]**. (Assume that each element in the list is different from all the others, i.e., there is only one **a**, one **b**, and so on.)

7) Write a Prolog program which has two arguments in the head goal. The first argument is a list of numbers, and the second is the sum of the numbers in the list, as calculated by the program. For example, if we ask

```
?- sum_of([3,5,6,7], What).
```

we should get the response **What = 21**. (Hint: Think in terms of a recursive definition of the sum of all elements in the list.)

8) Suppose we have two lists, which may have some common elements. For example, the first list may be **[a,b,c,d]** and the second list **[e,f,c,b,h]**. Write a Prolog program to combine these into a list which will list any element in either of the lists, but will not repeat any elements which are in both lists—in the above example, it will form a list **[a,b,c,e,f,h]**, without including **b** and **c** (which are in both lists) twice.

9) Write a program which will take two lists and form a new list which consists only of the elements in both lists. For example, given the two lists in the example above, it will give as the result **[b,c]**, since these are the elements found in both lists.

Chapter 7

Structures in Prolog

Let us start by reviewing what we have learned so far about Prolog programs.

What is the composition of a Prolog program?

Writing a Prolog program is the same as putting appropriate facts and rules into a database and asking a suitable question, or setting a goal. A fact is just a special kind of rule which has a head and no body.

Is there some kind of simple pattern in the rules as well as questions?

Yes. The key pattern is a sequence of characters, which for convenience we may call a *word,* followed by a number of words separated by commas. We called the first word a *predicate,* and the various items inside the parentheses are *arguments* of the predicate.

What kinds of words can be used as predicates?

For predicates, an atom is used. A typical atom is a series of characters starting with a lowercase letter. These are the only kind of atoms we have seen and these are what you would use most of the time. However, anything enclosed in single quotation marks is an atom.

So, something like* first-name('Reagan','Ronald') *could be used as a fact in the database?

Yes. Because of the single quotation marks, it will be treated as an atom with a fixed or constant value, and not as a variable, even though uppercase letters are used.

Could we use double quotation marks as well?

Double quotation marks round a sequence of characters means it is to be treated as a list of characters, i.e., a *literal.*

What would Prolog's response be to this question?

```
?- [Head| Tail] = "snow".
```

Write your answer before reading further.

Since the sequence of characters between double quotation marks is treated as a list, we would get **Head = s**, and **Tail = [n,o,w]**. However, this is one of the cases where there is a great difference between different Prolog implementations; it may not work on some.

What kind of words can be used as arguments of a predicate in a rule or fact?

We have seen different items which can be used as arguments:

1) atoms
2) numbers
3) variables, which we said are sequences of characters starting with an uppercase letter. We could also start the name of a variable with the underline character (_) instead of an uppercase letter.
4) an empty list, which is just the pair of symbols [ ].
5) lists of arguments, which consist of a number of items of types 1, 2, 3, and 4 above, and are enclosed between square brackets and separated by commas.

Are there any kinds of items other than these which can be used?

Yes. A general name for things which can be used as an argument is *term.* Atoms, numbers, variables and the empty list are all different types of terms. In addition, we can have terms which are called *structures*.

What is a structure?

In chapter 6 we discussed the concept of recursive definitions—defining something in terms of itself. The recursive approach is convenient for defining structures as well.

Recursively, we can define a structure as follows: A structure starts with an atom, which is called the *functor* of the structure. The functor is followed, in parentheses, by a series of structures separated by commas. These are called the *components* of the structure.

A structure, therefore, has the form:

```
{atom} (structure, structure, structure, . . ., structure)
```

As we saw in other recursive definitions, we need a boundary condition to avoid getting into an endless circle.

The "boundary condition" part of the definition follows: Any term counts as a structure, so an atom or number or variable or empty list is also a structure which can be thought of as having a functor and no components.

What is an example of a structure?

Look at **income(john,20)**. It starts with an atom, so it has a functor, as is required by any structure. It has an atom and a number between parentheses; since these qualify as structure, we see that **income(john,20)**, fits the definition of a structure.

But didn't we call something like this a fact or goal?

Yes. The facts and goals we considered are examples of structures. Predicates are examples of functors. We can have functors which are not predicates, and structures which are not facts or goals.

In addition to the atoms, numbers and variables we have seen as arguments for facts, rules, and goals, Prolog allows any structure to be used as an argument. For example, we can put a fact in the database:

```
income( person(john,smith), city(newyork), 30).
```

this is a fact with three arguments:

```
person(john,smith)
city(newyork)
30.
```

Each of the arguments in this fact is a structure which has its own functor and components. The first argument has the functor **person** and two components; the second has functor **city** and one component; and the third is a simple structure, with just a functor.

Could we describe a predicate as being the "outermost" functor in a fact, rule, or goal, whereas the other functors are just called functors?

Yes. Sometimes the predicate is called the *principal functor* of the structure. Another way of expressing this is to say that the predicate is the "top-level" functor, when we look at the structure in terms of a tree (Fig. 7-1).

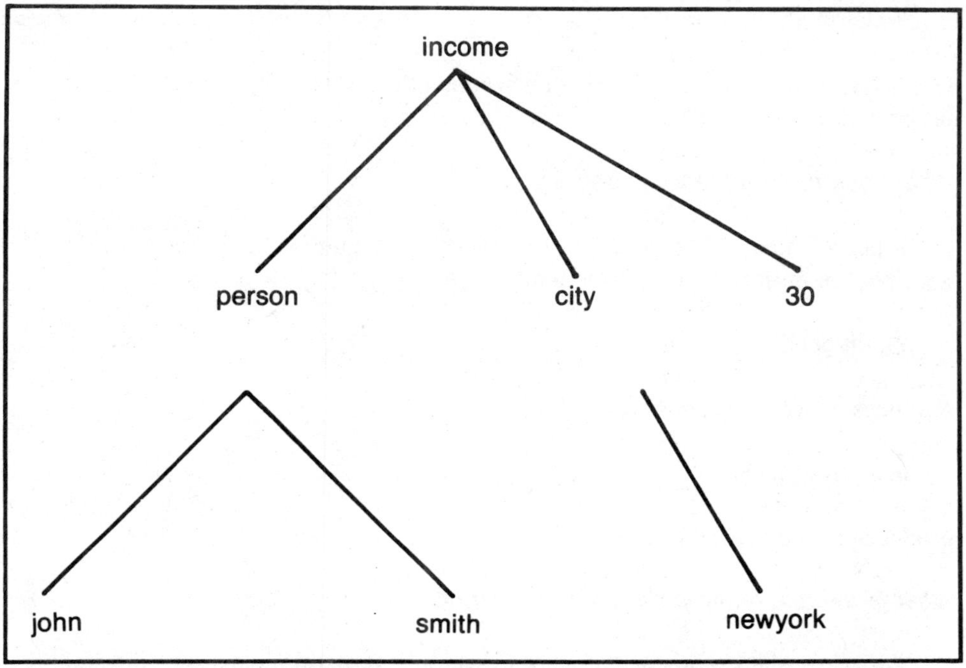

Fig. 7-1. A predicate is often called the "principal functor" of a Prolog structure.

Let us look at some built-in predicates that Prolog provides, which are based on structures. A built-in predicate is provided for some general purpose function by the system itself, as contrasted with the predicates designed by the user.

What is the built-in definition of the predicate atom?

It is defined as a predicate with one argument. It succeeds if the argument falls within the definition of an atom, otherwise it fails. For instance,

```
?-atom(income),
```

or

```
?-atom('Ronald Reagan'),
```

produce a "yes" response, while:

```
?-atom(Who),
```

or

```
?-atom([a,b,c]),
```

or

```
?-atom("abc")
```

would fail. If we wish to check that an argument is an atom for the rule or goal in our problem, we could use this built-in predicate.

What does the predicate integer *do?*

It has a similar role to atom. It, too, takes one argument, and checks whether the argument is an integer or whole number.

```
?- integer(3)
```

produces a "yes" response, and

```
integer(age)
```

produces a "no" response.

What is the role of the predicates var *and* nonvar*?*

Var takes one argument and checks whether the argument is an uninstantiated variable. We saw an example of how it may be necessary to carry out such a check in a program when we designed a program in chapter 4 as follows:

```
sum_of(First,Second,Third) :-
                var(Third),
                 Third is First + Second.
 sum_of(First,Second,Third) :-
              var(First), First is Third - Second.
 sum_of (First,Second,Third) :-
                  Second is Third - First.
```

We saw that if we want **sum_of** to work both for addition of First and Second to get Third, and for subtraction of First or Second from Third to get the value of Second or First, we have to take into account the fact that the built-in predicate **is** has the characteristic that there must be an uninstantiated variable to the left of **is**. We had to check which of the variables First,Second, or Third is uninstantiated, and then use **is** to instantiate it using the other two instantiated variables.

Nonvar is the complementary predicate to **var**. It is a goal which succeeds if its argument is *not* an uninstantiated variable.

Could we use nonvar *in the above definitions for* sum_of*?*
(Write your answer before reading further.)

Yes, but then we would have to check which are the instantiated variables. For instance, in the first clause we would replace **var(Third),** by **nonvar(First), nonvar(Second).**

What is the built-in definition of the predicate functor *which is usually provided in Prolog systems?*

Functor is defined as a predicate with three arguments. The predicate will succeed if the first argument is a Prolog structure, the second argument is the functor of the first argument, and the third argument is the number of arguments required by the first argument. This is also referred to as the *arity* of that structure. For example, if we ask:

```
?- functor(age(john,33), age , 2).
```

we would get a "yes" response. If we ask:

```
?-functor(age(john,33),What,Howmany).
```

we would get the response: **What = age,** and **Howmany =2.**

How would Prolog respond to this question?

```
?- functor(income,What,Howmany)?
```

Write your answer before reading further.

A simple atom is treated as a functor with no arguments, i.e., with "zero arity," so we would get the response: **What = income,** and **Howmany = 0.**

What is the definition of the predicate arg?

Arg is defined as a predicate with three arguments. The first argument is a number which specifies that you are looking for the 0th,1st,2nd . . . argument of a particular structure. The second argument is the particular structure, one of whose arguments we want to pick out. The third argument is what Prolog tries to match with what it finds using the first two arguments. If it is a variable, the variable is instantiated. If it is not a variable, Prolog tries to find a match.

For example, if we ask:

```
?-arg(2,address(john,100_main_street,anycity), What).
```

we would get the response:

```
What = 100_main_street.(tom_sawyer),
```

If we ask:

```
?- arg(2, income(john,30), 20).
```

we would get the response "no."

Some of the arguments we used in previous programs were lists. Where do they fit in the above definition?

We have included an empty list in the boundary condition definition of structures. Any other list is a special kind of structure with a functor, called the *dot constructor.* This functor takes two components, the *head* of the list and the *tail* of the list. A list with one element could be expressed in functor notation as:

```
.( a, [ ] ).
```

Similarly, a list with two elements would be:

```
.( a, .( b , [ ] ) )
```

and so on. This notation is awkward for longer lists, which is why the alternative notations [a,b,c] or [Head ¦ Tail] are also provided.

A list is always regarded as having the empty list as the last component of the structure.

Can we use the* functor *and* arg *built-in predicates to dismantle list structures the way we did with other structures?

Yes. If we ask:

```
?- functor( .(a,b), . , What).
```

we would get the response What =2, and if we ask:

```
?- arg(2,.(a, .(b,c) , What).
```

we would get the response What = .(b,c).

Can we use structures in the questions we ask in Prolog?

Yes, but keep in mind that Prolog tries to match the pattern or structure of the question to the clauses in the database. If we put the above fact in the database, and ask the question:

```
?- income(First,Second, Third).
```

Prolog will instantiate First to the first component of the functor income. It will give the response:

```
First = person(john,smith).
```

On the other hand, if we ask the question:

```
?- income(First(Fname,Lname), _ , _ ).
```

the response would be:

```
First = person, Fname = john, Lname = smith.
```

It is always a good idea to look at pattern-matching in terms of how the tree for the question and the tree for the clause in the database match. For the first question (Fig. 7-2A and 7-2B) We can see that First has to match with the whole structure **person(john,smith)**.

For the second question (Fig. 7-2C) we can similarly see by matching the two trees that First would be instantiated to **person**, Fname to **john** and Lname to **smith**.

Can we think of a rule as built up entirely from structures?

Yes, and what is more, we can think of a rule as not merely consisting of struc-

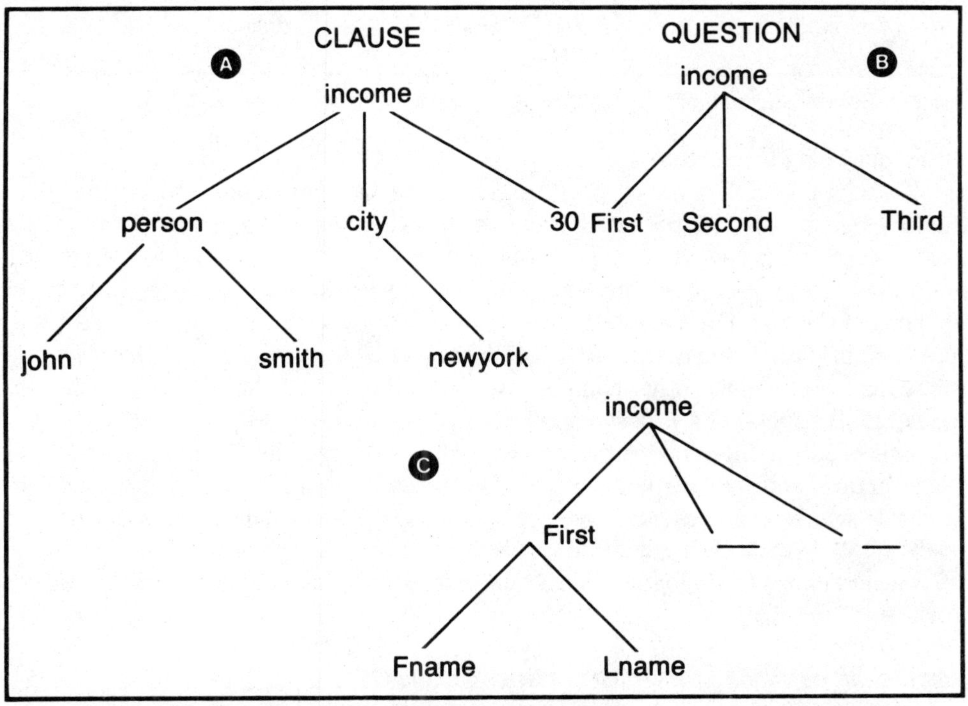

Fig. 7-2. Prolog pattern matching expressed as a tree comparison.

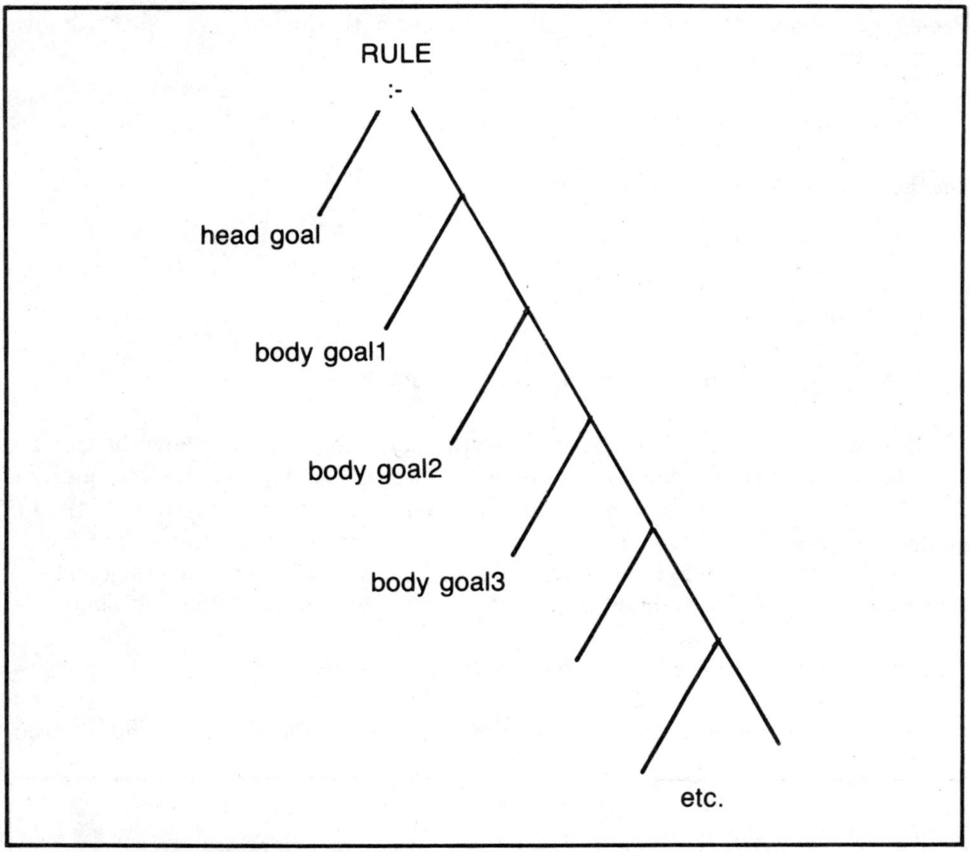

Fig. 7-3. General structure of a Prolog rule, showing the "if" symbol used as a functor.

tures, but being a structure itself.

We can think of the symbol :- ("if") as a functor which has a number of components, the first being a head or parent clause, and the others being the clauses in the body of the rule. This is shown in tree diagram form in Fig. 7-3. The thing to note is that not only is :- a built-in predicate, so is the comma used to separate different goals in the body of the rule. For convenience, instead of representing a rule in the usual structure form of putting the functor first, Prolog allows us to put the functor between the first component and the other components. Instead of **(goal1, goal2)**, we are allowed to use **goal1, goal2**, and proceed similarly for :-.

This is only a difference in the way we write it, but the idea is the same—the rule is a structure, and so is the body of the rule. Instead of using a comma as the built-in predicate which combines goals, we could also use the semicolon to show alternative goals: **goal1 ; goal2** in the body of a rule.

Most versions of Prolog provide a built-in predicate, **clause**, based on this aspect of rules.

What is the definition of the built-in clause "clause?"

It is defined as a predicate with two arguments. Prolog tries to match the first argument with the head of some clause in the database, and the second argument with the body of that clause. For instance, if we have in our database as the first clause:

```
young(Person) :-
      age(Person,Age), Age < 18.
```

and if we ask:

```
?- clause(age(X),What).
```

We would get some response like:

```
X = _22, and What = age(_22,_07), _07 < 18.
```

When we put in clauses for a program, we give the variable names starting with uppercase letters. Prolog stores them with some numbers, like _39,_22, _07, etc., to represent the variables, and that is why the response we get uses numbers instead of the names Person or Age, etc., which we use.

What is the importance of the fact that a Prolog program is made up entirely of structures?

We know that any information we use in various tasks does not generally consist of isolated pieces of knowledge; there are always relationships and connections. Prolog is suited for expressing these connections by using relationships between items of information which may themselves consist of other relationships. So, the use of structures is very helpful in representing information.

But what is even more important is the fact that there is no essential difference between the "data" or "information" processed and the "programs" which process them. Let us look at the simplest examples of Prolog we started with—facts in the database. When we put a fact into the database:

```
income(john,20).
```

from one point of view we can think of this as data, recording some information about the objects john and 20. But we can equally say that this is a program which tells us that to find out John's income, we should search the database to extract the second argument of a fact with predicate and john as the first argument. In other words, we can say that *implicitly*, in any declaration of information in the form:

```
predicate(argument1,  argument2,...)
```

there is an *embedded* description of a procedure for finding information.

There is a very important insight, attributed to Robert Kowalski, that says: When we record information in the form we have seen as used for facts and rules, there is a built-in description of a procedure. In a sense, we may say that Prolog is an implementation of this insight. A Prolog interpreter uses pattern-matching to extract the embedded procedure.

This form for representing information is referred to as *predicate logic.* Later in the book we will look at some of the history and background of the logic in general. But now the important point to remember is that any clause in Prolog can be looked at in two ways: explicitly, it is a declaration of certain logical statements, called the *declarative interpretation* of the clause—but when Prolog answers questions by pattern-matching, it is extracting from the clauses an implied *procedural interpretation* of the clause.

How does the description of any clause having an implied procedural interpretation apply to rules in a database?

We could say that declaratively a rule tells us the head goal is logically dependent on the goals in the body of the rule. The procedural interpretation is that in order to extract the information described in the head goal, in order to procedurally interpret the head clause, we need to procedurally interpret the clauses in the body of the rule.

Does this mean that a Prolog program is also based on the idea of a procedure or series of steps to be carried out by the computer, even though we make the distinction that Prolog is an assertional or declarative language, in contrast with conventional languages?

Yes. Make the careful distinction that the working of the computer does depend on procedures. The difference is that in conventional languages the user has to "think like a computer," and spell out the procedure, whereas in Prolog the interpreter's procedural interpretation of descriptions takes care of this requirement. The user has only to focus on the declarative or descriptive aspect.

Is the word "procedure" explicitly used in Prolog?

Yes, sometimes the whole set of alternative clauses for some predicate is called the *procedure* for that predicate. You can see that the meaning is essentially the same—a series of steps to be tried as alternatives, though the actual writing of each of the clauses is in declarative form.

Is the fundamental similarity of data and programs in Prolog significant in any other way, in addition to what we have seen above?

Yes. We have seen that data and programs are not different kinds of things, but consist of the same pattern of terms and structures, making it possible to interpret a declaration as a program, which makes it easier for the user to focus on the declaration. This characteristic has another interesting and important implication. It means that a program can modify itself, based on the results of the completion of the program, because any clause that may be inserted in the database as a result of the program is itself a program when interpreted procedurally, so the end result of the execution of a program is a modification of itself when the program puts in new clauses or removes old clauses as it runs. Prolog provides for predicates **asserta** or **assertz**, which can add new clauses to the database, and predicates like **retract**, which remove clauses from the database. If we have programs or clauses which include **assert** and **retract** goals, when these programs succeed one of the results is that the database is modified. Because of the unity of data and programs, we could as well say that the program as it was at the beginning has modified itself.

There is another built-in predicate in Prolog which is very useful in allowing a program to modify itself, for it can create structures in the process of execution of the program. This built in predicate is represented by an equals sign plus two periods (=..).

What is the definition of =.. ?

This is defined as a predicate with two arguments, one to each side of =..—it is an *infix predicate.* The term to the left of =.. can be any structure, and the term to the right of =.. is a list, in which the first item is the functor of the structure to the left of =.., and the other items are the various arguments of this structure.

For instance, if we ask:

```
?- age(a,10) =.. What.
```

We would get the response: **What = [age,a,10]**. To construct a structure as part of the execution of the program, all we have to do is to give the list consisting of the functor and the arguments we want for the new structure to the right:

```
? - New = [capital,peru,lima], assertz(New).
```

and New is instantiated to the value: **capital(peru,lima)**.

As we saw earlier, a rule is itself a structure with a functor :-, so we could generate new rules as a result of running a program, and add them to the knowledge or database. We would need to use a list in which the first element is the functor :- , and the other elements are the head and the tail of the rule:

```
Newrule =.. [:- , a,b] , assertz(Newrule).
```

This would add a new rule, **a :- b**, to our database, where **a** and **b** could be any predicates or structures.

Since these predicates would be of use only in advanced programming in Prolog, they may not work in the manner described above, in all versions of Prolog.

To put it in a more picturesque way, we could say that the ability to modify the database by actions taken by the program as it is executed enables a program to "learn" as it goes along; modifying itself amounts to changing its behavior, which is what learning is.

Why is the ability to "learn" a useful feature?

The whole field of artificial intelligence is concerned with trying to build programs which extend the current capabilities of computers. One of the things necessary for this is that we should be able to write programs for problems which we do not quite understand, but have some tentative ideas about, and use these programs as a first approximation, allowing them to learn and improve as they go along. Programs which can modify themselves are of great importance in this field.

Is Prolog the only language in which one can write programs which can modify themselves?

No. The great strength of the oldest and most widely used artificial intelligence language, LISP, is that it has this ability, and is regarded as one of the reasons for its dominance as the language of AI.

Chapter 8

Input/Output and Tracing

What is input and output all about?

We usually make a distinction between the program or set of instructions which process data to produce results and the data which are the material to be processed. Input and output usually refers to the *how* of providing the computer with data to process—by typing in at the terminal, or reading from a disk, and so on.

But this distinction between data and programs is not a useful one in Prolog. In working with Prolog it is preferable to think in terms of providing information to the computer, where (depending on the context) we think of the information as *the clauses or programs which are procedurally interpreted by the Prolog system,* or *the clauses viewed declaratively as containing the descriptive information.*

From this point of view we have already seen how input and output are provided for in Prolog systems. It is useful to visualize the Prolog database as part of the immediately accessible main memory of the computer, as distinct from supplementary information on disk which first has to be copied into the main memory before it can be used by the Prolog system. We have seen how, by using the "built-in" or "system" or "ready-made" predicates **asserta, assertz** and other variations of **assert** and **retract**, we can add or remove information from the Prolog database.

Should we think of these as predicates in the same sense we think of predicates in facts, rules, goals?

Yes. We can say that when we ask a question like:

?-assertz(income(john,30)).

we are asking the question to satisfy a goal with one argument (the clause **income(john,30)**). The system would respond with "yes." We would be able to verify that it is available in the database by using another built-in predicate we have seen:

?-listall. (* Prolog_V version *)

which displays all the clauses in the database. In both these cases, since these are also "goals" which have been satisfied, we would get a "yes" response at the end as well.

What is the major difference between the predicates like* assert, listall, *etc., which are provided with the Prolog system, and those we design or construct ourselves?

One difference is that we cannot alter them. If you try to put in a clause defining your own version of **assert**, you will get a message that you cannot redefine these built-in predicates. Also, we cannot get the definition as easily as we do with our user-designed predicates, which we do by just setting the goal listing.

Some versions of Prolog allow us, as an alternative to setting the goal **?- listall.**, to use a slightly different form like: **listall ?** or **listall !**. However, it is preferable to use the standard form: **?- <goal>**., so that you can use different versions of Prolog with a minimum of adjustment.

Is there anything special to keep in mind when using* assert *or retract to add or remove rules, rather than facts?

Even though *conceptually* facts are only a special case of rules, they do have a more complicated pattern. To make it clear that the head plus the :- symbol plus the body constitute one clause, in most versions of Prolog when one uses assert or retract for a rule an extra pair of parentheses are required.

To assert a fact, one may say:

?- assertz (income(john,30)).

But to assert a rule, typically one would say:

?-assertz((head of rule :- body of rule)).

***What is the major alternative to adding or removing clauses using* assert *or* retract?**

It is always possible to use a word processor to create a file of text, containing all the Prolog information, and store it on a disk, just as you would use a word processor to write and store a letter or a report. Then this file is brought into the database by using the built-in predicate **consult**. If you have stored a set of Prolog clauses in **file1.pro**, you would as usual get into Prolog and then respond to the prompt sign with:

?-consult('b:file1.pro').

This assumes the file is stored on Drive B of your computer. This is again a built-in predicate; after transferring the clauses in the file into the database, the system would respond with "yes" to indicate the goal has succeeded.

Many, but not all, Prolog systems provide another built-in predicate: **reconsult**. The difference between **reconsult** and **consult** is that when we consult a file the clauses in the file are added to what is already in the database. When we **reconsult** a file, if the file contains any alternative definitions for any clauses which are already in the database, the old definitions are replaced by the ones in the file.

Are assert *and* consult *enough for the operations of transferring information to the database?*

As long as you are dealing with sets of complete clauses, or single clauses, you can get by using these built-in predicates. However, you may want to exchange information in smaller units than a whole clause, and Prolog provides built-in predicates for this as well.

The most important of these built-in predicates are **read** and **write**, which operate with any Prolog term. Let us look at how they work by looking at some examples.

Suppose we add this predicate to our database:

```
greet__by__name: -
     write('Hello'),nl, write('What is your name?'), nl
     read(Person), write('Glad to meet you'), nl,
          write(Person),nl,nl.
```

Though this contains some expressions we have not discussed, does reading it give you a good idea of how it works?

I am sure you felt it is obvious that it will write a message, "Hello, What is your name?" and would respond with, "Glad to meet you." Let's look at the expressions we have not discussed so far.

Write is a built-in predicate which takes a single argument and displays it on the screen. Here we have given a phrase enclosed in single quotation marks. Remember, anything included in single quotation marks is an atom, in addition to anything without quotation marks that begins with a lowercase letter. The first goal is satisfied by displaying "Hello" on the screen.

The second goal we have not yet seen. It is the built-in predicate **nl**, which stands for "new line." This goal succeeds by moving one line down on the screen for the next display or output.

The third goal displays the message, "What is your name?" and the fourth goal gives a new line for the next output.

The important things to remember about the built-in predicate **read** are:

1) If the argument given is an uninstantiated variable, it instantiates the variable to whatever is typed in from the terminal.
2) What we type in from the terminal *must end with a period.* The system waits till the period is typed in.

The next two goals are **write** and **nl** goals. We can see that the system is going to give the message, "Glad to meet you," followed by an echo of the name the user typed in.

What happens if we use the* read *predicate with anything other than an uninstantiated variable as an argument?

The pattern-matching principles apply to this predicate, too. If we have a goal such as:

```
read(yes),
```

this goal will succeed if the user types in the atom *yes,* and will fail if anything èlse is typed in.

Since read and write and nl are predicates, can they be used as goals within a rule or program?

Yes. The important thing to keep in mind about these goals is that they can be satisfied only once, and cannot be resatisifed. Suppose we have a database containing a number of facts:

```
income(john,20).
income(mary,30).
income(anne,25).
income(jim,33).
```

and so on.

Now suppose we ask the question:

```
?- income(Who,Howmuch), write(Who), nl.
```

If we ask for multiple solutions, the output would be:

```
john
mary
anne
jim
```

Applying the usual principles of backtracking, we can see that the first time all three goals are satisfied, Who is instantiated to **john** and Howmuch to **30** by the success of the first goal; **john** is displayed on the screen by the success of the second goal; and a new line for display of the next output is created by the success of the next goal. When we ask for the next solution, we expect that the system should try an alternative solution for the third goal, **nl**. But for the built-in feature that **nl** cannot be resatisfied, the system would just go on printing new blank lines on the screen after displaying the first solution. Because of this built-in feature, the system backtracks to the second goal, **write**. Since this, too, is designed not to be resatisfied, the system backtracks to the first goal, and resatisfies it, and then tries to satisfy the second and the third goals.

The provisions like* read *and* write *look like predicates, but do not seem very different from giving specific commands to the computer. Isn't this supposed to be done only in imperative languages and not in declarative languages?

It is true that input/output predicates can be said to be nonimperative only by stretching the point. A better view is that these are what one might call "imperative aspects" of Prolog which are necessary for arranging for input and output. Sometimes they are referred to as "extralogical" features of Prolog. Whereas the heart of Prolog programs, as we have seen, consists of declarations of logical relationships, these extralogical features are helpful in order to make it convenient for use. Their presence in Prolog does not invalidate the fact that the essential programming tasks are carried out by declarative programs/clauses in the database.

We saw that Prolog programs can be created with a word processor and copied into the database using* consult *or* reconsult. *What about the reverse process—if we have added a number of clauses to the database using* assert, *can we save the whole set of clauses on a disk?

Yes. However, this is one of the features for which there is almost no standard predicate in the different versions of Prolog. Almost all versions of Prolog have the consult predicate built in, though some of them may have alternatives described in their specific manuals. For instance, one may be allowed to say:

```
?- load 'b:file1.pro'.
```

as an alternative to:

```
?- consult('b:file1.pro').
```

But most versions provide for something like:

```
?- save 'b:file1.pro'.
```

which will save the clauses in the database onto a file with the name **file2.pro** on disk drive B. It can be later copied into the database when necessary by

```
?-consult('b:file2.pro').
```

We have seen input and output of a file of clauses, or of individual clauses or of values for variables, by using* read *and* write. *Is it possible to so deal with other units, like lists or characters?

When we use **read(X)**, X is instantiated to any term of a kind used in Prolog. We could use **read** for reading in a list, by typing in the list in the usual form: **[a,b,c]**. Similarly, **write** can be used to display any term. For instance, **?-write([p,q,r])**. would work.

Typical Prolog implementations also provide for input and output of single characters by using the built-in predicates **get(X)**, for accepting a character and instantiating X to that value; and **put(X)**, for displaying on the screen the value to which the variable X has been instantiated.

The **get** and **put** predicates have the same characteristic as **read** and **write**—they can succeed only once. In other words, they are never resatisfied by backtracking. We saw above, in considering **write**, they are designed this way to avoid getting into an endless repetition.

Can input and output predicates be used only for accepting values from the keyboard and displaying on the screen?

No, they can be used for other purposes as well.

Initially you would want to use the keyboard as the standard input and the screen as the standard output. A **read** predicate comes up as a goal and the Prolog system waits for the user to type in something; when a **write** goal comes up, the result of satisfying this goal is displayed on the screen.

The standard input and the standard output are described as being the *current input stream* and the *current output stream* when you first invoke the Prolog interpreter. But Prolog implementations provide for *redirecting input and output*, that is, using alternatives for the standard input source and the standard output destination. This is described as "changing the current input or output stream."

How is input redirected?

The built-in Prolog predicate for changing the current input stream is **see( )**., where the name of the file to be treated as the source of input is given inside the parentheses. So, if one says:

```
?-read(X), write(X).
```

the system will wait for input from the keyboard and display it on the screen. But if one sets the goals:

```
?-see('b:filexxx.pro'),read(X), seen.
```

the computer will satisfy the first goal by "opening this file for input," as it is sometimes called. Following this, if we say the **read(X)** now reads a term from the file **b:filexxx.pro** rather than from the terminal, X will be instantiated to the first term found on the file **filexxx.pro** on disk B, and it is this value which is displayed on the screen. Having opened the file for input, subsequent reads and gets will go down this file treating it as the current input stream, so long as the parent goal which led to the see as a subsequent goal is not satisfied—so long as it is still part of the same program.

How do we return the keyboard to the input stream?

The built-in predicate **seen**, which has no arguments at all, closes the file and returns the current input stream to the keyboard.

How do we check at any stage what the current input stream is?

This is the purpose of the built-in predicate **seeing**. If we set the goal **?-seeing(X).** the system will instantiate X to the name of the current input stream and display this name on the current output stream.

What happens if we ask ?-seeing(X) *when using the keyboard as the input file?*

Typically, the keyboard is regarded by Prolog as a file called **user**, and we would get the response **X = user**.

How do we change the current output stream?

Corresponding to **see**, **seeing**, and **seen**, Prolog implementations provide **tell**, **telling**, and **told** to change the source of output, verify what is currently being used as the output file, and to close the current file.

To illustrate this, let us suppose we have created a database by using a number of **assertz** and **asserta** goals, and now want to save the new database as a disk file. One way to do this is to set the following goals:

```
?-tell('b:myfile.pro'), listall, told.
```

The effect of this is that the file **myfile.pro** on disk drive B is opened for output, and **listall** lists all the clauses in the working memory on this disk file instead of on the screen. In effect, we have saved the newly created database on disk. (Note: this works with the Prolog_V software, but may or may not work with the particular version you are using.)

To illustrate how some of these predicates work for input and output, let us consider the following problem: We have a database with information on the capitals of various countries, as follows:

```
capital(usa, washington).
capital(uk, london).
capital(france, paris).
capital(ussr, moscow).
capital(canada, ottawa).
```

Using the read, nl, *and* write *predicates, how would you design a program which would ask the user which country's capital the user wants to know about, and then extract the information from the database and display it?*

Let us consider the clause **find_capital**:

```
find_capital :-
     write('capital of which country?'),
     nl,
     read(Country),
     capital(Country,City),
     write(City),
     nl,nl.
```

You can see that we could use this as a model for writing many interactive programs in which the system first accepts some information from the terminal, and uses that information to guide its search of the database.

Let us consider one more illustration. The Michigan Lotto lottery prize is based on whether the six numbers on the ticket you buy match the six winning numbers announced by the Lottery Division of the State of Michigan. How can we write a Prolog program which will ask the user for his or her list of six numbers and give a suitable reply based on whether the six numbers match?

Consider the following program:

```
winner([1, 2, 3, 4, 5]).
lottery:-
     write('What is your number?'),
     nl,
     read(Your_list),
     check(Your_list),!.
check(Your_list):-
     winner(Your_list),
     write('Congratulations,you won'),
     nl,!.
check(Your_list):-
     write('Sorry,better luck next time'),
     nl.
```

We can see that if we ask the question **?-lottery.**, the program will first write a message asking for the user's number, and then wait for the number. Having read the number, the check clause is called. The check clause compares the list typed in with the winner clause to see if they match; if so, it prints a congratulatory message. If the first check clause does not succeed, the second check clause is tried, and a suitable message is displayed.

What would happen if we did not put cuts in this?

With a system which automatically produces all possible solutions, the winner would get both a congratulatory and a condolence message.

Do all built-in predicates deal with input and output functions?

Not quite. There are other general-purpose tasks required, whatever the subject about which one is writing programs. For instance, to list out the database—we have seen that a built-in predicate with no arguments, **listall**, or a predicate with one argument

listing(< *name of the particular predicate* >)

is likely to be provided.

Another general task is that of enabling us to watch step-by-step how Prolog goes through the database and tries to satisfy the goals, backtracks, etc. The standard predicate for this is **trace**.

What happens when one sets the goal **?-trace.**

The system would reply "yes," meaning that when any question is asked after this, the steps taken by Prolog to satisfy the goal would be shown at each stage. As an illustration, let us say we have put in the database these facts:

```
capital(usa,washington__d__c).
capital(ussr,moscow).
capital(india,new__delhi).
```

First we set the goal **?- trace**. and the system responds "yes." Next we set the goal:

```
?-capital(Country,City).
```

The typical sequence of displays on the screen would be something like this (this would vary from system to system; I have used as an example the Prolog-1 software from Expert Systems International):

```
?- capital(Country,City).
Goal capital(__44,__45)
Proved capital(usa,washington__d__c)
Country = usa
City = washington__d__c
More (y/n)? y
Proved capital (ussr,moscow)
Country = ussr
City = moscow
More (y/n)? y
Proved capital (india,new__delhi)
Country = india
```

```
City = new_delhi
More (y/n)? y
no
?-
```

As the system satisfies or "proves" the goal, it tells us it has done so, and when it is not able to prove the goal a fourth time, it tells us "no."

Now let us look at a case where the system has to backtrack to satisfy the goals. Let us take the example we considered in chapter 1, with a database as follows:

```
first_name(thatcher,margaret).
first_name(mitterand,francois).
first_name(reagan,ronald).
first_name(mulroney,brian).
first_name(gandhi,rajiv).
chief_exec(usa,president,reagan).
chief_exec(france,president,mitterand).
chief_exec(canada,prime_minister,mulroney).
chief_exec(uk,prime_minister,thatcher).
chief_exec(india,prime_minister,gandhi).
```

Let us see what happens when we try to trace the multiple goal question:

```
?- chief_exec(Country,prime_minister,Who),first_name(Who,What).
```

This time I used the trace command even before fetching the database by using **consult**, so the system traces the process of consulting as well:

```
?- consult('a:pres_pm.pro').
Goal consult(a:pres_pm.pro)
Goal assertz(first_name(thatcher,margaret))
Proved assertz(first_name(thatcher,margaret))
Goal assertz(first_name(mitterand,francois))
Proved assertz(first_name(mitterand,francois))
Goal assertz(first_name(reagan,ronald))
Proved assertz(first_name(reagan,ronald))
Goal assertz(first_name(mulroney,brian))
Proved assertz(first_name(mulroney,brian))
Goal assertz(first_name(gandhi,rajiv))
Proved assertz(first_name(gandhi,rajiv))
Goal assertz(chief_exec)usa,president,reagan))
Proved assertz(chief_exec(usa,president,reagan))
Goal assertz(chief_exec(france,president,mitterand))
Proved assertz(chief_exec(france,president,mitterand))
Goal assertz(chief_exec(canada,prime_minister,mulroney))
Proved assertz(chief_exec(canada,prime_minister,mulroney))
```

```
Goal assertz(chief__exec(uk,prime__minister,thatcher))
Proved assertz(chief__exec(uk,prime__minister,thatcher))
Goal assertz(chief__exec(india,prime__minister,gandhi))
Proved assertz(chief__exec(india,prime__minister,gandhi))

yes
?- chief__exec(Country,prime__minister,Who),first__name(Who,What).
Goal chief__exec(__45,prime__minister,__49)
Proved chief__exec(canada,prime__minister,mulroney)
Goal first__name(mulroney,__50)
Proved first__name(mulroney,brian)
Country = canada

Who = mulroney
What = brian
More (y/n)? y
Proved chief__exec(uk,prime__minister,thatcher)
Goal first__name(thatcher,__50)
Proved first__name(thatcher,margaret)

Country = uk
Who = thatcher
What = margaret
More (y/n)? y
Proved chief__exec(india,prime__minister,gandhi)
Goal first__name(gandhi,__50)
Proved first__name(gandhi,rajiv)
Country = india
Who = gandhi
What = rajiv
More (y/n)? y
no
?-
```

We can see how, when the first goal:

```
chief__exec(Country,prime__minister,Who),
```

has been satisfied, the instantiated value of the variable Who is passed on to the second goal to make it the first time **first__name(mulroney,What)**, etc. The messages given when tracing is carried out vary between the different versions of Prolog.

Some other systems trace the process by using the following explanations on the screen:

CALL	followed by the name of a goal, to show that the system is trying this goal.
EXIT	followed by the name of a goal, to show that this goal has been satisfied.

FAIL followed by the name of a goal, to show that it could not be satisfied.

REDO followed by the name of a goal, to show that the goal is being tried again on backtracking.

The explanatory messages of the "play-by-play" progress of Prolog trying to execute the goals are often helpful in trying to find out where a program is going wrong and not doing what you want it to do. To stop the tracing, most systems provide the built-in predicate **notrace**.

Are there any other built-in predicates helpful in input and output?

One very useful predicate is **fail**. As the name suggests, it just fails. It has no arguments. When a Prolog program encounters the **fail** goal, it backtracks. We may think of **fail** as a predicate which helps in the control part of programming.

For example, if we want to extract all possible answers automatically in one of the versions of Prolog in which answers are produced one at a time, try something like this:

```
keep_going :-
    capital(Country,City),
        write(Country),nl,
            write(City),nl,
                fail.
```

Remember, **write** succeeds only once so the backtracking from **fail** will take it back all the way to the first goal in the body. This will extract all possible solutions.

At this stage, I suggest you look at the appendix on baseball statistics using a Prolog database. It starts with a database containing facts relating to players, giving their names, number of times at bat, runs, etc. Using these facts it illustrates a number of rules for extracting various types of information. In the process it illustrates how the input/output predicates can be used. The appendix also contains some exercises which involve using input and output predicates.

Finally, you may like to keep in mind that if you are reading this book without using software, it is enough to have a general idea of the role of input and output. If you are using a particular version of Prolog, it is important to remember that input/output facilities are different in different versions. Check your manual carefully for any variations from the more-or-less standard predicates we have discussed above.

Chapter 9

A Variety of Programs

In this chapter we will consider programs which re-emphasize many of the points we have looked at. We will consider a classic example of recursion, called the Temple of Bramha or the Towers of Hanoi problem.

What is the Temple of Brahma problem?

It is a legend, mentioned in many books, that many years ago in a temple in the city of Varanasi, India, the priests were given a divine order to carry out the following task. There are 64 disks with a hole through the middle of each, placed on top of each other on a spike. Each disk is smaller than any of the disks below it (Fig. 9-1). The priests were required to transfer the disks to spike C, subject to the following rules:

a) They can move only one disk from one of the spikes to another at each move, and the disk which is moved must be the top-most disk on that spike. They may use all three spikes, though finally all the disks must end up on spike C.
b) A disk must never be placed on top of a smaller disk.
c) When the disks are finally on spike C, they must be in the same order as they were on spike A: the largest at the bottom, and each disk smaller than those below it.
d) If they make a mistake and put a larger disk on top of a smaller disk, they have to start from the beginning.

The legend continues that the world will end when the priests finish this task.

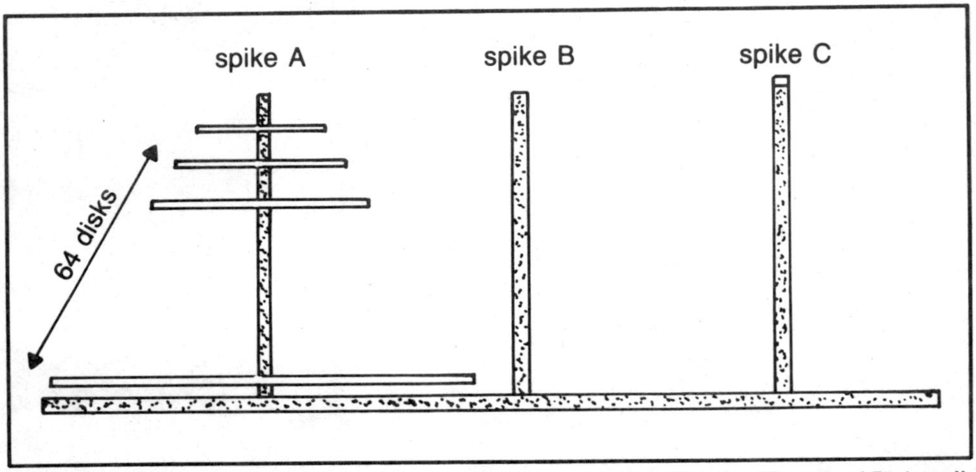

Fig. 9-1. The classic puzzle variously known as the "Towers of Hanoi" or the "Temple of Brahma."

This problem is usually given to illustrate the principles involved in calculating the number of moves required; we will consider that presently. The strategy for finding the best way of moving the disks is found by analyzing the problem using the recursive approach we have considered.

Let us think of the simplest case: one disk on spike A. We move it to spike C and are done. Now, suppose we have two disks. We move the top-most disk to B, move the lower (lowest) disk from A to C, and then move the disk on B to C. The two-disk problem is solved by two applications of the one-disk solution. When we consider three disks, we first move the top two disks to B, then move the lowest disk from A to C, and then move the two disks from B to C. Similarly, to move four disks, we would make two three-disk moves. First we would move the top-most three disks from A to B, then move the lowest disk from A to C, and then move the three disks from B to C . . . and so on, for 4,5,6,7 . . . disks. Once we see how to build up the solution for any number of disks using the solution for one less than that number of disks, we can easily express this as a recursive definition.

The approach to thinking recursively is to define the solution in terms of the solution of a simpler problem of the same type. We can express this approach here as follows: To move 64 disks from A to C, first move 63 disks from A to B, then move the last disk from A to C, and then move the 63 disks from B to C. We have recursively defined the problem of moving 64 disks from one spike to another in terms of two moves of 63 disks from the one spike to another, or in general, we have a definition of how to move N number of disks, in terms of how to move N – 1 disks, using the solution for moving N – 1 disks twice.

One point worth noting here: when we move the disks, say the 64 disks, from A to C, we need to use B as an intermediate, or spare, spike to achieve the goal. As we saw, this goal includes the subgoal of moving 63 from A to B, and for this move we will have to use the ultimate destination of the 64 as the intermediate or spare spike. Similarly, when the 63 are moved from B to C, it is the original spare spike which is the starting point, and the original starting point which is the spare spike. So, as we go recursively to apply moves of 63, 62, and so on, the spare spike for each of these calls are different; when we write a Prolog program we will have to take this into account.

We will have to think also of the boundary condition for the recursion. Since we think of 64-disk moves as two applications of 63-disk moves, 63-disk moves as two applications of 62-disk moves, etc., we can see that the boundary condition comes when we think of a one-disk move as consisting of two no-disk moves, which involve no action at all.

How can we express this in Prolog? Consider the following clauses:

a)

```
move(Number_of_disks,Start,Finish,Spare) :-
     Number_of_disks = 0,!.
```

b)

```
move(Number_of_disks,Start,Finish,Spare) :-
     All_but_last is Number_of_disks - 1,
move(All_but_last,Start,Spare,Finish),
move_last(Start,Finish),
move(All_but_last,Spare,Finish,Start).
```

c)

```
move_last(From,To) :-
write('move disk from'),write(From),
     write('to'), write(To),nl.
```

Since for each recursive use of the program we need to indicate the number of disks, the starting spike, the finishing spike, and the spike to be used as a spare, we need four arguments for the rule.

Clause (a) is the boundary condition; when the number of disks to move is zero, we have reached the end.

Clause (b) incorporates the considerations discussed above, that any move of N disks requires a move of N – 1 disks to a spare spike, treating the ultimate finish spike as a temporary spare for this operation; followed by a move of one disk from starting spike to finishing spike, provided as a message by clause (c); followed by a move of N – 1 disks from the spare spike to the finishing spike, treating the starting spike as a temporary spare for this operation.

If we ask **?- move(1,a,c,b)**, we would get the response:

```
move disk from a to c.
```

If we ask **?- move(2,a,c,b)**, we would get the messages:

```
move disk from a to b
move disk from a to c
move disk from b to c.
```

and so on.

If we do not want to have to specify the start, finish, and spare spike in asking our question, we could use a clause:

```
moves_for(Number) :-
    move(Number, start,finish,spare). { or move(Number,a,c,b) }.
```

We can then ask questions just as ?-moves_for(3), ?-moves_for(5), etc.

What would be the number of moves required to move 2,3,4,5. . . disks?

Calculating the answer to this is a good example of applying the recursive approach. We know that when we want to move any number of disks, N, we go through the following steps:

We move N – 1 disks from source to spare.

We move one disk from source to destination.

We move N – 1 disks from spare to destination.

So, the number of moves required for moving N disks is twice the number of moves required for moving N – 1 disks, plus 1.

We can now proceed inductively, starting with the fact that the number of moves for moving 1 disk is 1:

Number of disks	Number of moves needed
1	1
2	(2∗1) + 1 = 3
3	(2∗3) + 1 = 7
4	(2∗7) + 1 = 15
5	(2∗15) + 1 = 31

In general we can see that for N disks the number of moves is $2^N - 1$. For 10 disks this works out as 1023; for 20 disks, over a million; and for 64 disks—which is the number of moves to be made before the world ends—it is 18,446,744,073,709,551,615.

In chapter 6 we considered a Prolog program which deletes a given element from a list. For instance, if we say:

```
?-delete(john,[anne,john,mary], What).
```

we would get the response **What = [anne,mary]**. The Prolog program for this was:

```
delete(Unwanted,[ ],[ ]).
delete(A,[A|B],B).
delete(A,[C|B],[C|Result]) :-
    delete(A,B,Result).
```

However, this was based on the assumption that there was one or no instances of the unwanted element in the given list. If there were more than one instance, this program would remove only the first instance. For instance:

```
?-delete(a,[b,a,c,a,d], What).
```

would give us the response **What = [b,c,a,d]**.

How can we extend the foregoing program so all occurrences of the element to be deleted would be removed? Start by thinking in terms of what would be a recursive definition of the task we want to carry out.

We can see that this program has to be similar to the one for deleting an unwanted item when there is only one occurrence at most of the unwanted item. The difference is that once we have deleted the item we cannot stop there, we must look at the tail of the list to see if we have to delete again. We can use our **delete** program as a guide to build a **deleteall** program:

```
(1) deleteall(_, [ ], [ ]):- !.
(2) deleteall(Unwanted, [Unwanted|Tail], Result) :-
        deleteall(Unwanted, Tail, Result),!.
(3) deleteall(Unwanted, [Head|Tail], [Head|Result]) :-
        deleteall(Unwanted, Tail, Result).
```

The second clause tells us that if the unwanted element is the head of the list we should drop it and try to delete all occurrences from the tail of the list.

The third clause covers the case where the unwanted element is not at the head of the list. In that case we have to keep the head of the list for our result, but we also have to look at the tail of the list for any deletions required.

As we recurse, we would come to the boundary condition where we reach the empty list, and in that case all we have to do is keep the empty list as it is—what the first clause provides for.

How can we extend this further so we can remove all the elements in one list from another list?

We might want to remove everyone in the list **[john,mary, anne]** from another list **[jim,mary,liz,john, tom,anne, debbie]**, etc, and get only the remaining names **[jim,liz,tom,debbie]** as the result. We must start again by thinking in recursive terms of how we would do this, and how it connects with the ideas we have seen in **deleteall**.

We can connect this task with what we did in **deleteall** by thinking of it this way: we could take our first list and use deleteall to get rid of all occurrences of that element from the second list. But having done this, we have to do this for all the other elements in the first list until it becomes empty. The analysis suggests that we have to think in terms of representing the first list as a head and tail, and then proceed to use **deleteall**. This is the concept embodied in clause 2 below:

```
1) drop([ ], _, _ ):- !.
```

```
2) drop([Head Tail],SecondList,Result) :-
   deleteall(Head,SecondList,Result1),
   drop(Tail,Result1,Result).
```

As we recurse, ultimately the first list of items we want to drop out of the second list becomes empty and we reach the boundary condition represented by clause 1.

Now let us consider the following problem. We have in stock various quantities of a number of items, which we represent in our database using a predicate **stock**:

```
stock(b, 30).
stock(a, 20).
stock(c, 10).
```

We also have a policy that if the amount of stock in hand falls below a certain level we would like to place new orders to build up our stock. The level at which we feel it is necessary to reorder that item would be different for each item; let us record this information in our database using the predicate **rop** for "reorder point."

Also, we need a rule about how much we reorder. Let us say the policy of a particular company is to reorder enough to bring the quantity in hand after the order is received to 100 units above the recorder level.

For instance, suppose our database has the following facts for reorder point:

```
rop(a, 15).
rop(b, 40).
rop(c, 10).
```

We want to design a Prolog program which will do the following for us. If we ask:

```
?-placeorder(b,Howmuch,Newlevel).
```

it should figure out that since the stock of b is 30, which is below the reorder point of 40 units, it should tell us **Howmuch** is 110, because we need to order 110 units to bring up the new level to 100 units above the reorder level of 40.

How would you implement the solution to this problem in Prolog? Write out your answer before continuing.

The predicate **placeorder** I have given below is one possible way of handling the problem. It is possible you have designed an alternative program which would also work.

```
placeorder(Item, Quantity, Newlevel) :-
      stock(Item, Instock),
      rop(Item, Level),
```

```
Instock < Level,
Short is Level - Instock,
Quantity is Short + 100,
Newlevel is Instock + Quantity.
```

How can we design a predicate update, *which we attach as the last goal to the* placeorder *predicate above, and which will do the following: replace the existing data regarding stock available with the data regarding what the stock will be after receipt of the new order we are placing.*

We need to retract the old stock data and add the new stock data to the database. We could design a program as follows:

```
update(Item, Old,New) :-
     retract( stock(Item,Old) ),
     assertz( stock(Item,New) ).
```

To use this in the **placeorder** program, add a last goal:

```
update(Item,Instock,Newlevel).
```

Design a program which will take three arguments and check whether the first two arguments are elements located next to each other in the third argument, which is a list. For example, if we ask

```
?- next_to(b,d,[a,c,e,b,d,f,g]).
```

we should get the response "yes."

Consider the following:

```
1) next_to(First,Next,[First,Next|_]).
2) next_to(First,Next,[Head|Tail]) :-
   next_to(First,Next,Tail).
```

We can see that the second recursive rule checks the tail of the list until the boundary condition expressed in the head of the list (that the two are together at the start of the list) is satisfied. If the two items are not next to each other, both rules fail when the list becomes empty, and we get a "no."

If we ask the question:

```
next_to(a,What,[s,a,b,c,v,a,d,w,a,f,g]).
```

will the program produce only the solution What = b, *or will it find all the solutions for elements next to* a*? Analyze the problem before looking at the solution below, and write out your answer.*

This question provides more practice in tracing the way Prolog works. Prolog first tries to match the question with the first clause, fails, tries the second clause, which leads it to try the goal:

```
next__to(a,What,[a,b,c,s,v,a,d . . . ]).
```

This goal succeeds on the first clause, instantiating **What** = **b**. Now if we ask for a further solution, Prolog will try the second clause, and once again it will go on until it finds **What** = **d**. Once again this success is on the first clause, so it again tries the second clause if we ask for further solutions. It will find all the solutions.

Suppose we create a database with facts using the predicate **outer-planet** to signify that the relationship of the second argument is the next outer-most planet from the sun in relation to the first argument:

```
outer__planet(mercury,venus).
outer__planet(venus,mars).
outer__planet(mars,earth).
outer__planet(earth,jupiter).
outer__planet(jupiter,saturn).
outer__planet(saturn,uranus).
outer__planet(uranus,neptune).
outer__planet(neptune,pluto).
```

How can we write a Prolog program which will tell us which planets are farther from the sun than a given planet? For instance, we should be able to extract the information that Mars, Jupiter, Saturn, Uranus, Neptune, and Pluto are all further from the sun than Earth is. Design a suitable two-argument predicate, farther__from__sun, *which can be used for this purpose.*

Here is one possible solution to this problem:

```
farther__from__sun(First,Second) :-
     outer__planet(First,Second).
farther__from__sun(First,Second) :-
     outer__planet(First,Other).
     farther__from__sun(Other,Second).
```

There is an interesting point involved here which you might like to think about. Would the program work equally well if we put the goals in the following order?

```
farther__from__sun(First,Other), outer__planet(Other,Second).
```

Let us consider what would happen if we ask the question:

```
?-farther__from__sun(pluto,What).
```

We know that with the old order of the goals it would fail on both clauses and answer "no." But with the change in the order of the goals, when it tries the second clause, will generate the new goal;

```
farther__from__sun(pluto,Other).
```

To satisfy this goal it again comes to the second clause, which will lead it to try:

```
farther__from__sun(pluto,Other2).
```

(I am calling this **Other2** because it is a copy of the original program for this recursive use.) You can see what will happen—the program will keep calling itself again and again until it runs out of space due to putting too many copies on the stack, and give a message like "stack full."

This is called *the problem of left recursion.* When we have a goal which keeps calling itself as the first goal on the left, it could lead to an endless recursion in some circumstances. This is something to watch out for when designing recursive programs.

Reversing a list is an operation that can be defined recursively. Write down a recursive definition of how the reverse of a list is connected with the reverse of the tail of the list, and then formulate Prolog clauses for the recursive case and for the boundary condition.

We could say that the reverse of a list is the reverse of the tail of the list, with the head of the tail stuck onto the reversed tail. So, one could write a Prolog clause:

```
2) reverse([Head|Tail], Result) :-
     reverse(Tail,Result1), append(Result1,Head,Result).
```

We would need the boundary condition when the tail is ultimately reduced to the empty list:

```
1) reverse([ ], [ ]).
```

This would work perfectly well. However, Clocksin and Mellish (among others) mention that a program will use less storage for the stacks it uses to keep copies of a program in recursive calls if we can make the recursion part the last goal. Here, after **reverse** "calls itself," we have another goal, **append**. The **reverse** program can be modified to make the call to itself the last call by slightly changing our strategy for reversing the list.

We can think of it as follows: we do not have a built-in command for isolating the last element, as we have for picking out the head or first element. (If we had, it would be simple to move it as the head and then recursively do that to the rest of the list). Let us pick the first element and put it as the head of an empty list. Invoke the program by asking:

```
?- altreverse([a,b,c,d],[ ], What).
```

It is generally a good idea, as I pointed out earlier, to ask oneself how exactly would one want to invoke this program? That often gives a clue to designing it.

We want the program to attach the first element to the empty list, to get **[a]**, then attach the new head **b** as the head of **[a]**, which is the extent to which we have built up the Reverse list so far: to get **[b,a]**, and so on. We can express this as the Prolog program.

```
altreverse ([H|Tail], Rev__so__far,Result]) :-
    altreverse([Tail,[H|Rev__so__far]],Result).
```

When we have exhausted all the elements in our original list so that it has become empty, we need the boundary condition:

```
altreverse([ ],Anything,Anything).
```

you can see that if we invoke it with:

```
?-altreverse([a,b,c,d],[ ],What).
```

it successively invokes itself as:

```
altreverse([b,c,d],[a],What),
altreverse([c,d],[b,a],What),
altreverse([d],[c,b,a],What),
altreverse([ [ ],[d,c,b,a],What).
```

at which stage the boundary condition is reached.

Finally, let us consider a short program which will in a basic way illustrate the rudiments of how Prolog can be used for "natural language" processing—that is, understanding English or other human languages—and second, how we can have programs that "learn."

The situation we have is this: we have a very simple language with the following rules:

- ☐ Every sentence begins with an article: "a" or "the."
- ☐ The article is followed by a noun, which is followed by a verb.

"The dog barks" or "the man runs" would be an example of sentences in the language. Anything more complicated or with a different structure would not count as a sentence.

How can we write a Prolog program to recognize sentences of the "natural" language described above.

Consider the following program:

```
sentence([First,Second,Third]) :-
     article(First),
     noun(Second),
     verb(Third).

noun(Word) :- write(['is',Word,'a','noun?']),n1,
     read(yes),
     asserta(noun(Word) ).

verb(Word) :- write(['s',Word,'a','verb?']),n1,
     read(yes),
     asserta( verb(Word) ).

article(a).
article(the).
```

Let us see what would happen when we ask:

```
?-sentence([the,dog,barks]).
```

We can see that it will instantiate First to **the**, Second to **dog** and third to **barks**, and can succeed on the goal: **article(the)**. When it goes to the next goal, **noun(dog)**, the only clause is the rule for **noun**, so it will ask:

```
[is,dog,a, noun?].
```

If we reply yes, the system will add the fact **noun(dog)** to the database, and then ask if **barks** is a verb. If we confirm this, it will add **verb(barks)** to the database. Having succeeded on all three goals, it will reply "yes" to the original query.

The interesting thing is that if we now ask:

```
?-sentence([the,dog,runs]).
```

the only question it will ask is whether **runs** is a verb—it "knows" **dog** is a noun. Again, if we ask:

```
?-sentence([the,man,runs]).
```

Prolog has already "learned" that **runs** is a verb, so the only question it will ask is whether **man** is a noun.

We have a short learning program combined with a "simple language" understanding mechanism. The principles illustrated here can be extended to more complex languages and more complex learning processes. I hope by now you feel comfortable enough with Prolog to be able to develop your own applications.

Chapter 10

Etcetera

As the title indicates, this chapter deals with some miscellaneous matters. Having worked through this book, you should be in a position to program in Prolog. You might want to learn more about Prolog; I have included a bibliography of books about Prolog and logic programming. I suggest you look at the classic, Clocksin and Mellish's *Programming in Prolog.* Their book starts with the basics, so the first few chapters will give you a comfortable feeling of reinforcing what you have already learned from this book. In the latter part of the book they give more complicated examples than I have done, and go deeper into theoretical aspects. They also go into the question of using Prolog for natural language processing, which I have only briefly touched upon.

As we have seen, the strength of Prolog is in symbolic processing. You might like to explore the field of artificial intelligence and expert systems. I have included a short appendix as an introduction to this field. The bibliography contains suggestions for reading in this field. While there are many good books; but I suggest starting with P.H. Winston or Elaine Rich. The book by O'Shea and Eisenstadt gives succinct introductions to Prolog and LISP. You might find it interesting to compare them, using your knowledge of Prolog.

At various places in the book I have pointed out that Prolog as it is today is not a perfect realization of the ideal of a purely declarative language. We saw that to understand how Prolog works we do have to have awareness of the procedural aspects. Presumably, the "Prolog-based" languages which develop in the future will remedy this and more towards a more purely declarative style.

Connected with this is another issue which will interest you as a student of Prolog. When a language becomes purely declarative, the order of the goals should not matter. That would make such a language an ideal candidate for parallel problem-solving—carrying out different tasks, or trying to satisfy different goals concurrently, and then tying the results together. For an exploration of how standard Prolog is being modified to incorporate these ideas, you might like to look at an article by Robert Kowalski, entitled "Logic Programming," in the August, 1984, issue of *BYTE*.

To take full advantage of parallel problem-solving techniques, new types of computer hardware will be necessary. Computer systems as we know them are based on carrying out actions in the order in which we give the statements, rather than carrying out a number of statements at the same time by using a number of processors working on different tasks, and finally tying them together. One of the frontier areas of computer science is the development of parallel-processing machines, and developing suitable programming languages which can mesh with this style of processing. Japan's Fifth Generation Project has as one of its goals the development of such machines, and the software they will develop, starting on the basis of Prolog, will no doubt be oriented towards such machines.

Appendix A

Software

In this appendix are included reviews of some of the Prolog interpreters available for the IBM PC, with enough detail for the reader to decide which interpreter best suits his or her needs.

If you are familiar with software use, you will see from the Prolog interpreter manual that the procedure for getting the Prolog system working is similar to that you would use for any software package. You first boot the operating system and get the DOS prompt on your screen. If you are using a one-drive system, you would then replace the DOS disk with the Prolog disk and then give the appropriate command for copying the interpreter into the main memory of the computer (specified in the manual which comes with the Prolog disk). Prolog V stores the Prolog interpreter with the name **Prolog_V**; PROLOG_86 stores it with the name **Prolog**, and so on. Of course, you can always change the name using the RENAME utility in DOS.

If you have never used a software package and Prolog is the first one you are trying, the only thing to remember is that your computer will come with a disk containing a program known as the Disk Operating System (DOS). As the name suggests, this is a program which has to be used as a support for using any other program. You would first load the DOS into the working memory of the computer using the instructions which come with the computer for how to load DOS—in IBM PCs, typically you would put the disk containing DOS into the designated drive on the computer and press three keys: <Ctrl + Alt + Del>. The indication of a successful "booting" or copying of the DOS program into the working memory of the computer is that the screen would show the message: A>.

As mentioned above, you would then "boot" the Prolog disk. The program on the

Prolog disk is called the "Prolog interpreter." Think of it as a program which has to be in the main memory of the computer for the hardware to "understand" what is meant when you type in **?-assertz ( )** or **?-age(Who,What).** or **?-consult ( ).** or any other expression conforming to the rules of Prolog. This is in fact the general procedure for using any software package: first boot DOS, getting the "general prompt" on the screen. The "invoke" the particular package you are using, in the case of Prolog by entering whatever word the manual which comes with the disk says is to use to boot the Prolog interpreter. Similarly, if you are using a word processor program, you would use whatever work for booting is given by the manual for that program. Finally, each manual will always specify how to return to the general prompt, or exit from the particular package you are using. In most Prolog systems, this is a built-in predicate of the type **?-exit.** or **?-exitsys.** or **?-halt.** In word processor programs it is usually some variation of "quit."

With a word processor available, the most convenient procedure would be to put the word processor by using the **consult** predicate.
create the Prolog database, using the word processor, then exit from the word processor, invoke Prolog, and copy into working memory the database saved on disk by the word processor by using the "consult" predicate.

PROLOG FROM EXPERT SYSTEMS INTERNATIONAL

The Prolog-1 interpreter from Expert Systems International (1150 First Avenue, King of Prussia, PA 19406) is a very comprehensive implementation, with some features which make it extremely convenient and easy to use. It is available in MS-DOS/PC-DOS and CP/M-86 versions, and requires 128K RAM.

The interpreter comes with a very thorough manual. The manual explains at the beginning that it is not meant to be a tutorial. It does not contain many examples in the body of the manual, though there is an appendix with sample programs, also available on a supplementary disk. The sample programs cover a good range of areas, including a database and query language system, a parser-generator system, a symbolic differentiation program, and so on. The reader who looks only at the body of the manual along with a suitable introductory book would be able to benefit from the explanations in the manual of the basics of Prolog, as well as the various features of this implementation.

The language as implemented is essentially the Clocksin and Mellish version, which is the one I have followed in this book.

After booting the operating system, you invoke the Prolog interpreter. The disk supplied by ESI has two versions: one called Prolog86 and the other Proled86. The prompt sign which comes up in both versions is ?- . This is convenient and saves having to type in ?- for questions, which the manual also refers to by the alternate name of *directives*.

The "ed" in the second Prolog version indicates that a built-in editor for editing programs can be called upon from within Prolog. This is one of the very special features of this implementation.

The manual suggests that it would be convenient to use the built-in editor for databases of up to about 40 clauses for the same predicate; for longer programs, you might want to create a file using a word processor and then transfer it to the Prolog interpreter.

When using the ESI version, you have many ways of adding clauses to the database. You may use the standard method of adding clauses by using the **assert** predicate, in any of three ways of positioning the clause: **asserta( )**. will add the clause at the beginning of all other clauses with the same predicate, and **assertz( )**. will add the clause at the end. If you imply **assert**, and follow the text of the clause with a number, the clause is added in-between the clauses with the same predicate, at the position indicated by the number. If one says:

```
assert( income(john,30), 3).
```

the clause **income(john,30)** is added after the third clause for **income** which is already in the database. Of course, if there are fewer than three, it means the clause is added at the end.

You may also create a file (**prog1.pro**, for instance) using a word processor. Now the file can be transferred for use by the Prolog program by using the directive or question:

```
?-consult( 'b:prog1.pro').
```

As we have seen, **consult** is the standard Prolog predicate for loading a file. The related directive available is **reconsult**. The difference is that **consult** adds the file to the working space, whereas **reconsult** replaces any clauses in the working space which have a particular predicate with the clauses with the same predicate in the file which is reconsulted. **Reconsult** would be a convenient way to change some of the clauses.

The third way is to bring a number of files into the workspace by giving the names of the files in a list. For instance, typing in:

```
?- [file1,file2,file3].
```

has the effect of "consulting" all three files. If you want to reconsult instead of consult a file, precede the name of the file with **$**; in the above example, using **$file2** instead of **file2** would cause the system to reconsult that file.

The most convenient way is by using the built-in clause editor, which works as follows. When you enter Prolog by using **Proled86**, you get a message showing the editor has also been loaded, and then the usual prompt: ?-. To use the editor, type in **edit**. The indication that the editor is now available is that the prompt changes to **ed**>.

The editor allows a number of options. Typing **a**, for add, changes the prompt to :, indicating that the system is waiting for additions to the database. After adding all the clauses you like, <Ctrl + Z> is used to get back the **ed**> prompt. From here any of the other options available in the editor can be chosen. The most important of these are:

- ☐ **g** followed by the name of a file, for get or load the file.
- ☐ The options for saving all clauses with a specific predicate, or all clauses in the database, (options **s** and **S**).

Other options relate to listing the names of the predicates. Finally, **q** is used for quitting the editor and getting back to the Prolog interpreter prompt.

A *Program Clause Editor Manual* supplied along with the main manual explains all options in detail. This editor is a very attractive, extremely handy feature which would be useful at the early learning stages as well as later.

The next feature of Prolog-1 worth commenting on is its provision for error messages. Not only do you get an error message when you make an error in syntax or when something goes wrong in the program, you also get a message asking if you want an explanation of the error. For example, suppose you give the directive **?-consult(X)**. This is a mistake, because the name of a file to be consulted must be given specifically, not as a variable. The error message tells us this is an error (because the argument for **consult** is uninstantiated) and asks if you want an explanation. if you say yes, it explains that the argument must be a valid filename. For different types of errors there is first a short explanation, and the option for a more detailed one. This facility is provided for through an additional file called **prolog86.err**, which is on the distribution disk. This file contains the messages giving the detailed explanations.

While the usual system predicates (according to the Clocksin and Mellish standard) are provided for, in addition Prolog-1 provides a number of predicates/directives which make the system easier to use. For example, **open-read** lets you open a file for reading; There's also **open-write**, and **open read-write**. These alternatives are available along with the standard directives like **see, tell, seen, told, write, user**, etc., which we have seen in chapter 8. There is also provision for using random access files, using predicates **seek-read** and **seek-write**.

In regard to arithmetic, integers in the range 0 to $(2^{14} - 1)$ can be handled, and real numbers in the range $\pm\ (3.6 \times (10^{308})\ )$.

Another feature worth mentioning is the provision for interrupting execution by using <Ctrl+Y>, which then gives you the option of aborting, continuing, existing etc.

There is a provision for tracing execution of a program through the directive **trace**. For instance, suppose you have already given the directive **trace** and then ask a question like **?-age(Who,What)**. The database would have the fact **age(a,10)**. The system prints out something like:

```
goal age(-44,-45)
proved age(a,10)
Who  = a
What  =  10
```

It shows us the stages by which it solves or proves the goal. The -44 and -45 indicate that they are uninstantiated variables.

The **trace** directive is cancelled by the **notrace** directive. You may also trace only some or not all predicates by what is called setting 'spypoints,' explained in the manual.

When a question has multiple answers, after printing out the first solution, the system asks: **more(y/n) ?** and, depending on the response, looks or does not look for alternative answers.

These are the most attractive features of this version. This commentary should give you an idea of how convenient the system is to use. There are other features which would be of interest to advanced programmers, such as the capability of linking up with machine code using the **external-code** predicate.

Although this version is somewhat more expensive than others, it is undoubtedly excellent value for money for the serious user of Prolog on the IBM PC because of the features which make it very easy to use. One other plus is that the same organization produces the expert system package, ES/P Advisor (see next review), and the two together are a good combination for those who want to go from Prolog into more extensive applications of declarative programming, including expert systems.

The version of Prolog-1 which I had tested was version 2.2. ESI also has a more advanced Prolog compiler and interpreter package, Prolog-2.

ES/P ADVISOR

ES/P Advisor is an expert system development tool, created by Expert Systems International, makers of Prolog-1. The price is approximately $900. There are two key programs in this package, both written using Prolog.

The first important task in building an expert system is to create a knowledgebase which contains the relevant information regarding the problem in hand. In particular, the most widely used approach to representation of knowledge in a knowledgebase is by the use of *production rules*, that is, rules of the type: IF condition A and/or condition B, etc., THEN draw the following conclusions or take the following actions. We saw also that information of this type can be represented using suitable Prolog clauses, wherein a regular Prolog interpreter is used as the *inference engine* to draw inferences using the knowledgebase.

The first key program in this package, the KRL compiler, aims to make the representation of knowledge in the knowledgebase even easier than a representation in Prolog, by using a language called Knowledge Representation Language that is closer to English than Prolog. Chapter 3 of the manual which comes with the package is a detailed guide to the rules of KRL. Once information has been expressed according to the grammar of KRL, the KRL Compiler translates it into a form executable by the computer.

The second essential component of an expert system package is the inference engine, which uses the knowledgebase to draw conclusions or answer questions from the user. The second program in the package, the consultation shell, plays the role. It is a very sophisticated inference engine, providing excellent facilities for explaining the process by which it is answering questions. In the example below I will highlight these facilities.

Some idea of the way a knowledgebase is built up in KRL, as well as what happens when one invokes the consultation shell, can be best seen by considering the very simple illustration below. The listing BHARATH.KRL (Fig. A-1) is a representation in KRL of the relevant knowledge base for the following problem:

In our university, students can enroll in the course CP440 if they have taken a prerequisite course CP110. If not, they can still enroll if they get special permission from the instructor who teaches the course. This problem will suffice to illustrate the nature of the language and to show how it tries to be as "natural-language-like" as possible.

The following features of this representation in KRL are worth noting:

```
/*                    BHARATH.KRL                    */
/*              Always start with a title                   */
title            'advice on enrolling in cp440 '.
'  This is control section, so          ' &
'it will be displayed always          ' &
'DECIDING ELIGIBILITY FOR CP 440'.

reference pre_reqs.

/*Control section ends because new section is declared below*/
/*     SECTION            PRE_REQS                 */

section pre_reqs:
  'Check first if person has taken cp110   '.

/*EXAMPLE OF PARA TO BE DISPLAYED IF A CONDITION IS MET*/

{has_prereq}
  OK, you can enroll in cp440'.

has_prereq: 'has taken cp110'
fact
explanation
'a student who has taken cp110 is eligible to enroll'
askable
'hello, ' . . @student . .', Have you completed cp 110?'.

student: 'name of the student'
phrase
askable 'What is your name?'.

{not has_prereq}
/*  REFERENCE  PASSES  CONTROL  TO ANOTHER  SECTION  */
reference permission.

/*  NEW  SECTION        PERMISSION              */

section permission: 'checks if instructor has given permission'.

{has_permission}
'OK, you can enroll'.

has_permission: 'has taken permission of instructor'
fact
askable
'Well, '. . @student . .', Have you got permission from the' &
     'instructor teaching the course?'.

{not has_permission}
'Sorry, you cannot enroll. You ;need either' &
'cp 110 or special permission of instructor'.
```

Fig. A-1. Listing of BHARATH.KRL, a simple expert system created using ES/P Advisor and its Prolog-like language, KRL.

1) A knowledgebase starts with a title, which explains what it is about.
2) The first part is called the *control section*, which is where the processing of the knowledgebase always starts. If a string of characters between single quotation marks are entered here, they will display on the screen. In my example, the screen will display **This is control section . . . ELIGIBILITY FOR CP440.**
3) An important feature of a KRL knowledgebase is that it is divided into sections, each of which has a heading (in the example, there is a section called **pre_reqs** and another called **permission**).
4) The knowledgebase is structured by "references" to relevant sections. In this example, we see that starting at the beginning or control section, we are given a reference to the **pre_reqs** section.
5) The fundamental units in a knowledgebase in KRL are pieces of text which are "animated," that is, displayed on the screen as advice or guidance, *if the condition for their display is satisfied*. These are called *paragraphs*. (The knowledgebase can be annotated with comments enclosed in **/* */**, which have no effect whatever and are only for explanatory purposes in the text of the knowledgebase.)

In item 5 above, the piece of text "**OK, you can enroll**", following the comment

/* EXAMPLE OF PARA TO BE DISPLAYED IF CONDITION IS MET */

has a condition, {**has pre_reqs**} above it. So, when we look at the knowledgebase to see what it means to say the condition {**has pre_reqs**} is satisfied, we see a typical conditional test. We see a definition of **has_prereqs**, and a cursory reading of the definition conveys the general idea that a question, "Have you taken CP110?" would be asked. Depending on the answer, the system would decide if the condition is met, allowing it to display, "OK, you can enroll now."

Looking at the definition in more detail, the key facets of this definition are that it says:

a) The expression **has_prereqs** is a fact.
b) It is described as "askable," and followed by "Have you taken CP110?". You can guess that the system is going to ask this question; if the person says yes, it will decide to give the message, "OK, you can enroll in CP440."
c) We see also that there is another conditional message, {**not has_prereqs**}. Once again you can guess that if the person says no to the **has_prereqs** question the system is going to try the **not has_prereqs** paragraph. This refers us to another section, **permission**.

In item (c) the design of the permission section is very similar. There is another question asked, "Have you got permission from the instructor?" Depending on the answer, the student gets permission to enroll or not. A paragraph with no condition would be displayed without checking, as in the case of the paragraph in the control section.

It is impossible to go into detail on all aspects of constructing a knowledgebase and the various rules governing how to express information, but I hope this simple example gives you an intuitive feel of how KRL aims to make recording information in a knowledgebase more like natural language.

Once the KRL Compiler program is invoked to convert this representation into a form that can be processed by the computer, the system generates a new file called BHARATH.KBS. A knowledgebase created by the user is designated **xxx.KRL**, and the system keeps the same name and creates a file **xxx.KBS** for further processing; we may think of the latter as the information which is processed by the *consultation shell*.

The distinguishing features of the consultation shell program are that in addition to following the database, and asking questions, and following the references to different sections as provided in the knowledgebase, there are a number of features which make this process as close to a person-to-person dialogue as possible. Suppose you ask the consultation shell to operate with the BHARATH.KBS file. The system prints out the initial display and asks, **What is your name?** It is instructive, instead of immediately typing in your name, to respond with the question **Why?** The consultation shell program replies:

> **I am asking because I wish to establish what is the name of the student mentioned either in an advice paragraph or in . . . a question which is to be displayed.**

You can see that the question it asks involves a student, and it has to get a value for this by asking the "What is your name" question.

Now suppose I type in **bharath**. The system responds:

> **hello, bharath, have you completed cp 110?**

If, instead of replying "yes" or "no," if I ask "why?" the system again gives an explanation:

> **I am asking because I wish to establish whether**
> **has taken cp110" (has_prereq) which is a necessary pre-condition for the display for the following paragraph:**
> **"OK, you can enroll in cp 440."**

The ability to ask "Why?" at any stage, and give an explanation in terms of the structure of conditions in the database, makes the consultation shell a real pleasure to use. You should be able to guess that if you reply no to the question, the knowledgebase will reference the section **permission** and ask: **Well, bharath, have you got permission from the instructor?**

This is a simple simplification of the construction and use of a knowledgebase. The principal aspects other than those we have seen in this example are that questions can be asked not merely to get yes/no answers to what were described as "facts." It is also possible to use rules to assign values to variables of different kinds, and use them for deciding which section to reference next. (The manual describes all these different variables as *fact parameters, number parameters, phrase parameters*, and *category parameters*).

A particular reason this package will be of interest to students of Prolog is that the KRL Compiler program, as well as the Consultation Shell program, were written using Prolog. Because of this the system allows sections of the knowledgebase to be written in prolog if the user so wishes. The user therefore has the flexibility of using a mix of KRL and Prolog. However, the user needs the Prolog-1 interpreter as well as the ES/P ADVISOR package, which can otherwise be used on its own, to do this.

The manual is well-written, and includes a tutorial section. This section takes a section of regulations in Britain regarding the paperwork an employer has to do when hiring a new employee. The actions required vary according to various circumstances, such as whether the employment is for less than a week, or whether the employee has a certificate from the previous employer, and so on. The package also comes with other sample knowledge bases.

Constructing a knowledgebase using KRL seems to be a step nearer natural language than constructing it in Prolog, though it still requires careful attention to the do's and don'ts of how to express the information. A helpful feature is that when one uses the KRL Compiler to convert the knowledgebase file into a file which can be run on the computer, the Compiler program checks for internal consistency, and points out any errors it finds. The consultation shell, and especially its explanatory facilities, are impressive. I have described the facility for asking "Why?"; there are other facilities, of which two deserve special mention. One is the ability to turn a tracing mechanism on so that at each stage the program gives a "play-by-play" description of how it is processing the knowledgebase.

The second noteworthy feature is the ability to keep a record of all transactions by turning a "logging" facility on, which creates a disk file containing a full record of the questions asked by the system, the response given by the user, etc.

For the casual user who is using knowledgebases designed by someone else, the consultation shell is excellent. For anyone planning to graduate from Prolog to using expert systems shells and expert system development packages, the facilities for design of the knowledgebase are also important. Because of the array of facilities provided, this Prolog-based package might be the natural choice for the next step forward into design of expert systems.

PROLOGS FROM AUTOMA DESIGN ASSOCIATES

Automata Design Associates (1570 Arran Way, Dresher, PA 19025) has introduced a number of versions of Prolog for different levels of requirement.

To start with they are to be congratulated for having made available a public domain version of Prolog. PDPROLOG, available for downloading from *BYTE* magazine's BYTEnet (*BYTE*, August 1985, page 149). PDPROLOG is also available from Automata Design Associates when you purchase their educational Prolog, or EDPROLOG. The main features of EDPROLOG which distinguish it from PDPROLOG are that it allows tracing (discussed in Chapter 8), and it also lets you link up with a text-editor from within Prolog by using an "exec" function.

Educational Prolog costs $29.95. EDPROLOG comes on a disk which also contains documentation to print out and use as the user guide. I found it an excellent introductory package with which a user would be quite satisfied until reaching the stage of making very specialized applications.

The syntax used is described as a variant of the Clocksin and Mellish standard. It is perhaps inevitable that all implementers would want to make changes they feel are helpful, but it is very convenient in EDPROLOG that the core Prolog associated with the C&M is found. It would be suitable to use this package as an adjunct to this book.

There is no built-in text editor, but using the disk with a word processor, either by using the "exec" function or by the usual process of getting out of Prolog and into the word processor, this lack is surmounted.

One feature I like is that unlike some other implementations, all possible solutions are not printed out automatically; you are given the option of replying "yes" or "no" to the prompt **More?** after the first solution has been displayed.

The user guide includes a brief Prolog primer, but I doubt it is really adequate for a real beginner. It is a handy reference once you have acquired a minimum background in Prolog.

If you want to experiment with Prolog before deciding whether to acquire a package like the ESI Prolog/ESP Advisor combination, it is a good idea to acquire EDPROLOG.

Automata Design Associates also produces a number of other versions of Prolog, incorporating features like random access file capability, virtual memory, and so on—relevant for those wishing to go deeper in the study of Prolog.

PROLOG V INTERPRETER

This interpreter of Prolog for the IBM PC, from Chalcedony Enterprises (5580, La Jolla Blvd, Suite 126, La Jolla, CA 929037), is very attractively prices (around $70). The claim made in the manual—that they have tried to make it "affordable, without cutting corners"—is justified.

Prolog V requires 128K and one disk drive. It runs on machines with PC-DOS/MS-DOS, versions 1.4 or later. The interpreter version on which my comments are based is version 1.10.

A *Primer and User's Manual* is provided. I found the initial tutorial introduction as well as the later reference section well-written. The interpreter is invoked after booting DOS by typing in **prolog_v**; the prompt which appears is >. As in all versions which do not use the **?-** as prompt, queries have to be prefaced by typing **?-**. Clauses are added to the database by just typing them in response to the prompt, and can be viewed by using **?-listing.**

The alternative form of typing in the question mark at the end of the question, in the form:

```
income(john,Howmuch) ?,
```

instead of:

```
?-income(john,Howmuch).
```

is provided for. I believe that in this, as well as in similar interpreters when this alternative is available, it is preferable to stick to the standard ?- .

Databases can be saved by:

```
save 'b:file1.pro' ?
```

or by

```
?-save 'b:file1.pro'.
```

Files can be brought into the working space by using:

```
?-load 'f:file1.pro'.
```

or the standard:

```
?-consult('b:file1.pro').
```

In Prolog V there is no difference between **load** and **consult**. Both add the clauses in the relevant file to the existing database, whereas in some implementations (such as Prolog 86), **load** and **consult** work slightly differently.

When multiple solutions can be obtained for a question, Prolog V will normally display all the answers instead of displaying them one by one and asking if the user needs a further search. A nice thing about Prolog V is a built-in function called **solveone**. If you give the directive **?-solveone.**, thereafter the system will ask **MORE>** after displaying each solution of a multiple-solution question, giving you the opportunity to respond yes or no. Giving the directive **?-solveall**. reverts to the condition of displaying all alternative solutions without pause.

For lists, both alternative notations, **[Head ¦ Tail]**, and **[Head, .. Tail]** are provided.

Arithmetic is restricted to whole numbers or integers. Addition, subtraction, multiplication and, integer division giving only the whole number part of division are provided. There is also a modulo operator which will give the remainder after integer division. The goal **?- X is 20/3** would give X = 6, and the goal **Y is 20 mod 3** would give Y = 2.

For input output operations the standard predicates **read, write, getc,** and **putc** are provided. The predicates **see, tell,** etc., for redirecting the input and output from the keyboard and screen to alternative files are provided. The **trace** predicate for tracing execution of a program, as well as the spy points are provided.

Section I of the manual is a tutorial introduction. Section II lists all the built-in predicates. There is an alphabetically arranged glossary of Prolog vocabulary in Section III. Another section gives explanations of the error messages. The manual one is of the best I have seen.

There is no built-in editor, so the user has to use this Prolog in conjunction with a suitable word processor for programs where the editing possibilities of using **assert, retract**, etc., are not sufficient.

PROLOG-86 INTERPRETER

The PROLOG-86 interpreter for IBM PCs is made by Micro-AI (P.O. Box 91,

Rheem Valley, CA 94570); the manual says it is adapted from the University of New South Wales version of Prolog implemented by Claude Sammut. It is available for IBM PCs in MS-DOS/PC-DOS and CP/M-86 versions. The review below is of version 1.12 for MS-DOS. It requires at least 128K and one disk drive. This is a very reasonably priced piece of software (about $100).

The manual is very helpful. In addition to installation instructions, it has a tutorial section and a more detailed reference manual section. It gives the basics of Prolog and leads comfortably into the fundamentals of creating databases, asking questions, etc.

When the interpreter is booted by using **prolog**, the prompt sign appears, it is a colon rather than a **?-**. This is different from most other versions. The user must type in **?-** to ask questions. The advantage is that when adding clauses to the database you do not have to say **asserta**. If you type in a clause in response to the prompt, the clause is added to the database at the end of existing clauses.

As an alternative to the standard way of asking a question or setting a goal. PROLOG-86 lets you use the alternative notation of adding the question mark at the end of the goal:

```
income(john,Howmuch) ? .
```

This is one of the variations from the Clocksin and Mellish standard. The manual has a appendix listing the major differences from the Clocksin and Mellish standard. Since both notations work, it may be preferable for the user to stick to **?-**, since most of the literature and sample programs he or she is likely to come across would use this form.

To return to the operating system PROLOG-86 uses <Ctrl+C>, as well as the standard prolog predicate **?-halt**.

When a question has multiple answers PROLOG-86 produces all alternative solutions automatically. You can use the cut operator (!) to cut off further search. Comments can be added to programs by prefacing them by a percent (%) sign. This again is different from the standard.

Regarding arithmetic, only integers or whole numbers are handled. They can be in the range −32765 to 32764. The add (+), subtract (−), and multiply (*) operations are provided. Since only integers are used, the divide(/) operation is only integer or modulo division, giving only the whole number part of division: **X is 20/3** would instantiate X to 6. a mod operator is also provided to give the remainder resulting from integer division: **Y is 33 mod 4** would instantiate Y to 1.

Unfortunately, there is no provision for editing programs. You can add and remove clauses from the database using the **assert** and **retract** predicates, but the most convenient way would be to use it in conjuction with a word processor. Create a text file and then bring it in from PROLOG-86 by using some of the commands discussed below.

The **asserta** and **assertz** for adding clauses at the beginning and end are provided in standard form. There is also an **assert** provided, but it has the same effect as **assertz**. To remove clauses, **retract** is provided, as well as a **retractall** for removing everything.

A variation in PROLOG-86 is that when using predicates which are commands to manipulate the database, you can give the command in the form:

```
retract( income(john,20))! .
```

Again, for conformity to the general standard, it may be preferable to use the standard form rather than the special alternative. This also applies to the procedures for saving or loading a whole database. You can save the contents of the working space by:

```
save( 'b:file1.pro' ) !  .
```

or by:

```
?-save( 'b:file1.pro' ).
```

To bring a file into the database, you can use the standard:

```
?-consult('b:file1.pro')
```

or:

```
load 'b:file1.pro'.
```

The difference between is that **consult** adds the clauses from the file at the end of the database, and **load** replaces the database with the contents of the file. PROLOG-86 does not provide for the reconsult operation. Nor is giving a list of files as an alternative way of consulting a series of files provided.

A nonstandard alternative notation for formatting lists is provided: **[Head,..Tail]**.

The **read** and **write** predicates for input and output of terms are provided as well as predicates **getc** and **putc** for characters. **See**, **tell**, etc., for changing the file for input and output instead of the terminal for input and screen for output are also provided.

The manual describes in detail the sample programs on the distribution disk. There are sample programs for a natural language interface, symbolic differentiation, implementation of LISP functions, a simple expert system using the game "animals," and a planning program. The samples are all very interesting and helpful.

The first part of the manual explains most of the terms with suitable examples; there is a reference section which systematically defines the various predicates included in the implementation. There is also an appendix which lists the major differences from the Clocksin and Mellish version.

MICRO-PROLOG PACKAGE

The micro-PROLOG version of Prolog for microcomputers is made by Logic Programming Associates (10 Burntwood Close, London SW18 3JU, England); it is available in CP/M versions for Z-80 computers, as well as MS-DOS/PC-DOS and CP/M-86 versions for IBM PCs and compatibles. The version described below is version 3.1 under MS-DOS. It requires at least 128K.

I have called it the micro-PROLOG package rather than micro-PROLOG interpreter because the distribution disk has what one might call three languages on it. When you boot the disk by invoking the basic micro-PROLOG interpreter (by using the invocation **prolog**) the prompt which appears on the screen is an ampersand plus a period (&.). The syntax you use to communicate with the basic micro-PROLOG system is different from the Clocksin and Mellish standard or the Edinburgh version. However, it should not be too difficult to adjust. The distribution disk has a file called DEC.LOG, which you load by entering **LOAD DEC**, in response to the **&**. prompt, or at the beginning: **prolog load dec**. When the DEC.LOG file has been loaded the prompt which appears is **?-**., and you are in effect using a version which is practically the same as the Clocksin and Mellish standard.

We will look at the fundamental "language" in the micro-PROLOG package and then look at the supplementary programs which let us use the two other languages. The first is the DEC program which lets us use the standard Prolog language, and another is a program called SIMPLE which lets us communicate using what the manual calls a "sugared easy-to-read syntax."

The key feature about the standard micro-PROLOG syntax is that everything is expressed as a list. To enter what we think of as a fact in standard Prolog, enter it as a list with the predicate as the first item in the list and the arguments as the other items; **income(john,30).** is entered in micro-PROLOG as **(income john 30).** Similarly, a rule which in standard Prolog might be:

```
parent_of(Father,Son) :- father_of(Father,Son).
```

would be entered in micro-PROLOG in the form:

```
( (parent_of x y) ( father_of x y ) ).
```

A rule is also treated as a list, with the head clause as the first item, and any clauses in the body as the other items, with each clause itself in list form. ( ) rather than [ ] are used to enclose lists. The manual explains that the standard micro-PROLOG syntax, which is close to the list syntax of LISP, was adopted to allow a compact and efficient implementation. Clauses are added by just typing them in response to the prompt.

Chapter 2 of the manual gives the basic syntax, and chapter 3 describes the various methods of adding clauses to the database, removing from the database, loading and saving files, etc. The discussions in the manual are very thorough, going into depth explaining the underpinnings of micro-PROLOG. However, it is not in tutorial form, and recommending Clark and McCabe's book, *micro-PROLOG: Programming in Logic* as the book to read as you use the instructions in the manual.

The standard syntax of micro-PROLOG is something which the user is likely to come to only at a later stage. When first using it you are more likely to benefit by using the SIMPLE program development system, which is what is called a "front-end" program. (When it is loaded, users have a "virtual machine" at the front end connecting them to the system, to which they can talk in a language different from standard micro-PROLOG, and the SIMPLE program takes care of translating the user's communications into standard micro-PROLOG.)

Load the SIMPLE program by typing: **LOAD SIMPLE** in response to the prompt after entering **prolog**, or at the beginning by typing: **prolog load simple.** The message that SIMPLE has been loaded appears, and the prompt is still the **&.**

The adjustment you have to make between standard Prolog and the language of the SIMPLE front-end program is fairly easy. Look at the following major differences in the next few paragraphs.

Facts with one argument can be represented in either of the two different ways shown below: with the predicate first as in standard Prolog, or with the predicate last.

```
expensive(rolls_royce).
rolls_royce expensive.
```

Facts with two arguments could also be entered in two different ways: predicate at the beginning or predicate between the arguments:

```
age( john 30)
(john age 30).
```

A minor difference is that arguments are separated by blanks rather than commas.

To add facts to the database, the built-in predicate is **add** rather than **assert**:

```
&. add(   age(john 30)   )
```

add is the equivalent of **assertz**, adding at the end, but there is also an option to add at a designated place, e.g., **add 3 ( )**. to put the new clause third in the list of clauses for the predicate.

In line with the general aim of the SIMPLE front-end there is a built-in predicate **accept**. This echoes back the predicate, so that you have to type in only the arguments. If you enter **&.accept age**, the system keeps coming back with prompts **&.age**. The system reverts to a normal prompt if you type in the word **end**.

Removing clauses uses the predicate **delete** rather than **retract**.

In regard to rules, the SIMPLE system explicitly puts in the words **if** and **and**. A rule with one goal in the body might be:

```
(x parent_of y) if (x father_of  y)
```

and a goal with two rules in the body might be:

```
qualified (x) if lives_in(x Michigan) and veteran(x)
```

This brings up differences in the way variables are treated. In micro-PROLOG any of the six symbols **X,Y,Z ,x,y,z** are variables, and so are any of these symbols followed by a whole number: **x32** or **Z11**. Anything else is a constant. However, in formulating rules there is a provision for using other sequences of characters as variables by specifically saying so. One could say:

```
parent_of(Person1 Person2) if father_of(Person1 Person2) and (Person1
Person2) vars
```

For querying the database, micro-PROLOG provides a number of alternatives. The predicates **which** and **all** have the same effect, and produce all possible solutions:

```
all(x  y : age(x y) )
```

display in turn all possible solutions to **age(x y)**. Another nice touch is that you can make the output even more readable by inserting any words you want:

```
all( x 's age is y : age(x y) )
```

produces output in the form: **john 's age is 30, mary's age is 25**, etc.

As an alternative to **all** or **which** you can use the word **one**. In this case, after displaying each solution the system asks **More(y/n) ?**. Depending on your answer, it may display alternative solutions.

The SIMPLE system is much closer to English than standard Prolog, but is capable of all the tasks you might want. The manual says that after acquiring experience with the SIMPLE front-end, users tend to go on to the standard micro-PROLOG syntax. The disk has a program which has various extensions to the standard micro-PROLOG. These are accessed by loading a program called MICRO. Using the standard syntax and the MICRO program may be something which attracts programmers who want to go into more theoretical applications.

Another front-end, DEC, allows you to use practically the same language as the Clocksin and Mellish standard. There is also a built-in line editor, but it is somewhat restricted, and use with a word processor may be more convenient.

Overall this is an extremely sophisticated package with a variety of interesting options. If you want to go in-depth into standard Prolog and are not attracted by the other options, it may be better to go for ESI Prolog. These two packages are in about the same price range. Micro-Prolog provides a lot of options of value for the non-casual user.

One other plus for micro-PROLOG is an expert system package written in micro-PROLOG, a natural application for the user of this package to graduate. I have not tried the package, which is called APES, or Augmented Prolog for Expert Systems, but have only looked at the manual. It seems a very interesting way of designing and building modest-sized expert systems.

Appendix B

Artificial Intelligence, Expert Systems and Prolog

The aim of this appendix is to look at Prolog in relation to the general field of artificial intelligence, particularly with reference to so-called "expert systems."

What is artificial intelligence, or AI?

Over the years, one of the major goals of computer scientists has been to improve communication between computers and human beings. This doesn't mean merely making it possible for people to communicate with computers in natural languages like English, although of course that is one of the things involved in better communication. It also involves expanding the range of things computers can do. This process seems to involve a trend towards telling computers what we want done and letting the computer work out step-by-step procedures—an emphasis on the *declarative* or *descriptive* mode rather than the imperative mode.

This field is usually referred to as artificial intelligence, or AI. The generally accepted definition of AI is the one given by Professor Marvin Minsky, one of the pioneers and leaders in the field. He described AI as being concerned with getting computers to do things, which, if they were done by human beings, would be regarded as intelligent. What is regarded as intelligent is a relative rather than absolute classification.

In the old days, when arithmetic was something known only to a few scholars, anyone who could add, subtract, multiply, or divide would have been rated as intelligent. But today we regard it as a trivial skill which anyone with a pocket calculator can do, and which is taught routinely in schools. In a sense, we could say that AI is concerned with finding ways to convert currently rare or difficult skills into routine operations. From that point of view, we can think of AI as something whose content changes from time to time, because when a way has been found to "routinize" something which is rated as intelligent, AI goes on to try to find a way of transforming some other skill. However, while the problems AI deals with change this way, the activity of AI remains the same—seeking to extend the range or repertoire of computers, and finding ways for computers to be used to solve new types of problems. A program for more effective recognition of human speech broadens computer applications, and qualifies as AI.

AI has had varying success. For instance, the human backgammon champion of the world was beaten by a computer program in 1978. Earlier, a computer program found a better proof for one of the theorems in a classical mathematical book, *Principia Mathematica,* by Whitehead and Russell. And chess playing programs have advanced to grand master levels, though not to world champion levels.

One aspect of the efforts to make computers smarter is the development of what are called "expert systems," programs which can substitute at least in part for a human expert. In a sense, all computer programs have this characteristic. A program for calculating averages can be thought of as taking over the kind of job that skilled and trained statisticians used to do in the precomputer age. A database program which retrieves the information we ask for is partly replacing the file clerks or other record keepers who used to organize files in a way suitable for quick access to information. But the term "expert system" is applied only to some such programs.

There seems to be a difference between two categories of skills we usually call "expert." The first is where we understand in principle how the job is done, but the expert seems to be able to do it much more quickly than most people. This would describe somebody who is good at payroll calculations, or doing arithmetic in their head.

In the second category of expertise it is not clear what the underlying facets of the skill are. An example would be the way in which an expert on automobile engines can diagnose what is wrong, using the same information available to the non-expert; similarly, information about symptoms is meaningful to the doctor, but the layperson cannot use the information. Often the expert is not able to spell out the basis on which he or she make an expert judgement.

Programs which can replicate this second category of expertise are the ones usually referred to as expert systems. This is also a relative term; a few years ago anyone who knew how to use a microcomputer would have been regarded by most people as an expert, but now the boundary defining expertise in this area has changed. Because of this fuzziness about what exactly an expert system is, some computer scientists prefer to use alternative descriptions. In *Artificial Intelligence,* Winston says he prefers to call such programs *design and analysis systems.* Other computer scientists use names like *intelligent assistants.*

There is one broad classification of decisions it is helpful to keep in mind. There are some decision-making processes for which the procedure or technique for processing the input information is well-defined. These are usually referred to as *highly structured,* and designing computer programs for such decisions is in principle a task which can be carried out using well-understood methods. There may be a lot of detailed work to be done and considerable scope for creative and insightful design when the task is very complex.

But many important decision processes are what are called *ill-structured*, where the procedure to be used is not well-defined or clear. The medical diagnosis situation mentioned earlier is a typical example. Another example is decision-making for economic policy. These are often handled by what are called *heuristic* methods of problem-solving. A heuristic method can be thought of as something which usually works well, but involves rules of thumb or "good judgement." Most important, a heuristic sometimes may go wrong. The greatest value of expert systems programs is in handling problem where heuristic approaches are required. A heuristic method is contrasted with an *algorithm*, a term we have seen before, which describes procedures consisting of a finite number of steps which we know for sure will find the best solution for the problem at hand.

In the search for ways to extend the range of tasks in which computers can help us, there has been a change in approach between the period up to the 1960s and the period from the 1970s onwards. In the first phase it was thought that some powerful principles of problem-solving could be discovered and taught to computers, which could then apply these techniques to problems in any area whatever. Some very powerful general principles of problem-solving were identified, such as systematic methods of reducing the necessary trial and error or search when there were a large number of possible solutions available. Applications of these principles led to impressive results in areas such as proving mathematical theorems. However, this approach did not lead to as much progress as was initially hoped for.

A feeling grew that the best way to solve problems in a particular discipline was closely linked to the special kinds of knowledge required in that area, what is referred to as *domain-specific knowledge.* From the 1970s onwards great attention has been paid to the importance of the *knowledgebase* required by a program, as well as the methods by which conclusions are drawn. The term *knowledge engineering,* and the description of programs as *knowledge-based systems,* have come into use for emphasizing the importance of the background knowledge. This is what was embodied as folk wisdom in the old saying, "Knowledge is power."

One final aspect of AI in general and expert systems in particular is worth mentioning. The search for ways to make computers more helpful in more areas of human thought and action has led computer scientists to explore fundamental questions more deeply. These include such questions as: What is knowledge? What does solving a problem involve? What are the characteristics of experts which enable them to do things most people cannot do? The field of AI has led to creative interaction with studies of fundamental questions about human thinking and psychology; we might say that in part AI is a field which is deeply philosophical as well as action-oriented.

One result of this is that AI has inevitably led to controversy about whether computers "really" can be called intelligent, or whether a computer will ever be able to do everything a human being can do, whether the fact that a program successfully simulates the working of the human mind implies that we understand the human mind better, and so on. These are important questions, no doubt, but from a pragmatic point of view, it may be more convenient to regard AI as a field which tries to get computers to carry out more and more of the intellectual activities that human beings carry out. It does not commit us to a position on how far this process can go, or whether it can go beyond the frontiers of what humans are at present capable of doing.

What are the fundamental principles underlying knowledgebase design and analysis systems or "expert" systems?

An expert system is usually regarded as having the following components, connected as shown in Fig. B-1. Let us look at the different parts of the system.

The two important principles involved in knowledgebased systems are:

- ☐ They are knowledge-intensive. Their power comes from the amount of background information available to the system.
- ☐ They are oriented towards using heuristic knowledge.

There has to be some provision for holding this knowledge; the *knowledgebase* is what holds the information. Then we need some kind of computer program to use the knowledgebase and apply it to a problem, to draw useful conclusions and frame recommendations or advice on what should be done. This program is usually referred to as an *inference engine.* We also need some mechanism for deciding which rules are applicable in the current case. In other words, we require a control mechanism for operating the production system. This is also part of the inference engine.

It is generally regarded as desirable that an expert system should be able to explain why it drew certain conclusions or recommends certain actions. It would also be convenient if the knowledgebase could be modified without too much trouble, by adding new knowledge and deleting knowledge which does not seem so useful.

The diagram shows the need for two-way communication between the user and the inference engine. The inference engine accepts the user's questions, including the information supplied by the user about the current problem, and interacts with the knowledgebase to draw conclusions and return them to the user. The two-way communication between the user and the knowledgebase through the "knowledge refiner" is the mechanism for the user to examine or update the database.

Because the knowledgebase is the source of the power of a knowledgebased system,

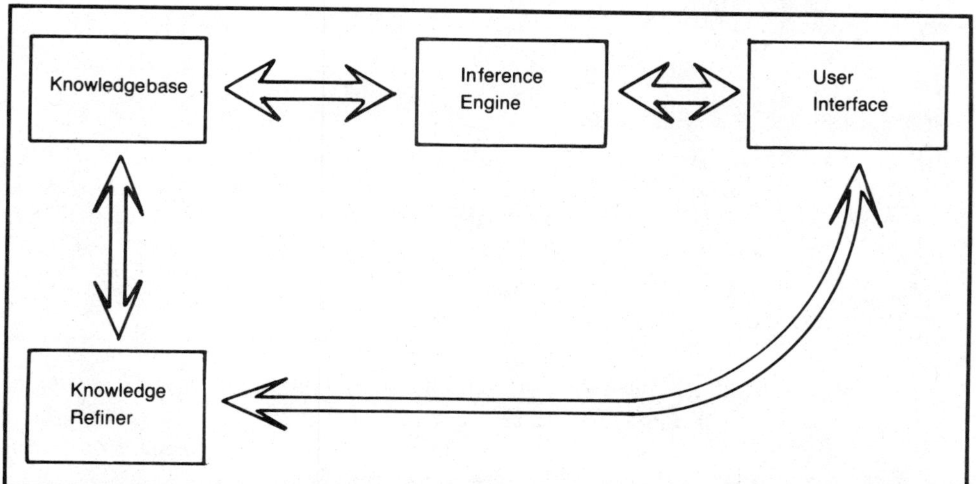

Fig. B-1. Components of an expert system.

a very important issue arises: how should the knowledge the system uses be represented or structured for use by the system? There have been a number of approaches, but one which has proved very successful and is relevant for us in regard to the usefulness of Prolog as a language for AI and expert systems is the representation of knowledge in the form of *production rules* or a *production system.*

What is a production system?

We can think of a production system as a way of looking at the task of information processing as transforming input data into output results by using a number of conditional rules. From this point of view, when we are trying to solve a problem there are two different types of information we deal with:

1) We have information about the facts and circumstances of the problem with which we are dealing.
2) To process this data, we use general principles and rules. Very often these are not "logically cast-iron" rules, but heuristic rules which have proved effective in practice. We have to put all this in the knowledgebase we use to solve the problem.

When the question of how the knowledge should be represented in the knowledgebase is considered, it is remarkable that by trying to express the knowledgebase in the form of a set of "conditional rules" people have found that really powerful systems can be built. The conditional rules are referred to as the *production rules* or part of the *production system.*

The structure of a conditional rule might look something like:

IF *some condition* A *is true about this case,*
AND (*or* OR) *some condition* B *is true;*
AND (*or* OR) *some condition* C *is true;* . . .
•
•
•
THEN *take actions* P *and* Q *and* R, *etc.*

The actions P, Q, etc., could be recommendations for action or conclusions to be drawn. Most successful expert systems in use today are based on the model of production systems.

This idea of conditional rules seems a fairly simple idea.

It is, but the insight that it is a tool for building very powerful systems has proved one of the most useful of ideas. It reminds me of the character in the movie (and Jean Anouilh's play) *Becket,* who says something to the effect that the best ideas often are very simple, but it takes a very clever person to think of them!

Let us consider this question of the effectiveness of production systems by con-

symptom1	symptom2	symptom3	disease
yes	no	no	disease1
no	yes	no	disease2
no	no	yes	disease3
yes	yes	no	disease4
yes	no	yes	disease5
no	yes	yes	disease6
yes	yes	yes	disease7

Fig. B-2. One way of representing knowledge in an expert system. The simple symptom-disease matrix shown here illustrates "production rules."

sidering the classic example of a powerful knowledgebased system, the MYCIN system developed at Stanford. This is a system for diagnosing bacterial infections. It was designed using a large number of If-Then rules. Typical rules from MYCIN are reproduced in many of the textbooks on expert systems, giving rules which include statements like: "IF the morphology of the organism is rod," or "IF the stain of the organism is Gramneg," "THEN there is evidence that the identity of the organism is Pseudomonas-aeruginosa." These technical terms are meaningful only to those who work in the field, but what we should remember is that they are really some conditions to be checked to see if they are true, and conclusions to be drawn based on checking the conditions.

To understand how a set of production rules can be useful for medical diagnosis or other decision-making, and how Prolog is particularly suitable for use, let us consider a very simplified situation.

Say there are three symptoms, called "sym1," "sym2," and "sym3," and we know that different combinations of these symptoms are indicative of different diseases, which we will label "disease1," "disease2," etc. The connection between the pattern of symptoms and the diseases could be as shown in Fig. B-2.

How could we write a production rule which could be used for, say, disease 5?

We could express it as:

```
IF symptom1 is present
     AND symptom2 is absent
     AND symptom3 is present
THEN diagnose disease5.
```

We could put in six more production rules, and we can see that it is immediately possible to translate a production rule into a Prolog program.

How could we set up the relationship between patterns of symptoms and diseases, using a predicate cause*? Write your answer before reading further.*

Something like this would fill the bill:

```
cause(disease1, [sym1]).
cause(disease2, [sym2]).
cause(disease3, [sym3]).
cause(disease4, [sym1, sym2]).
cause(disease5, [sym1, sym3]).
cause(disease6, [sym2, sym3]).
cause(disease7, [sym1, sym2, sym3]).
```

Now suppose we enter the specific information about each patient using a predicate suffers_from. For instance, we might have:

```
suffers_from(john, [sym1,sym3]).
suffers_from(mary,[sym2]).
```

How can we design a rule with the head goal as diagnose *and two arguments; one where we will supply the patient's name and the other for the program, to instantiate to the name of the disease?*

You would, I am sure, have immediately written down a rule like this one:

```
diagnose(Person, Disease) :-
      suffers_from(Person, Symptoms),
      cause(Disease, Symptoms).
```

We can see from this example that Prolog meshes beautifully with the production rule approach to designing knowledgebased systems.

However, you might want a knowledgebased system to be somewhat more interactive. It should be able to ask for the relevant information about the patient, and so on. On the basis of what we have seen of the "extra-logical" features of Prolog we could easily expand our skeleton program above along the following lines:

```
hi_doctor :-
      diagnose(Person,Disease),
      write(Person),
      nl,
      write(Disease),
      nl.
suffers_from(Person,Symptoms),
      write(' Patient name ? '),
      read(Person),
      write(' Give list of symptoms '),
      read(Symptoms).
```

Based on what we have seen of various features of Prolog, you see that if the user invokes the program by typing:

```
?-hi_doctor.
```

the program will ask for the patient's name and then the symptoms, and use its knowledgebase to draw conclusions.

You would want the program to ask for more patients' names, rather than end after diagnosing just one patient. You can easily extend the program by introducing a predicate which makes it repeat again and again. Attach a final goal to **hi_doctor**, which says **again**, where **again** is defined as:

```
again :- write('More ?') , read(yes), hi_doctor.
    again :- !.
```

Suppose you have six or seven or eight symptoms to check on. Clearly, the simple way we put in all lists above would not work. Instead of seven possible lists as above, there would be 255 possible lists with eight symptoms, or 1023 with ten symptoms and so on. You would have to investigate more efficient ways of representing the information.

For what other type of problem can we use this approach?

The important point in the above example is that many expert tasks are tasks of *classification*, using a number of criteria and associating different patterns of responses to the criteria for arriving at different conclusions. As another example, consider the problem of geological prospecting, one of the areas in which a famous expert system has been notably successful. (The program PROSPECTOR, developed in the late 1970s at Stanford Research Institute.)

Even though the field of geology is very different from that of medical diagnosis, from the view of production systems we can look at the similarity in structure of the process of arriving at conclusions. We could say this is also a *classificatory problem*, only the criteria used are no longer "symptoms," but various geological features which can be observed in an area. Different combinations or patterns of these features are to be associated with the different minerals whose presence the pattern makes likely. We can see that the same type of production rules could be designed, and the same type of Prolog program would work well.

What about rules about which we are not absolutely certain? For instance, a geological expert knows the presence of certain features in most cases leads to finding say, molybdenum, but sometime it doesn't work out. How can we use such rules?

Programs like MYCIN or PROSPECTOR make use of heuristic rules. I won't go into detail about how they handle such cases of less than 100 percent certainty. But we can consider the general principle, and see how it is very easy to incorporate into a Prolog program. Let us say that in our program above, the diagnosis that the list of symptoms **sym1** and **sym3** tends to indicate (but not invariably) **disease5**. We could change our database to:

```
cause(disease5,[sym1,sym3], 75).
```

and our rule for diagnosis to:

```
diagnose (Person,Disease,Certainty) :-
      suffers_from(Person,Symptoms),
      cause (Disease,Symptoms,Certainty).
```

We would get an answer that the disease is **disease5** and the "certainty" is 75. For each diagnosis, we could attach a *certainty factor* (CF) on a scale of 0 to 100, to indicate level of confidence one can have in the diagnosis.

One other aspect of expert systems we should note is the idea of "expert system shells."

What are expert system shells?

The idea is something we have implicitly looked at above: that expert systems for different tasks may be similar, with changes as in our example from "symptoms" to "geological features" and "diseases" to "minerals likely to be found." A shell is a common program which can be adapted to any expert system of a certain type by adapting the general structure to the specifics of that system. As an example, there is the ESP/ADVISOR shell, which I described in the appendix on software; reading that description will help you understand what a shell does.

What about other languages? Can they be used for expert systems, too?

In fact, most of the famous expert systems were written in a variety of languages, notably LISP, and some in Fortran or Forth or other languages. The point is that the features we would want in an expert system are an inherent feature of Prolog.

Prolog is not the only language which can be used, nor is it clear that it will be better than LISP, which also has many of the same virtues (allowing us to modify or refine the knowledgebase without having to disturb the inference engine, and providing for explanations easily). In a recent book, *Research and Development in Expert Systems*, Dr. M. A. Bramer points out that while there are a large number of working expert systems in LISP, comprehensive expert systems in Prolog are still rare. But what we can say is that Prolog is a convenient language for building knowledgebased systems, and with the further development of Prolog-based languages in the Fifth Generation Project, we may have languages with additional convenient features as well.

References

I highly recommend the following reading for further exploring the relationship of Prolog to expert systems, and for learning more about expert systems in general:

1) Clark, K. L., and McCabe, F. G. "Prolog as a Language for Expert Systems." In *Machine Intelligence 10.* New York: Ellis Horwood/John Wiley.
2) Forsyth, Richard, ed. *Expert Systems: Principles and Case Studies.* New York: Chapman and Hall, 1984.

Appendix C

Background on Logic

This appendix will look at the historical and theoretical background of the concept of "programming in logic." Let us start by looking at a brief history of logic.

What is logic?

Logic is the study of the principles and rules which tell us how to draw inferences or conclusions from given statements or *premises.* A *logically valid* procedure is one which has this property: IF the statements or facts we start with are true, and we apply a logically correct or valid procedure, THEN the conclusions are true.

In other words, we have a *conditional guarantee* when we use a logically valid procedure. We do not know whether our conclusion will be true or false if we start with statements or facts which are not true. This is sometimes described by saying that a *valid* argument is when we use a logically correct, or valid, or reliable process of drawing conclusions. If, in addition, the statements we start with are definitely true, our argument is not merely valid, it is also *sound.*

What is an example of a logically valid process of reasoning or drawing conclusions?

Perhaps the most famous example of valid logical arguments—almost everyone has heard of it—is this:

All men are mortal.
Socrates is a man.
Therefore, Socrates is mortal.

The person who is regarded as the father of logic is the Greek philosopher Aristotle (384-322 B.C.); the example above illustrates one of the various valid "forms of reasoning" which he tried to identify. He called the 19 valid forms he discovered *syllogisms*, and gave them different names.

The key concept here is that they are valid forms of reasoning. That is, it is not the *content* of the statements which is important, but the structure or form:

All X are Y.
Z is an X.
Therefore Z is Y.

If we have a valid form of reasoning, whatever values we give to the variables, it becomes an instance of that valid form.

Instead of instantiating X to **men,** Y to **mortal**, and Z to **Socrates,** we could instantiate X to **Americans**, Y to **1000 pounds in weight**, and Z to **John**, and get another instance:

All Americans are 1000 lbs in weight.
John in an American.
Therefore John weighs 1000 lbs.

This is a valid argument, but not a sound one, because the first statement we start with is not true. All this syllogism guarantees us is that *if* the first two statements are true, the last must be true.

Although this key idea of finding valid forms which could be used to check whether one is reasoning correctly was a great contribution, the 19 valid syllogisms found by Aristotle and his followers were not able to provide forms, or templates, for all the kinds of reasoning that were necessary. There were some types of facts which did not fit the template of any of the syllogisms. The next important breakthrough in finding valid forms of reasoning is credited to the 19th century mathematician George Boole.

What was Boole's major contribution?

In brief, Boole discovered a way to combine statements, or propositions, to make combined statements, using what are called the *logical operators*: AND, OR, and NOT. When we have statements of the type:

IF A is true AND B is true

or

IF A is true OR B is true

or

IF C is NOT true

there was no way to fit any of these into the syllogism templates of Aristotlean logic. Boole's discoveries enabled logicians to design valid forms of reasoning which could be used to check the correctness of reasoning when such statements were used.

However, there was still a problem. Boole's discoveries are usually referred to as *propositional logic* because they deal with how to combine propositions or statements using the logical operators. The statements which could be used had to be about some object or class of objects, and could be true or false statements. But Boole's system did not allow for statements which said something about "some" of the objects of a certain class of objects, as distinct from "all" the objects in that class. The system could not provide any guidance on valid forms of reasoning in such situations.

The position was that Aristotle's syllogisms gave rules for certain valid forms of reasoning, and Boole's propositional logic gave valid forms for some types of reasoning for which no syllogism existed, but there were situations where neither of the systems applied. The major advance that solved this problem is credited to the German mathematician Gottlob Frege. All the valid rules which the theory of syllogisms and the theory of propositional logic provided were part of Frege's system as well, but in addition it provided valid rules for types of reasoning which could not be handled by the other two systems. Frege's system, developed over the years by many others, is known as *first-order predicate logic.*

What is first-order predicate logic?

The predicates we have been using in Prolog are in fact the forms used in first-order predicate logic—that is, expressing statements in the form of relationships between objects. Essentially, what Frege showed was that all the valid forms of reasoning contained in the syllogisms and in propositional logic could be derived equally well by using predicates and certain rules for drawing conclusions.

Our interest is not so much in predicate logic in general, as in a subsequent discovery:

a) All predicate logic statements can, by following certain rules, be converted into a simple form known as *clause form.*
b) When you have statements in clause form you need only one rule for correctly drawing conclusions, instead of a number of correct rules which apply to different forms of statements.

A specially simple form of clauses is known as *Horn clause form.*

What is a Horn clause?

Roughly speaking, a Horn clause is a statement of the type:

```
IF predicate1(object1,object2, . . . ) is true
AND predicate2( obj3,obj4, . . . ) is true
AND predicate3( . . . ) is true
```

AND . . .
AND . . .
THEN predicateh (objecta, objectb, objectc, . . .) is true.

You see that the facts and rules we have been using in Prolog are in fact Horn clauses. They are called that in honor of the mathematician Alfred Horn, who first discovered that different forms of statements could be converted into this common form by using various rules for making the manipulations.

Why is it that all statements are put in Horn clause form in Prolog?

The second important discovery in the theory of logic which is of interest to us is the one that IF all the statements are in clause form, THEN only one simple rule for how to draw correct conclusions is required. The reason this is important is that if we have only one rule for drawing correct conclusions, then writing a computer program to draw conclusions is that much easier—we have to "teach" the system only that rule. That is precisely what a Prolog interpreter or translator does; it applies the one rule over and over again. It is these theoretical discoveries in logic which provide the underlying power of Prolog.

What is this single rule for drawing conclusions, and how have we seen it working in Prolog?

The rule is called *Robinson's resolution principle*, in honor of the mathematician and computer scientist J.A. Robinson, who first discovered it; others also have contributed to its development and refinement into the form in which it is used in Prolog. Again, without going into all the finer points, let us consider its connection with Prolog. The single rule for drawing inferences, the resolution principle, led to the development of a systematic procedure, or algorithm, which could be implemented on a computer. This is called the *unification algorithm.*

What does the unification algorithm give as the method for drawing inferences?

Suppose we have a series of statements of the form:

1) A is true if B1 is true AND B2 is true
2) B1 is true
3) B2 is true IF B3 is true
4) B3 is true

If we want the computer to see if the statement A is false or correct, the following rule is the only one we have to program into the system.

Suppose your goal is to prove that A is true. Look for the conditions on which the goal depends. In this case, we have the conditions *B2 is true* and *B3 is true.* Look for any other rules which match these conditions. In our case, we have the condition *B2 is true.* Thus we can reduce our original statement to the simpler form, *A is true IF*

B3 is true. We may say that we have "resolved" the two statements (1) and (2) and thereby eliminated B2.

Now try to "resolve away" the next condition: *B2 is true.* Looking for any other statement, we find *IF B3 is true B2 is true.* We can reduce our original goal to the form: A is true IF B3 is true. Now try to resolve B3.

We have the statement, *B3 is true,* so our original statement becomes *A is true.*

Is this resolution the same as what we thought of as pattern matching, replacing the head goal in a rule by the conjunction of goals in the body?

Yes. Technically, a Prolog interpreter is described as a *resolution theorem prover.* In describing how resolution works, I have changed it to a form where it fits in best with what we have already seen of how Prolog works. The formal description of the resolution principle would be slightly different in the books I have listed in the bibliography. I have followed the computer-oriented description which Robinson gives in his article in the book *Intelligent Systems,* edited by Hayes and Michie.

Appendix D

Illustrations and Problems in Prolog–86

by Margaret M. Sklar

The sample problems in this appendix are written in Prolog86, which is close enough to standard Prolog to make this a good choice. The appendix is divided into three main sections. The first section contains a discussion of baseball statistics using Prolog. The second is a mixture of whimsy and practicality. The last section discusses Prolog concepts as applied to relational databases. The entire appendix is meant to illustrate the principles introduced in the book and to give you further practice in dealing with Prolog.

A BASEBALL DATABASE

To illustrate a few of the basic Prolog techniques, let us start with an all-American database of baseball facts. The reader will have to pardon the author her admitted prejudices. It's a proven fact that baseball fans remain loyal whether their favorite team is winning or not. So, we start with a database of team members from the world-famous Marquette Mustangs:

```
player(mustangs;white,396,126,15,318).
player(mustangs,gribbs,366,107,20,292).
player(mustangs,lime,326,88,5,270).
player(mustangs,tram,394,106,8,269).
player(mustangs,garcon,164,44,5,268).
player(mustangs,perry,340,88,15,259).
player(mustangs,brooks,290,72,4,248).
player(mustangs,hearn,324,80,9,247).
```

```
player(mustangs,sanders,89,22,6,247).
player(mustangs,everard,306,75,23,245).
player(mustangs,melon,50,10,0,200).
player(mustangs,grimes,93,16,1,172).
player(mustangs,berg,78,13,2,167).
player(mustangs,flanagan,27,4,0,148).
player(mustangs,cassell,54,7,0,130).
```

Each fact in the database contains the team name, player name, at bats, number of hits, number of runs, and batting average. Since Prolog86 does not use decimal numbers, the batting average is multiplied by 1000 to give it an integer value.

We add to the facts above a pitcher relation:

```
pitcher(mustangs,harry,5,4,75,16,192).
pitcher(mustangs,tanning,4,3,58,15,233).
pitcher(mustangs,o_reilly,5,3,62,20,287).
pitcher(mustangs,murrow,12,6,174,60,309).
pitcher(mustangs,peters,12,10,178,68,343).
pitcher(mustangs,terrence,10,6,149,67,403).
pitcher(mustangs,shear,1,1,37,18,430).
pitcher(mustangs,smokey,1,7,60,30,448).
pitcher(mustangs,burns,2,3,40,26,575).
pitcher(mustangs,barn,2,0,41,31, 675).
```

Each fact contains information on team name, pitcher name, wins, losses, innings pitched, hits, and earned run average.

Simple queries can be made on either relation, such as:

```
?-player(mustangs, N, AB, H, R, AVG).
```

which would, of course, respond with a listing of Mustang player's names, at-bats, and so on. Since Mustangs are the only team in the relation, all the existing information will be retrieved.

To retrieve only the names and batting averages of the players, the query could be phrased:

```
?-player(mustangs, N, _, _, _, AVG).
```

The underscores represent anonymous variables, or variables in which we have no interest, and which will not be part of the answer. The above query results in:

```
N = white        AVG = 318
N = gribbs       AVG = 292
N = lime         AVG = 270
N = tram         AVG = 269
N = garcon       AVG = 268
```

```
N = perry          AVG = 259
N = brooks         AVG = 248
N = hearn          AVG = 247
N = sanders        AVG = 247
N = everard        AVG = 245
N = melon          AVG = 200
N = grimes         AVG = 172
N = berg           AVG = 167
N = flanagan       AVG = 148
N = cassell        AVG = 130
```

To search the database for only those averages over a certain value, say above 250, the query would be:

```
?-player(mustangs,N,_,_,_,A), A > 250.
```

The database would be searched for all names of players on the team. Remembering how Prolog instantiates variables, it should be obvious that the first value of N would be **white** and that A would be instantiated to 318. Since 318 is over 250, the response: **A = 318 N = white** would be printed, followed by the rest of the response:

```
A = 292            N = gribbs
A = 270            N = lime
A = 269            N = tram
A = 268            N = garcon
A = 259            N = perry
```

In like manner, we could ask for the names and win-loss records of pitchers who have an earned run average of 2.5 (listed as 250 in the database) or less:

```
?-pitcher(Team,Name,Wins,Losses,_,_,ERA), not (ERA > 250).
```

or, alternately:

```
?-pitcher(Team,Name,Wins,Losses,_,_,ERA), ERA <= 250.
```

and the response would be:

```
ERA   = 192          Team = mustangs
Name  = harry        Wins = 5      Losses = 4
ERA   = 233          Team = mustangs
Name  = tanning      Wins = 4      Losses = 3
```

Although Prolog is not primarily a number-cruncher, it can be used to do calculations on values within the database entries, as in the following example, which calculates batting averages:

```
batting_average:-
   player(T, N, AB, H, R, AVG),
   Average is H * 1000/AB,
   write(Average).
```

Since Prolog86 does not allow for decimal positions, and the average is desired to three decimal places, the number of hits is first multiplied by 1000 and then divided by the times at bat to get the batting average. Unfortunately, the version of Prolog86 I am using does not allow for products in excess of 32000, so the above rule will give incorrect results. Prolog86 does, however, allow for modular division, so that: **Y is A mod B** sets Y to the remainder when dividing A by B.

The response to:

```
?-Y is 343 mod 90.
```

is: Y = 73, since 343 divided by 90 is three with a remainder of 73. Using this feature, the batting average rule could be rewritten:

```
batting_average:-
   player(T, N, AB, H, R, AVG),
   X is H * 100/AB,
   Y is H * 100 mod AB,
   Z is Y * 10/AB,
   Average is X * 10 + Z,
   write(Average).
```

To clarify this rule , let's step through it one line at a time:

```
batting_average:-
```

is the format for indicating that this is the head of the rule.

```
player(T, N, AB, H, R, AVG)
```

retrieves from the database a fact of the form specified, and instantiates the specified variables to correspond to values in the fact; that is, looking at the above database, the first player entry is:

```
player(mustangs,white,396,126,15,318).
```

so that the variables are instantiated as follows:

```
T = mustangs
N = white
AB = 396
H = 126
```

```
R = 15
AVG = 318.
```

It should be noted that the batting average is already in the database, but the above calculations will be necessary when it comes time to update the batting average, which is by no means a constant value in real life.

```
X is H * 100/AB
```

instantiates the variable X to the value 126 times 100 divided by 396, or 31 (since Prolog86 uses integer division only).

```
Y is H * 100 mod AB
```

instantiates the variable Y to the remainder when H * 100 (12600) is divided by AB (396), or 324.

```
Z is Y * 10 /AB
```

instantiates the variable Z to the value received by dividing 10 times the remainder by the times at bat (3240 / 396), or Z = 8.

```
Average is X * 10 + Z
```

instantiates the variable Average to the sum of Z and X times 10, or 318.

```
Write(Average)
```

prints the value of the variable Average.

The above can be used to calculate and show on the screen batting averages from values within the database. When the query

```
batting_average?
```

is entered, the response will be:

```
318** yes
292** yes
269** yes
269** yes
268** yes
258** yes
248** yes
246** yes
247** yes
245** yes
```

```
200** yes
172** yes
166** yes
148** yes
129** yes
```

It should be understood that while the averages are calculated, this command does not affect the actual values in the database in any way! To change the values in the database, the predicates **retract, retractall, assert, assertz,** and **asserta** can be used. Thus:

```
asserta(player(T, N, AB, H, R, AVG))
```

places a new player fact at the top of the player relation, while

```
assert(player(T, N, AB, H, R, AVG))
```

or

```
assertz(player(T, N, AB, H, R, AVG))
```

places the same fact at the bottom of the player relation.

In some applications the exact placement of the new clause is not important, but in the following example we will see that placement can be a crucial factor in determining whether the query has correct results. Suppose we want to update all the batting averages for the team. In a sample game, in which each player on the team had three hits and five at-bats, the following rule is designed to update the team's batting averages:

```
update__batting__average:-
     player(T, N, AB, H, R, AVG),
     AB1 is AB +5,
     H1 is H + 3,
     X is H1 * 100 / AB1,
     Y is H1 * 100 mod AB1,
     Z is Y * 10 / AB1,
     Average is X * 10 + Z,
     retract(player(T, N, AB, H, R, AVG)),
     assert(player(T, N, AB1, H1, R, Average)).
```

This rule will result in the response:

```
**yes
**yes
**yes
```

and so on, until you manually stop execution. When each average is updated, the **re-**

tract in the rule removes the old player fact from the relation, but the **assert** adds the updated fact to the end. Since the rule continues until the end of the player relation is reached, and at each step another fact is added to the end, the result is an endless loop. This endless loop will not occur in all versions of Prolog. Prolog86, unlike some other versions, automatically finds all alternative solutions. Some versions present the user with one solution and ask if another is desired. In Prolog86, this situation can be corrected by changing **assert** to:

```
asserta(player(T, N, AB1, H1, R, Average)).
```

This places the new fact at the beginning of the player relation. Since Prolog keeps a marker at the last position checked, and ends when it reaches the end of the relation, these new facts will not be updated a second time. The result of:

```
?-update__batting__average.
```

(using the revised rule) will be one ****yes** for each player in the relation. The important thing is that this time, the rule is able to stop at the end of the relation, since updated facts are placed at the beginning of the relation. Looking at the player relation now we would see:

```
player(mustangs, cassell, 59, 10, 0, 165).
player(mustangs, flanagan, 32, 7, 0, 219).
player(mustangs, berg, 83, 16, 2, 195).
player(mustangs, grimes, 98, 19, 1, 194).
player(mustangs, melon 55, 13, 0, 230).
player(mustangs, everard, 311, 78, 23, 254).
player(mustangs, sanders, 94, 25, 6, 260).
player(mustangs, hearn, 329, 83, 9, 256).
player(mustangs, brooks, 295, 75, 4, 258).
player(mustangs, perry, 345, 91, 15, 267).
player(mustangs, garcon, 169, 47, 4, 276).
player(mustangs, tram, 399, 109, 8, 276).
player(mustangs, lime, 331, 91, 5, 279).
player(mustangs, gribbs, 371, 110, 20, 290).
player(mustangs, white, 401, 129, 15, 325).
```

Note that the facts in the relation are in the reverse order from the original due to **asserta** in the rule. The first fact entered will be at the bottom, and the last fact at the top.

The above example is not representative of a true baseball game, where different players will have varying numbers of at-bats, hits, and runs. To make it more realistic, we need to have a way of accepting input from the keyboard and using this input to perform the calculations. The read predicate can be used to accept input. The statement:

```
read(N)
```

will stop execution and wait for information from the keyboard. This can be coupled with the **write** predicate to make it clearer to the person entering data exactly what is required.

There are two methods to solve the problem of inputting values in this type of update. The first involves the programmer entering the name of the player, while the other method involves the program printing out the players' names one by one and the user indicating whether a given player has changes or not. Both methods require entering the pertinent information (at-bats, hits, runs).

The following rule will ask for player information and search the relation for the given name and team name. The new batting average is calculated as above, and the fact replaced with the batting average, hits, runs, and at-bats updated.

```
update_batting_average :-
   write(update),
   read(A),
   A = y,
   bat_avg,
   update_batting_average.

bat_avg :-
   write(team),
   tab(11),
   read(T),
   nl,
   write(name),
   tab(11),
   read(N),
   nl,
   write(times_at_bat),
   tab(3),
   read(Bats),
   nl,
   write(number_of_hits),
   tab(1),
   read(Hits),
   nl,
   write(runs),
   tab(11),
   read(Runs),
   player(T, N, AB, H, R, AVG),
   H1 is H + Hits,
   AB1 is AB + Bats,
   X is H1 * 100 / AB1,
   Y is H1 * 100 mod AB1,
   Z is Y * 10 / AB1,
   Average is X * 10 + Z,
```

```
retract(player(T, N, AB, H, R, AVG)),
asserta(player(T, N, AB1, H1, R, Average)),
nl,
write(N),
tab(5),
write(Average),
nl,nl,nl,
!_
bat_avg :-write('this player is not on the team'),nl.
```

The above, which is really two rules, one calling on the other, needs some explanations. Taking the rule **update__batting__average** first, we will go through it line by line:

```
update__batting__average :-
```

the head of the rule.

```
write(update),
```

will write what is within the parentheses, the word "update" on the screen.

```
read(A),
```

waits for information from the keyboard. In this case, the only information needed is "y" for yes.

```
A = y,
```

checks for the correct input; "y" is desired if the update is to take place.

```
bat_avg,
```

calls on another rule, **bat__avg**. After that rule has been executed, control will come back to the following statement.

```
update__batting__average.
```

sets up a loop. **Update__batting__average** is called from itself. In recursive rules it is necessary to make sure there is a loop exit. In this case, the exit is in the input update. A "y" will continue the process. Any input other than "y" will result in a failed rule and termination.

Now, looking at the rule **bat__avg**, which actually does the work of updating:

```
bat__avg :-
```

the head of the rule.

```
write(team),
```

prints out the word "team" (to give the programmer some idea what information is called for).

```
tab(11),
```

skips 11 spaces before the >. This is just for readability.

```
read(T),
```

asks for information from the keyboard. T will be instantiated to the value input; in this example, T should be the name of the team.

```
nl,
```

goes to a new line before proceeding. This, also, is for readability.

```
write(name),
```

prints the word "name" on the screen.

```
tab(11),
read(N),
nl,
```

as before, skips 11 spaces, asks for the players' name, and goes to a new line.

```
write(times_at_bat),
tab(3),
read(Bats),
nl,
write (number_of_hits),
tab(1),
read(Hits),
nl,
write(runs),
tab(11),
read(Runs),
```

asks for times at bat, hits, and runs, getting the information from the keyboard. Remember that the variables begin with capital letters, and that the **write** statements are there to give the person entering the information a clue as to what is wanted. This is preferable to having a series of prompts without clues.

```
player(T, N, AB, H, R, AVG),
```

asks if a fact exists in the player relation matching the above data. Since T and N have been instantiated (via the reads above) these are the only variables that need to be matched. The uninstantiated variables can be any value.

```
H1 is H + Hits,
```

instantiates a variable, H1, to the sum of H, the number of hits already recorded, plus Hits, the input value which represents the number of new hits to be included in the new batting average.

```
AB1 is AB + Bats,
```

adds the new at-bats to the recorded at bats.

```
X is H1 * 100 / AB1,
Y is H1 * 100 mod AB1,
Z is Y * 10/AB1,
Average is X * 10 + Z,
```

calculates the batting average.

```
retract(player(T, N, AB, H, R, AVG)),
```

removes the old player fact from the relation.

```
asserta(player(T, N, AB1, H1, Runs, Average)),
```

enters the new information into the relation. Note that T and N are unchanged and are the same as in the **retract** statement but that AB1, H, R, and Average are the new values that have been calculated.

```
nl,
write(N),
tab(5),
write(Average),
nl,nl,nl,
```

writes out the name and new average. This is for user reassurance.

```
!.
```

the cut operator stops **bat_avg** at this point if the above has been successful.

```
bat_avg :- write('this player is not on the team'),nl.
```

This second clause in the rule is to inform the user that the name or team entered are not in the database. It will be executed only when the first clause fails, because of the cut operator in the first clause.

The query:

```
?-bat_avg.
```

causes the bat_avg rule to be executed. This results in exactly one player fact being updated. The query:

```
?-update_batting_average.
```

continues updating batting averages until the update clue gets an "n" response. (Actually, any response other than "y" terminates the program.)

In the second method, the program steps through the database facts one by one and then presents the team and player name to the user. This gives more reliable results by preventing the user from omitting, through oversight, some of the information. It is just as efficient if the number of entries to be made is a significant percentage of the facts in the database. The following program illustrates this method:

```
new_batting_average:-
     write(update),
     read(A),
     A < > y,
     !.
new_batting_average:-
     player(T, N, AB, H, R, AVG),
     write(N),
     nl,
     write(any_changes),
     read(A1),
     A1 = y,
     retractall(temp(T1, N1)),
     asserta(temp(T, N)),
     change_the_batting_average.
change_the_batting_average:-
     temp(T, N),
     player(T, N, AB, H, R, AVG),
     write(team),
     tab(5),
     write(T),
     nl,
     write(name),
     tab(5),
     write(N),
     nl,
     write(at_bats),
     tab(2),
```

```
read(AB1),
nl,
write(hits),
tab(5),
read (H1),
n1,
write (runs),
tab (5)
read (R1),
n1,
ABnew is AB + AB1,
Hnew is H + H1,
X is Hnew * 100 / ABnew,
Y is Hnew * 100 mod ABnew,
Z is Y * 10 / ABnew,
Average is X * 10 + Z,
retract(player(T, N, AB, H, R, AVG)),
asserta(player(T, N, ABNEW, Hnew, R1, Average)).
```

This rule has some characteristics which distinguish it from the previous method, and are worth considering. First, note that the rule does not handle recursion in the same way; that is, it does not call on itself. Rather, Prolog's natural method of stepping through the database one fact at a time is used. Since the second clause calls on the facts within the database, the rule will continue as long as the condition:

```
player (T, N, AB, H, R, AVG)
```

is true. That is, as long as there are any facts remaining in the database with predicate **player** and six arguments. The first clause:

```
new__batting__average:-
    write(update),
    read(A),
    A < > y,
!.
```

allows the user to decide whether to continue (or start if the first player has not yet been updated). An answer is given to the prompt "update," and the rule fails if A (the input value) is "y." In this case a positive response causes the rule to fail. This is because of the cut operator (!) in the first clause.

The second clause:

```
new__batting__average:-
    player(T, N, AB, H, R, AVG),
```

```
write(N),
nl,
write(any__changes),
read(A1),
A1 = y,
retractall(temp(T1, N1)),
asserta(temp(T, N)),
change__the__batting__average.
```

is executed only if the first fails: if A = "y." It first calls on a player fact, and asks for a response to the question, "any changes." A1 is the response; if no, this part of the rule fails, but if there are facts remaining in the player relation, the rule goes on to check them all.

If there are changes, the statements below are executed:

```
retractall(temp(T1, N1)),
asserta(temp(T, N)),
change__the__batting__average.
```

Retractall and **asserta** set up a temporary relation holding the team and name of the player to be updated before calling on the rule **change__the__batting__average**. This temporary fact is used in **change__the__batting__average** to locate the proper fact in the player database. This is necessary since the variables become uninstantiated when going from one rule to the next. When **player(T, N, AB, H, R, AVG)** matches a fact in the **new__batting__average** rule, there is no guarantee that the same (or any) fact will be matched with the next rule. The fact **temp(T, N)**, however, is in the database and is matched with **temp(T, N)** in **change__the__batting__average**. This has nothing to do with the variables being instantiated! There is only one fact in **temp**, so there can be no mistake as to the name of the player being updated. The team is also included, since player name alone need not uniquely identify a player.

In a database which contains other teams, the combination of team name and player name would uniquely identify a fact. Let's look at **change__the__batting__average**:

```
change__the__batting__average:-
   temp(T, N),
   player(T, N, AB, H, R, AVG),
```

matches a fact in the relation, **player**, with the team name (T) and the player name (N) from the relation **temp**. If no such match exists, the rule fails, otherwise, the following are executed:

```
write(team),
tab(5),
write(T),
nl,
```

```
write(name),
tab(5),
write(N),
nl,
```

which is just a reminder to the user exactly which player is being updated.

```
write(at_bats),
tab(2),
read(AB1),
nl,
write(hits),
tab(5),
read(H1),
nl,
write(runs),
tab(5),
read(R1),
nl,
```

asks for the necessary information (as in the previous example).

```
ABnew is AB + AB1,
Hnew is H + H1,
X is Hnew * 100 / ABnew,
Y is Hnew * 100 mod ABnew,
Z is Y * 10 / ABnew,
Average is X * 10 + Z,
```

calculates the average as before.

```
retract(player(T, N, AB, H, R, AVG)),
asserta(player(T, N, ABNEW, Hnew, R1, Average)).
```

deletes the old fact and inserts the updated information in the player database.

This method is really less work for the user and reduces the chance that the database will contain erroneous data after the update. Also, note that there is no built-in data validation. If bad data is entered, incorrect results may occur or the rule may fail. For example, if the prompt "hits" is answered by something other than a numeric value, when the attempt is made to calculate Hnew by adding Hits to H, the rule will fail. But if R1 (runs) is entered incorrectly, the new value (even if nonnumeric) will be stored, since there is no distinction between numeric and nonnumeric variables except when used in arithmetic. A sample run follows:

```
update> y.
white
any_changes> n.
gribbs
any_changes> y.
team      mustangs
name      gribbs
Mat_bats          >4.
hits              >3.
runs              >1.

**yes
lime
any_changes> n.
tram
any_changes>y.
team      mustangs
name      tram
at_bats           >5.
hits              >3.
runs              >1.

**yes
garcon
any_changes>n.
perry
any_changes>n.
brook
any_changes>n.
```

and so on, until the end of the relation is reached, which must happen since the **asserta** places the updated entries at the beginning rather than at the end of the relation. The resulting **player** relation is:

```
player(mustangs, tram, 399, 109, 9, 273).
player(mustangs, gribbs, 370, 110, 21, 297).
player(mustangs, white, 396, 126, 15, 318).
player(mustangs, lime, 326, 88, 5, 270).
```

followed by the original(non-updated) entries.

Using similar techniques, programs can be written to recalculate new earned run averages, or indeed to update any argument within the database relations. Here is a program for updating earned run averages:

```
new_era :-
```

```
        write(update__era),
        read(A), A < > y,!.
    new__era :-
        write(team__name),
        read(T),
        write(name),
        tab(5),
        read(N),
        pitcher(T, N, W, L, IP, ER, ERA),
        nl,write(win),
        tab(6),
        read(W1),
        nl,
        write(loss),
        tab(5),
        read(L1),
        nl,
        write(runs),
        tab(5),
        read(R1),
        nl,
        write(innings),
        tab(2),
        read(IP1),
        nl,
        Wnew is W + W1,
        Lnew is L + L1,
        IPnew is IP + IP1,
        ERnew is ER + R1,
        ERAnew is ERnew * 90 / IPnew * 10,
        retract(pitcher(T, N, W, L, IP, ER, ERA)),
        asserta(pitcher(T,N,Wnew,Lnew,IPnew,ERnew,ERAnew),
        new__era.
```

A real disadvantage of some versions of Prolog is the lack of any editing features whatever. As the main body of the database can be the facts that need to be entered, a program that "builds" the database by asking for the information to be entered and places that information in the database is very useful. The following program asks for and places player information into the database:

```
    build__team :-
        player__info,
        new__el(T, N, AB, H, R, A),
        not(N = 0),
```

```
        not(player(__, N, __, __, __, __)),
        assertz(player(mustangs, N, AB, H, R, A)),
        build__team.
    build__team :-
        new__el(T, N, AB, H, R, A),
        not(N = 0),
        build__team.
    player__info :-
        write('name    '),
        read(N),
        nl,
        write('at bats'),
        read(AB),
        nl,
        write('hits '),
        read(H),
        nl,
        write('runs '),
        read(R),
        nl,
        write('bat avg')
        read(A),
        retractall(new__el(T,Name,AtBats,Hits,Runs, Bavg)),
        asserta(new__el(mustangs, N, AB, H, R, A)).
```

The rule **player__info** is a series of prompts and inputs to build a fact that will be placed in a temporary relation, **new__el**. If the name entered is "0," the program terminates.

Note that **build__team** has two clauses. The first, calls upon **player__info** to place information entered by the keyboard into the **new__el** temporary relation. It will succeed only if all of these conditions are true:

(1) There is an element in the **new__el** relation.
(2) The name is not "0."
(3) There is not a player fact with the same name already entered.

If the rule succeeds, the information in **new__el** is entered at the bottom of the player relation, and **build__team** is repeated. If any of the above conditions is not met, the first clause of the rule fails and the second clause is tried. This clause handles the case of a duplicate name. As long as the name in **new__el** is not "0," the **build__team** rule will be repeated. But if this clause is reached, the name already exists and will not be entered again.

Here is a sample program run:

```
'name       '>jones.
'at bats    '>54.
'hits       '>54.
'runs       '>9.
'bat avg    '>1000.
'name       '>white.
'at bats    '>10.
'hits       '>5.
'runs       '>0.
'bat avg    '>500.*
'name       '>0.
'at bats    '>0.
'hits       '>0.
'runs       '>0.
'bat avg    '>0.
**no*
```

If there have not been any previous entries, the above run will result in:

```
player(mustangs, jones, 54, 54, 9, 1000).
player(mustangs, white, 10, 5, 0, 500).
```

It should be noted in the problem above that parts of the information could be entered and other parts calculated and entered into the relation in the same program. For example, the batting average could be calculated from the other input data by combining the **build_team** rule with a rule for calculating the appropriate average.

With any procedure that allows for input into the database, there should be a way of correcting entries that may have been entered incorrectly. The next program deals with correcting erroneous data:

```
correct_team :-
    player_info,
    new_el(T, N, AB, H, R, A),
    not(N = 0),
    player(_, N, _, _, _, _),
    retract(player(_, N, _, _, _, _)),
    asserta(player(T, N, AB, H, R, A)),
    correct_team.
```

Notice that the procedure **player_info** is used in this rule as well as in the **build_team** rule. After getting the information, the name in **new_el** is checked against the player relation. If there is an entry, it is replaced by the **new_el** data and **correct_team** is repeated. If not, **correct_team** is repeated with no change made.

A CHANGE OF PACE

Let's go on to what seems to be an entirely different type of problem. My sons are particularly fond of what are called "logic" problems. These problems give a list of statements and ask you to deduce from the "facts" given certain conclusions. The following example is typical of this type of problem.

1) John, Mary and Robin are the pilot, navigator, and engineer on a space shuttle, but not necessarily in that order.
2) There are three representatives on the space shuttle named Congressperson John, Congressperson Mary, and Congressperson Robin. We shall use the title "Congressperson" only when we refer to one of these representatives.
3) The pilot lives in Georgia.
4) The pilot's namesake (the representative who has the same name as the pilot) lives in Maryland.
5) Congressperson Mary earns $50,000 per year.
6) Congressperson Robin lives in New Jersey.
7) One of the three representatives is the pilot's next-door neighbor.
8) The pilot earns in cash each year exactly one third the salary of his next-door neighbor.
9) John beats the navigator at billiards.

The problem is to identify the pilot, the engineer, and the navigator.

The solution, although not readily obvious, has a rather straightforward approach using Prolog. Since Prolog is an *assertional* rather than a procedural language, what is necessary is to express the "facts" given above in a more exact manner and in the proper syntax. Then the questions:

```
?-pilot(Who).
?-engineer(Who).
?-navigator(Who).
```

should give the names of the pilot, engineer, and navigator respectively. The problem becomes one of stating the facts given, along with some simple deductions that can be drawn from these facts. Attempt to solve this problem before continuing.

From the list of statements above, we will systematically extract Prolog facts and rules. Statement 2 gives us the names of the representatives. We can express this by the set of facts:

```
representative(mary).
representative(john).
representative(robin).
```

Statements 3, 4, 6, and 7 give information about where different people live. Using the relation form:

```
plives(Representative__name, State)
```

we can write:

```
plives(robin, new__jersey).
```

to indicate that Robin lives in New Jersey. The information given about the representative who lives in Georgia (that his salary is exactly three times that of the pilot) can be summarized by:

```
plives(X, georgia) :-
      income(X, Y),
      not(integer(Y / 3)),
      fail.
```

which indicates that a representative living in Georgia must have an income divisible by three. Since we know that Robin lives in New Jersey, John must live in either Maryland or Georgia, and Mary must live in the other state. This can be expressed by:

```
plives(john, maryland) :-
      plives(mary, georgia).
plives(mary, maryland) :-
      not(plives(john, maryland)).
```

or John lives in Maryland if Mary lives in Georgia; and Mary lives in Maryland if John does not live in Maryland.

Statement 5 gives information about Mary's income, namely:

```
income(mary, 50000).
```

Last, we will express what we know about each of the three space shuttle workers. Statement 4 tells us that the representative with the same name as the pilot lives in Maryland, or:

```
pilot(X) :- plives(X, maryland).
```

We know that the navigator is not John, from statement 9, and that the representative with the same name as the navigator cannot live in Maryland (since the pilot's namesake does):

```
navigator(N) :-
      representative(N),
      not(N = john),
      not(plives(N, maryland)).
```

The navigator's name must be among the facts in the relation **representative**. The above is sufficient to find the navigator and the pilot. To find the engineer, we merely need to state that the engineer's name is in the relation **representative**, but must not be the same as either the pilot's or the navigator's name:

```
engineer(E) :-
    representative(E),
    not(pilot(E)),
    not(navigator(E)),
    !.
```

The cut operator is included in the rule to eliminate unwanted backtracking.

Verify that the questions and responses below are accurate:

```
?-navigator(Who).
Who = robin

?-engineer(Who).
Who = john

?-pilot(Who).
Who = mary.
```

A MORE TRADITIONAL APPROACH

The next example is more of a textbook type. The practical applications of this type of problem should be easily recognized.

A Prolog database has facts of the type:

```
flight(Dept_city, Dest_city, Leave, Arrive).
```

representing the information that there is a plane flight from **Dept_city** to **Dest_city**, leaving at time **Leave** and arriving at time **Arrive**. The problem is to write a program which will respond to a question of the type:

```
?-route(Dept_city, Dest_city, Sequence).
```

with a list of connecting flights, where there is at least a 30-minute gap between flights. For example, if a database contains the facts:

```
flight(marquette, detroit, 800, 1000).
flight(detroit, chicago, 1020, 1200).
flight(chicago, milwaukee, 1230, 1400).
flight(detroit, chicago, 1200, 1330).
flight(chicago, milwaukee, 1400, 1600).
```

then a query:

```
?-route(marquette, chicago, Sequence).
```

should produce the response:

```
Sequence = [ [marquette, 800], [detroit, 1000], [detroit, 1200], [chicago, 1330] ]
```

Again, attempt the solution before looking at the solution given below.

Solving this problem is a matter of describing the list, Sequence, the desired result. Remember the **append** operation? In considering the form of the rule:

```
route(Dept_city, Dest_city, Sequence)
```

we must take into consideration the two possible cases. The easier case (which is also the boundary condition) is that there is a direct flight. In this case, the solution to a route query is simply the information contained in the **flight** fact rearranged in list format, or:

```
route(Dept_city, Dest_city, Sequence) :-
    flight(Dept_city, Dest_city, Leave, Arrive),
    append [[Dept_city, Leave] ], [ [Dest_city, Arrive] ], Sequence).
```

This rule will be used for queries such as:

```
?-route(marquette, detroit, Sequence).
```

where the response would be:

```
Sequence = [ [marquette, 800], [detroit, 1000] ].
```

We need a second rule to describe how to build the list, Sequence, when there is no direct flight. Here we call upon recursion in order to step through the database, adding an element to the list when a former destination city is seen to be the departure city in another **flight** fact. The second rule necessary is given in full directly below, and then broken down and analyzed:

```
route(Dept_city, Dest_city, Sequence) :-
    flight(Dept_city, Temp_dest, Leave, Arrive),
    Gap is Arrive + 29,
    route(Temp_dest, Dest_city, [ [Temp_dest,
    Earliest_leave], [A | TAIL] ]),
    Earliest_leave > Gap,
    append([ [Dept_city, Leave] ], [ [Temp_dest, Arrive] ], R1),
    append(R1, [ [Temp_dest, Earliest_leave], [A | TAIL] ], Sequence).
```

This rule looks more difficult than it actually is, as seen below:

```
route(Dept_city, Dest_city, Sequence) :-
```

is simply the head of the rule.

```
flight(Dept_city, Temp_dest, Leave, Arrive),
```

finds a fact in the database with the specified format

```
Gap is Arrive + 29,
```

defines Gap to be a time 29 minutes past the arrival time of the flight above, since we want at least 30 minutes between flights.

```
route(Temp_dest, Dest_city, [ [Temp_dest, Earliest_leave],
[A | TAIL]),
Earliest_leave > Gap,
```

ensures that a Sequence element has the **earliest-leave** time at least 30 minutes from the previous arrival time.

```
append([ [Dept_city, Leave] ], [ [Temp_dest, Arrive] ], R1),
append(R1, [ [Temp_dest, Earliest_leave], [A | TAIL] ], Sequence).
```

adds the **[city, time]** element that meets the conditions specified above to the list, Sequence.

Here are several sample runs to illustrate the above rule. You should answer each of the sample queries before looking at the responses.

```
?-route(marquette, detroit, Sequence).
```

The response will be:

```
Sequence = [ [marquette, 800], [detroit, 1000] ]
```

since there is a direct flight between Marquette and Detroit. To the query

```
?-route(marquette, detroit).
```

the response will be: ** **no**; even though there is a direct flight between Marquette and Detroit, there is no route entry with the given format (i.e., only two attributes). For

```
?-route(detroit, los_angeles, Sequence).
```

the response will be: ** **no**, since there is no flight entry (either direct or connecting) between Detroit and Los Angeles.

Now consider the query:

```
?-route(detroit, chicago, Sequence).
```

Since there are two ways to go from Detroit to Chicago, Prolog will respond:

```
Sequence = [ [detroit, 1020], [chicago, 1200] ]
Sequence = [ [detroit, 1200], [chicago, 1330] ]
```

For the query

```
?-route(marquette, milwaukee, Sequence).
```

there is not a direct flight between Marquette and Milwaukee, so the second route rule will be used, giving the response:

```
Sequence = [ [marquette, 800], [detroit, 1000], [detroit, 1200], [ [chicago, 1330],
[chicago, 1400], [ [milwaukee, 1600] ] ] ]
```

The brackets are inserted according to the way we told Prolog to build the list. The list can be understood without going into an explanation of why there are multiple brackets. Notice that the fact

```
flight(detroit, chicago, 1020, 1200).
```

is overlooked when building the list. This is due to the specification that there must be at least a 30-minute gap between connecting flights.

The final query we ask on this database is dedicated to my students, who sometimes overlook the beauties of Michigan's upper peninsula and are ready to go *anywhere* other than Marquette.

```
?-route(marquette, Anywhere, Sequence).
```

asks for route information on any destination from Marquette. The response to this is, of course,

```
Anywhere = Detroit
Sequence = [marquette, 800], [detroit, 1000] ]

Anywhere = chicago
Sequence = [ [marquette, 800], [detroit, 1000], [detroit, 1200], [ [chicago, 1330] ] ]
Anywhere = milwaukee
Sequence = [ [marquette, 800], [detroit, 1000], [detroit, 1200], [ [chicago, 1330],
           [chicago, 1400],[ [milwaukee, 1600] ] ] ]
```

PROLOG AND DATABASE CONCEPTS

To illustrate the applications of Prolog to traditional data manipulation concepts, let us examine a set of Prolog facts and rules as a relational database. Suppose the

Advising Department of a college stores this information for each student:

> student number, last name, first name, street, city, state, major, minor, class taken, time, class credit hours, class meeting time, class grade, total credit hours, total honor points, and honor point average

There may be multiple occurrences of the attributes pertaining to individual classes (class taken, time, class credit hours, class meeting time, class grade). A database system should be able to handle queries about any combination of fields pertaining to an individual student—which, of course, Prolog can do very well. In addition, there should be the possibility of extracting information from the database pertaining to groups of students, such as a list of students in a given class, a list of students with a given major, a list of students living in a particular state or city, or a list of students (perhaps within a major) arranged in some order (alphabetical, by honor point average, etc.).

In addition, there must be some way of performing the traditional file maintenance processes of inserting, deleting, and modifying the data in the database. Since the database system should be able to handle queries on several different fields, and perform the several maintenance operations, a single relation with all the multiple attributes mentioned above would be inappropriate. The attributes will be divided into three relations: student, class, and major, having the formats following and with key fields indicated by all capital letters.

```
student(STUDENT_NUMBER, Last_name, First_name,
    Street_address, City, State)

class(CLASS_NAME, STUDENT_NUMBER, Credit_hours,
    Meeting_time, Grade)

major(STUDENT_NUMBER, Major_subject, Minor_subject,
    Total_credit_hours, Total_honor_points,
    Honor_point_average)
```

No attempt is being made to normalize relations beyond first normal form. These formats could contain the sample data:

```
student(1001, brown, sam, happy_way, marquette, mi).
student(1022, andrews, andy, king_olaf_st, marquette, mi).
student(1099, cummings, maria, gray_rd, marquette, mi).
student(2000, xylon, fred, greenview_ave, lansing, mi).
student(3022, franklin, georgia, burrow_way, detroit, mi).
student(4001, green, nancy, greenview_rd, mt_pleasant, mi).
student(5000, green, sam, greenview_rd, mt_pleasant, mi).
student(5055, pershing, xerxes, happy_way, marquette, mi).
student(6000, petersen, olaf, blackstone_blvd, detroit, mi).
student(6087, sklarson, bill, center_blvd, milwaukee, wi).
student(7001, timmons, timmy, twin_st, minneapolis, mn).
```

```
student(7555, young, chiquita, felton_st, philadelphia, pa).
student(8005, herring, cremora, briggs_blvd, detroit, mi).

class(elem_math, 1001, 3, m900, g).
class(elem_math, 2000, 3, m900, g).
class(elem_math, 4001, 3, m900, g).
class(elem_math, 7555, 3, m900, g).
class(elem_math, 8005, 3, m900, g).
class(intro_comp, 1001, 3, m1100, g).
class(intro_comp, 2000, 3, m1100, g).
class(intro_comp, 5000, 3, m1100, g).
class(intro_comp, 6087, 3, m1100, g).
class(intro_comp, 7555, 3, m1100, g).
class(english_comp, 3022, 4, t800, g).
class(english_comp, 4001, 4, t800, g).
class(english_comp, 5000, 4, t800, g).
class(english_comp, 6000, 4, t800, g).
class(english_comp, 6087, 4, t800, g).
class(english_comp, 7001, 4, t800, g).
class(english_comp, 8005, 4, t800, g).
class(intro_bus, 1001, 3, t1200, g).
class(intro_bus, 4001, 3, t1200, g).
class(intro_bus, 5000, 3, t1200, g).
class(intro_bus, 6000, 3, t1200, g).
class(intro_bus, 7001, 3, t1200, g).
class(intro_bus, 7555, 3, t1200, g).

major(1001, business, economics, 0, 0, 0).
major(1022, business, economics, 0, 0, 0).
major(1099, business, economics, 0, 0, 0).
major(2000, computer_sci, math, 0, 0, 0).
major(3022, accounting, business, 0, 0, 0).
major(4001, business, accounting, 0, 0, 0).
major(5000, computer_sci, business, 0, 0, 0).
major(5055, computer_sci, economics, 0, 0, 0).
major(6000, economics, accounting, 0, 0, 0).
major(6087, economics, computer_sci, 0, 0, 0).
major(7001, accounting, economics, 0, 0, 0).
major(7555, accounting, business, 0, 0, 0).
major(8005, economics, accounting, 0, 0, 0).
```

The "g" in the relation **class** and the zeroes (total credit hours, total honor points and honor point average) in the relation major can be considered null values and be left to the system to fill in when modifying the database. To aid in calculations, it is also helpful to have facts pertaining to the honor points in the database. These are included:

```
honor_points(a, 400).
honor_points(b, 300).
honor_points(c, 200).
honor_points(d, 100).
honor_points(f, 0).
```

The honor points are multiplied by 100, so that honor point averages can be understood to contain two decimal places.

The following sets of exercises are designed to illustrate the query and maintenance abilities of Prolog. As before, to get the full benefit of the exercises, the reader should work each before looking at the answers. Solution and responses follow the questions.

Exercise Set 1
Sample Queries on the Database

Write Prolog queries which will do each of the following:

a) Find the complete address (street, city, state) of student Sam Brown.
b) Find the student number of student Xerxes Pershing.
c) Find Olaf Petersen's major and minor fields.
d) List the names of all students living in Michigan (MI).
e) List the student numbers of all lower peninsula students (i.e., students living in Michigan, but not in Marquette).
f) List the student numbers of all students taking **elem_math**.
g) List the names of all students taking **elem_math**.
h) List the names of all students with business as their major field.
i) List the names and address of all students with economics as their minor field.
j) List the student numbers and honor point averages of students in the **intro_bus** class.
k) List the names of all students taking a class at noon on Tuesdays (**t1200**).
l) Calculate and list the honor point average for a particular student, say, Fred Xylon.
m) Update the honor point average for Fred Xylon if he receives an A in **elem_math**.

Solutions to Queries

To find the address of a particular student (a) is simply a matter of extracting information from the student relation. Remember that although the name given is Sam Brown, the data is stored in the relation as two fields: Lastname, Firstname. The student number can be represented by the anonymous variable (_) since we are not concerned with this field. The query:

```
?-student(_, brown, sam, Street, City, State).
```

produces the response:

```
Street = happy_way    City = marquette    State = mi
```

Finding a student number (b) is, again, a matter of extracting information from the student relation:

```
?- student(Student_number, pershing, xerxes, _, _, _).
```

produces:

```
Student_number = 5055.
```

Getting the major and minor fields (c), given the student name, deals with the two relations, **student** and **major**, since the name appears in the **student** relation, but not the **major**. The student number field will allow for correspondence between the relations.

```
?-student(Student_number, petersen, olaf, _, _, _),
   major(Student_number, Major, Minor, _, _, _).
```

responds with:

```
Student_number = 6000    Major = economics
Minor = accounting
```

The student number is given even though it is not part of what was originally wanted. This is because the variable is instantiated as part of the query. (We cannot treat it as an anonymous variable since **Student_number** is the key field for both the **student** and the **major** relations.)

To get the names of students living in a particular state (d) involves a query on the relation student, with the state as a constant.

```
?-student(_, Lastname, Firstname, _, _, mi)
```

will yield the responses:

```
Lastname = brown        Firstname = sam
Lastname = andrews      Firstname = andy
Lastname = cummings     Firstname = maria
Lastname = xylon        Firstname = fred
Lastname = franklin     Firstname = georgia
Lastname = green        Firstname = nancy
```

```
Lastname = green          Firstname = sam
Lastname = pershing       Firstname = xerxes
Lastname = petersen       Firstname = olaf
Lastname = herring        Firstname = cremora
```

Please note that the author realizes that there are cities other than Marquette in the upper peninsula of Michigan, but for simplicity question (e) was phrased to correspond to entries in the database. Here we are asked for a query on the student relation which has two further conditions: that the state field be a specific value, **mi**, and that the city field cannot have a specific value, namely **marquette**:

```
?-student(Student_number,_,_,_, City, mi), City /= marquette.
```

or, alternately:

```
?-student(Student_number,_,_,_, City, mi),
    not(City = marquette).
```

Either of these queries will respond:

```
City = lansing            Student_number = 2000
City = detroit            Student_number = 3022
City = mt_pleasant        Student_number = 4001
City = mt_pleasant        Student_number = 5000
City = detroit            Student_number = 6000
City = detroit            Student_number = 8005
```

Listing student numbers based on the name of a class (f) involves a query on the relation class:

```
?-class(elem_math, Student_number, _, _, _).
```

produces:

```
Student_number = 1001
Student_number = 2000
Student_number = 4001
Student_number = 7555
Student_number = 8005
```

To list the names of individual students based on a class name (g) involves a query on two relations. We are asking for names, but since we need to extract information from both the **student** and the **class** relations, we will get information on student numbers as well. The answer to question (d) in the second exercise set will show how to do this type of listing giving neater output.

```
?-class(elem__math, Student__number, __, __, __),
 student(Student__number, Lastname, Firstname, __, __, __).
```

responds:

```
Student__number = 1001     Lastname = brown
Firstname = sam

Student__number = 2000     Lastname = xylon
Firstname = fred

Student__number = 4001     Lastname = green
Firstname = nancy

Student__number = 7555     Lastname = young
Firstname = chiquita

Student__number = 8005     Lastname = herring
Firstname = cremora
```

Listing the names of students with a given major field (h) is very similar to (g), but we want information from the relations **major** and **student**.

```
?-student(Student__number, Lastname, Firstname,
     Street, City, State),
 major(Student__number, business, __, __, __, __).
```

yields:

```
Student__number = 1001     Lastname = brown
Firstname = sam
Student__number = 1002     Lastname = andrews
Firstname = andy
Student__number = 1099     Lastname = cummings
Firstname = maria
Student__number = 4001     Lastname = green
Firstname = nancy
```

Listing names and addresses of students with a particular minor field (i) is very similar to (g) and (h), but asks for more information:

```
?-student(Student__number, Lastname, Firstname, Street,
     City, State),
 major(Student__number, __, economics, __, __, __).
```

yields responses of the form:

```
Student__number = 1001
```

```
Lastname = brown      Firstname = sam
Street = happy_way     City = marquette
State = mi.
```

Asking for student numbers and honor point averages (j) involves a query on the **class** as well as the **major** relation. This is a query that might be asked often of data such as we have, but as the database stands now, the query:

```
?-class(intro_bus, Student_number, _, _, _),
major(Student_number, _, _, _, _, HPA).
```

yields rather boring results. This query should be tried after the honor point average is updated—question (b) in exercise set 2. With the data in the database as presented, the student numbers 1001, 4001, 5000, 6000, 7001, and 7555 will be listed, each with an honor point average of 0.

In (k) we want the names of students taking a class at a specific time, **t1200**. Again, we are asking for information based on two relations. Once more, the student number is the field that allows correspondence between the relations.

```
?-class(_, Student_number, _, t1200, _),
student(Student_number, Lastname, Firstname, _, _, _).
```

produces:

```
Student_number = 1001
Lastname = brown      Firstname = sam
Student_number = 4001
Lastname = green      Firstname = nancy
Student_number = 5000
Lastname = green      Firstname = sam
Student_number = 6000
Lastname = petersen     Firstname = olaf
Student_number = 7001
Lastname = timmons     Firstname = timmy
Student_number = 7555
Lastname = young      Firstname = chiquita
```

To get the honor point average of a particular student (l), we need information from the relation **major**, namely, the total credit hours and the total honor point fields. If the total credit hours is not zero, the honor point average can be calculated. The query:

```
?-student(Snum, xylon, fred, _, _, _),
major(Snum, _, _, Tot_cr_hrs, Tot_hr_points, _),
not (Tot_cr_hrs = 0),
Honor_point_avg is Tot_hr_points / Tot_cr_hrs.
```

will not calculate the **Honor_point_avg** for Fred Xylon because the condition

```
not (Tot_cr_hrs = 0)
```

fails. Suppose the **major** relation contained the fact:

```
major(2000, computer_sci, math, 2400, 8, 0).
```

Then the result of the above query would be:

```
Honor_point_avg = 300
Tot_honor_points = 2400
Tot_cr_hrs = 8
Snum = 2000.
```

In question (m), updating the honor point average when new information is given for a relation would be better stated as a rule, which we will do in exercise set 2. If the question is to be asked for only one student, however, it is acceptable to phrase it as a query and not make it a permanent part of the database. The query:

```
?-student(Student_number, xylon, fred, _, _, _),
class(elem_math, Student_number, Credits, _, _),
honor_points(a, HP),
major(Student_number, _, _, TCH, THP, HPA),
Tot_cr_hrs is TCH + Credits,
Tot_honor_pts is THP + HP * Credits,
New_hpa is Tot_honor_pts / Tot_cr_hrs.
```

will not update the honor point average field in the relation itself, but will yield the information:

```
New_hpa = 400
Tot_honor_pts = 1200
Tot_cr_hrs = 3
THP = 0
HP = 400
TCH = 0
Credits = 3
Student_number = 2000
HPA = 0
```

Note that the order in which the variable values are given is from the last calculated to the first, and that all the variables used in the query are listed. By formulating the query as a rule, we could get just the information wanted.

Exercise Set 2

Using Prolog Rules for Database Queries

Write the Prolog rules that will do each of the following:

```
asserta (class(Class, Student__number, CH, Time, G))
```

a) Assign grades to each student in each class. This should be done by having the system write out the class name and the student number and accept input from the keyboard. The input grade should then be stored in the grade field of the class relation.
b) Update the honor point averages after the class grades have been assigned.
c) Find pairs of students having the same major field.
d) Write out a list of all major fields of study in the database.
e) Write out a listing of students in a given class by their student numbers. The rule should have the format:

```
class__list(Class, L)
```

where Class is the name of the class and L is the list of student numbers in that class.
f) Write out a listing of students in a given class by their names. This is similar to the exercise above, but slightly more complicated.
g) Write a list of students who made the dean's list, defined as HPA above 300.

Solutions to Exercise Set 2

In question (a), assigning grades to each student in a class is a matter of inputting the letter grade for a student and storing it as the Grade field of the relation. This is an example of modifying a particular field in the database, and is accomplished by deleting the current fact and inserting a new fact with the appropriate information. This is accomplished by the following steps:

Locate a fact in the database:

```
class(Class, Student__number, CH, Time, Grade)
```

Write out the class name and the student number(this is a prompt to the user):

```
write(Class),
tab(5),
write(Student__number),
nl
```

Accept input from the keyboard:

```
read(G)
```

Delete the current fact:

```
retract(class(Class, Student__number, CH, Time, Grade))
```

Insert the new information:

```
asserta (class(Class, Student_number, CH, Time, G))
```

Altogether, the rule looks like:

```
assign_grades:-
   class(Class, Student_number, CH, Time, Grade),
   write(Class),
   tab(5),
   write(Student_number),
   nl,
   read(G),
   retract(class(Class,Student_number,CH, Time, Grade)),
   asserta(class(Class,Student_number,CH, Time, G)).
```

It would be quite inappropriate to use anonymous variables in this problem even though the Class and student number fields are all that are actually being used for locating the relation, and Grade is the field being changed. If anonymous variables were used for CH and Time, these values would not be instantiated and would be lost when the fact is retracted.

Here is a sample run:

```
?-assign_grades.
elem_math     1001
> a.
** yes
elem_math     2000
> a.
** yes
.
.
.
intro_bus     7001
> c.
** yes
intro_bus     7555
> b.
** yes
```

You should recognize that the resulting relation is:

```
class(intro_bus, 7555, 3, t1200, b).
class(intro_bus, 7001, 3, t1200, c).
class(intro_bus, 6000, 3, t1200, a).
class(intro_bus, 5000, 3, t1200, d).
class(intro_bus, 4001, 3, t1200, a).
class(intro_bus, 1001, 3, t1200, f).
```

```
class(english_comp, 8005, 4, t800, b).
class(english_comp, 7001, 4, t800, b).
class(english_comp, 6087, 4, t800, a).
class(english_comp, 6000, 4, t800, c).
class(english_comp, 5000, 4, t800, b).
class(english_comp, 4001, 4, t800, c).
class(english_comp, 3022, 4, t800, a).
class(intro_comp, 7555, 3, m1100, b).
class(intro_comp, 6087, 3, m1100, c).
class(intro_comp, 5000, 3, m1100, d).
class(intro_comp, 2000, 3, m1100, a).
class(intro_comp, 1001, 3, m1100, a).
class(elem_math, 8005, 3, m900, d).
class(elem_math, 7555, 3, m900, a).
class(elem_math, 4001, 3, m900, c).
class(elem_math, 2000, 3, m900, b).
class(elem_math, 1001, 3, m900, a).
```

Asserta in the rule places each new fact at the top of the relation. This is necessary to avoid endless looping which will occur when Prolog86 keeps searching the database. The end will never be found if additional facts are added to the end.

After assigning grades, the next logical step (b) is to update the relation **major**, which holds information regarding honor point average. It is also appropriate to update the total credit hours and total honor points fields as well, since they are used in calculating honor point average. Updating the honor point average involves finding the grade and credit hours fields from the class relation:

```
class(_, Student_number, CH, _, Grade)
```

finding the fact in the major relation which matches the data in the class relation (the link is **Student_number**):

```
major(Student_number, Major, Minor, TCH, THP, HPA))
```

finding the fact in the honor_points relation which matches the Grade in the class relation:

```
honor_points(Grade, HP)
```

Next, we must accumulate the credit hours for this class (CH) into the total credit hours(TCH), and the honor points for this class (HP) into the total honor points (THP). Note: honor points for a class are found by multiplying the honor points associated with a letter grade by the number of credit hours assigned to the class. We then divide the total honor points by the total credit hours to get the honor point average. Care must be taken when dividing to avoid division by zero, which is possible if there are students listed who have not yet taken any class (new admissions, for example), so a check is included to make sure that total credit hours is not zero:

```
Tot__cr__hr is TCH + CH,
Tot__honor__pts is THP + HP * CH,
not(Tot__cr__hr = 0),
New__hpa is Tot__honor__pts / Tot__cr__hr,
```

Last, we will delete the old fact and insert the fact with the updated information:

```
retract(major(Student__number, Major, Minor, TCH, THP, HPA)),
asserta(major(Student__number, Major, Minor, Tot__cr__hr
  Tot__honor__pts, New__hpa))
```

The complete rule is:

```
update__hpa:-
  class(__, Student__number, CH, __, Grade),
  major(Student__number, Major, Minor, TCH, THP, HPA)),
  honor__points(Grade, HP),
  Tot__cr__hr is TCH + CH,
  Tot__honor__pts is THP + HP * CH,
  not(Tot__cr__hr = 0),
  New__hpa is Tot__honor__pts / Tot__cr__hr,
  retract(major(Student__number, Major, Minor, TCH, THP, HPA)),
  asserta(major(Student__number, Major, Minor, Tot__cr__hr, Tot__honor__pts,
New__hpa)).
```

A sample run is just a series of ** yes responses, one for each updated fact in the database, but the relation major is changed to:

```
major(1001, business, economics, 9, 2400, 266).
major(2000, computer__sci, math, 6, 2100, 350).
major(4001, business, accounting, 10, 2600, 260).
major(7555, accounting, business, 9, 3000, 333).
major(8005, economics, accounting, 7, 1500, 214).
major(5000, computer__sci, business, 10, 1800, 180).
major(6087, economics, computer__sci, 7, 2200, 314).
major(3022, accounting, business, 4, 1600, 400).
major(6000, economics, accounting, 7, 2000, 285).
major(7001, accounting, economics, 7, 1800, 257).
major(1022, business, economics, 0, 0, 0).
major(1099, business, economics, 0, 0, 0).
major(5055, computer__sci, economics, 0, 0, 0).
```

There are three facts as in the original relation, namely those pertaining to the three students who have not taken any classes. The order in which the update takes place should also be noted. Depending on the size of the relations **class** and **major**, and the percentage of **major** facts needing updating, it may be more efficient to find the **major** fact before the **class** fact in the rule **update__hpa**. In order to eliminate the need for real numbers, the total honor points and the honor point average are both to be considered as having two decimal positions; that is, 2400 total honor points should be understood to represent 24.00 and an honor point average of 266 should be understood to be 2.66.

Finding pairs of students with the same major field (c) is a matter of comparing two **major** facts and checking to see that the majors are the same, and the student numbers are different (so that a fact does not match itself). The rule below will do the job:

```
major__same(Student1, Student2, Major):-
   major(Student1, Major, _, _, _, _),
   major(Student2, Major, _, _, _, _),
   not(Student1 = Student2).
```

This rule can be used to print out all pairs of students having the same major. This query will be in the form of:

```
?-major__same(Student1, Student2, Major).
```

where all three fields are treated as variables, or it can be used to print out all pairs of students having a given major, such as:

```
?-major__same(Student1, Student2, computer__sci).
```

The response to this query would be:

```
Student1 = 2000    Student2 = 5000
Student1 = 2000    Student2 = 5055
Student1 = 5000    Student2 = 2000
Student1 = 5000    Student2 = 5055
Student1 = 5055    Student2 = 2000
Student1 = 5055    Student2 = 5000
```

Notice that the same amount of information could be condensed into three responses, but that Prolog reinstantiates Student1 (and consequently Student2) each time a fact is checked for conformity to the rule. Readability can be improved by writing the responses in list form, which is the object in question (d).

In (d), the easiest way to build a list in Prolog is by use of the **findall** operator. The general format is:

```
?-findall(Item, Goal, List).
```

and the result is the list of items which satisfy the goal. The query:

```
?-findall(Major, major(_, Major, _, _, _, _), List).
```

asks for a listing of values of the variable Major which are in the second attribute position of any fact in the **major** relation. The response, when querying the original database, will be in list format:

```
List = [business, business, business, computer_sci,
     accounting, business, computer_sci, computer_sci,
     economics, economics, accounting, accounting, economics].
```

While it is possible to write a rule that will eliminate the redundancy evident in this response, the **findall** operator does not do this automatically.

Listing the student numbers of all students in a given class (e) is an application of the **findall** operator. We can place it within a rule, **class_list**:

```
class_list(Class, L):-
     findall(Student_number, class(Class, Student_number,
     _, _, _), L).
```

When the Class is identified, L returns a list of all student numbers in that class. For example:

```
?-class_list(elem_math, L).
```

responds:

```
L = [1001, 2000, 4001, 7555, 8005]
```

It should be noted that the question:

```
?-class_list(Class, [1001, 2000, 4001, 7555, 8005]).
```

will *not* give the response:

```
Class = elem_math.
```

This is not the way the **findall** operator works. It should be used only to build a list.

In (f), to get a list of student names instead of student numbers, we need a list based on two relations, **class** and **student**. The complications arise because we really need to build two lists: a list of student numbers in the given class, and then a list of student names matching the student numbers. This can be done by first getting a list of student numbers for a given class. We can use the rule **class_list** to do this. We must then find each fact in the student relation where the Student_number of the fact is a member of the list, L, produced by **class_list**. For this, we need the rule **member**, which can be written:

```
member(X, [X|_]).
member(X, [_|Y]):- member(X, Y).
```

and which states simply that a value, X, is a member of any list having X as its head, or X is a member of any list having any element as its head, and X as a member of the tail of the list. The two statements:

```
member(Student_num, L),
student(Student_num, Lastname, Firstname, _, _, _)
```

will find such facts.

Now we can build a temporary relation, **classlist**, which will hold the names (Lastname and Firstname as a unit) that satisfy the statements above:

```
asserta(classlist([Lastname, Firstname]))
```

After all the names have been found, we will again use the **findall** to build a list of these names:

```
findall(Names, classlist(Names), Listing).
```

Putting all of the above together, we have:

```
class_listing(Class, Listing):-
      class_list(Class, List),
      member(Student_number, L),
      student(Student_number, Lastname, Firstname, _,_, _),
      asserta(classlist([Lastname, Firstname])).
class_listing(Class, Listing):-
      findall(Names, classlist(Names), Listing).
```

This rule calls on **member** and **class_list**, as defined previously.

Note that the second part of the rule occurs only when the first fails, when there are no more matching student numbers in L and in **student**. The query should be phrased giving the Class name and asking for the Listing. Notice also that as long as the first rule succeeds, Listing will not yet have a value. Therefore, the response to the query:

```
?-class_listing(elem_math, Listing).
```

is:

```
Listing = _0
Listing = _0
Listing = _0
Listing = _0
```

```
Listing = _0
Listing = [ [brown, sam], [xylon, fred], [green, nancy],
    [young, chiquita], herring, cremora] ].
```

There will also be a new relation, **classlist(Names)**, entered into the database. This can be removed by:

```
?-retractall(classlist(Names)).
```

In (g), writing a dean's list (defined as honor point average over 300) can be done using the rule:

```
deans_list([Lastname, Firstname]):-
    student(Student_number, Lastname, Firstname, _, _, _),
    major(Student_number, _, _, _, _, HPA),
    HPA > 300.
```

When used in a query:

```
?-deans_list(Who).
```

will respond:

```
Who = [xylon, fred]
Who = [franklin, georgia]
Who = [sklarson, bill]
Who = [young, chiquita]
```

based on the relation as updated in question (b). Another way of approaching this problem is to write out the response in list form, which can be accomplished by using a rule, **deanslist**:

```
deanslist(Namelist):-
    findall(Names, deans_list(Names), Namelist).
```

which calls on the **findall** operator and **deans_list** (from above) to build a list (Namelist) of Names. The response to the query:

```
?-deanslist(Who).
```

is the same information as above, but in the list format:

```
Who = [ [xylon, fred], [franklin, georgia],
    [sklarson, bill], [young, chiquita]]
```

OTHER DATABASE CONSIDERATIONS

In addition to answering queries, a relational database should be able to handle the typical file maintenance operations of inserting, deleting and modifying a fact. The traditional relational algebra operators *select, project,* and *join* need also be considered. **Retract** or **retractall** serve as delete operators, and forms of the **assert** predicate serve as insert operators.

For example, suppose it is desired to enter information about a new class, **pol_sci.** If the class has three hours of credit, meets on Wednesdays at 2 P.M. (w200), and has the students with student numbers 1099, 4001, and 7555 enrolled, we can insert this information with the three statements:

```
?-assertz(class(pol_sci, 1099, 3, w200, g).
?-assertz(class(pol_sci, 4001, 3, w200, g).
?-assertz(class(pol_sci, 7555, 3, w200, g).
```

If there is a large amount of data to be entered, or if class data is to be entered regularly, a rule could be written to ask for the class name and number of credits along with a list of students to be entered in the database. This is very similar to operations performed above (see the baseball database) and will not be repeated here.

If we wanted to delete all the class information (suppose it is the end of the term and the stored data is no longer relevant), this can be done with the statement:

```
?-retractall(class(Name, Student_number, Cr, Time, G)).
```

Removing the facts concerning student number 7555 from the relation class (suppose this student has dropped all her classes) can be accomplished by:

```
?-retract(class(Class, 7555, Cr, Time, G)).
```

Rules could be written to delete facts for each of the relations in the database.

Modifying a fact is a matter of finding the relevant fact in the database, deleting (**retract**) this fact, changing the update information, and then inserting (**assert**) the fact into the database.

Modifying, or even reorganizing the database, can be accomplished with the **assert** and **retract** statements. For example, suppose you wish to further normalize the class relation. You have probably noticed by now that data in the relation **class** is dependent on both the class name and on the student number. It should be noted that this means that if a class is to be offered, no information for this class can be entered into the database until a student is enrolled. The problems inherent in this situation should be immediately obvious. How can a student enroll if there is no information available as to class name, time, and credit hours; and how can the information be available if there is no student registered? Further normalizing of the relation would alleviate this problem. The solution would be to break **class** into two separate relations, **classdata** and **classlist**, where **classdata** holds information regarding class name, credit hours, and time; **classlist** contains information about the student, namely class name, student number, and grade. This involves finding a **class** fact:

```
class(Name, Snum, Cr, Time, Grade)
```

building two new facts from this fact:

```
asserta(classlist(Name, Snum, Grade))
not(classdata(Name, _, _)),
asserta(classdata(Name, Cr, Time)),
```

and deleting the **class** fact from the database.

```
retract(class(Name, Snum, Cr, Time, Grade))
```

To avoid duplicate facts in the **classdata** relation, we include the check in the second step. The result of the rule:

```
reorg_class:-
     class(Name, Snum, Cr, Time, Grade),
     asserta(classlist(Name, Snum, Grade)),
     not(classdata(Name, _, _)),
     asserta(classdata(Name, Cr, Time)),
     retract(class(Name, Snum, Cr, Time, Grade)).
```

would be, then, removing all **class** facts from the database and insert instead the two relations below (if we start from the original database):

```
classdata(intro_bus, 3, t1200).
classdata(english_com, 4, t800).
classdata(intro_comp, 3, m1100).
classdata(elem_math, 3, m900).

classlist(intro_bus, 7555, g).
classlist(intro_bus, 7001, g).
classlist(intro_bus, 6000, g).
classlist(intro_bus, 5000, g).
classlist(intro_bus, 4001, g).
classlist(intro_bus, 1001, g).
classlist(english_comp, 8005, g).
classlist(english_comp, 7001, g).
classlist(english_comp, 6087, g).
classlist(english_comp, 6000, g).
classlist(english_comp, 5000, g).
classlist(english_comp, 4001, g).
classlist(english_comp, 3022, g).
classlist(intro_comp, 7555, g).
classlist(intro_comp, 6087, g).
classlist(intro_comp, 5000, g).
```

```
classlist(intro__comp, 2000, g).
classlist(intro__comp, 1001, g).
classlist(elem__math, 8005, g).
classlist(elem__math, 7555, g).
classlist(elem__math, 4001, g).
classlist(elem__math, 2000, g).
classlist(elem__math, 1001, g).
```

In relational database operations, the SELECT, PROJECT and JOIN operators should result in relations. That is, in Prolog terms, one of these operators should produce a new relation in the database. In strict terms, a relation should have no duplicate facts. As we have seen, Prolog has no restrictions on duplication, but we will attempt to avoid duplicates.

The SELECT operator constructs a horizontal subset of a relation. For example, if you wished to retrieve all the **major** facts where the major field was business, the statement:

```
SELECT major where Major = business
```

corresponds to the Prolog:

```
?-major(Snum, business, Minor, TCH, THP, HPA).
```

except that no new relation is formed. To fully correspond to the select statement, Prolog would need a rule such as:

```
select__major(Major):-
     major(Snum, Major, Minor, TCH, THP, HPA),
     assertz(majornew(Snum, Major, Minor, TCH, THP, HPA)).
```

with the query:

```
?-select__major(business).
```

resulting in the relation:

```
majornew(1001, business, economics, 0, 0, 0).
majornew(1022, business, economics, 0, 0, 0).
majornew(1099, business, economics, 0, 0, 0).
```

if the original database was used as a starting point.

Similarly, if it was necessary to find student facts within a particular range of student numbers, we could write:

```
select__student(Slow, Shigh):-
     student(Snum, Lname, Fname, Street, City, State),
```

```
Snum >= Slow,
Snum <= Shigh,
assertz(studentnew(Snum, Lname, Fname, Street,
    City, State)).
```

Verify that the query:

```
?-select_student(3000,6000).
```

would add to the database the relation:

```
studentnew(3022, franklin, georgia, burrow_way, detroit, mi).
studentnew(4001, green, nancy, greenview_rd, mt_pleasant, mi).
studentnew(5000, green, sam, greenview_rd, mt_pleasant, mi).
studentnew(5055, pershing, xerxes, happy_way, marquette, mi).
studentnew(6000, petersen, olaf, blackstone_blvd, detroit, mi).
```

The PROJECT operator is used to construct a vertical subset of a relation. That is, certain arguments are chosen and others are ignored. For example:

```
PROJECT student over Snum, State
```

should produce a new relation consisting of student numbers and states. This corresponds to the Prolog query:

```
?-student(Snum, _, _, _, _, State).
```

if duplicates are allowed. Of course, the query does not enter a new relation into the database. This can be done with the rule:

```
project_student(State):-
    student(Snum, Lname, Fname, St, City, State),
    not(proj_st(Snum, State)),
    assertz(proj_st(Snum, State)).
```

and the query can be expressed either to get a full projection of student over the fields Snum and State, or to get a partial projection where the value of the State field is expressed. For example:

```
?-project_student(State).
```

produces:

```
proj_st(1001, mi).
proj_st(1022, mi).
proj_st(1099, mi).
```

```
proj__st(2000, mi).
proj__st(3022, mi).
proj__st(4001, mi).
proj__st(5000, mi).
proj__st(5055, mi).
proj__st(6000, mi).
proj__st(6087, wi).
proj__st(7001, mn).
proj__st(7555, pa).
proj__st(8005, mi).
```

while:

```
?-project__student(mi).
```

would produce a similar relation, but having only those facts with state field of **mi**:

```
proj__st(1001, mi).
proj__st(1022, mi).
proj__st(1099, mi).
proj__st(2000, mi).
proj__st(3022, mi).
proj__st(4001, mi).
proj__st(5000, mi).
proj__st(5055, mi).
proj__st(6000, mi).
proj__st(8005, mi).
```

The class reorganization example given above is another example of a PROJECT operation.

The JOIN operator produces a new relation from two relations with a field in common. For example,

```
JOIN major with classlist over Snum giving temp
```

would produce a new relation, **temp**, with all of the information from the relations **major** and **classlist** combined. Notice that this is accomplished only if the common field, Snum, has a matching value in each relation.

While slightly more complicated than SELECT or PROJECT, this can be handled in Prolog without too much difficulty. For example, the Prolog rule **major__classlist** will produce the same relation as the JOIN statement given.

```
major__classlist:-
    major(Snum, Major, Minor, TCH, THP, HPA),
    classlist(Classname, Snum, Grade),
    not(major__class(Snum, __, __, __, __, __, __, __, Classname,__)),
```

```
assertz(major_class(Snum, Major, Minor, TCH, THP,
    HPA, Classname, Grade)).
```

The result of the query

```
?-major_classlist.
```

is:

```
major_class(1001, business, economics, 0, 0, 0, intro_bus, g).
major_class(1001, business, economics, 0, 0, 0, intro_comp, g).
major_class(1001, business, economics, 0, 0, 0, elem_math, g).
major_class(2000, computer_sci, math, 0, 0, 0, intro_comp, g).
major_class(2000, computer_sci, math, 0, 0, 0, elem_math, g).
major_class(3022, accounting, business, 0, 0, 0, english_comp, g).
major_class(4001, business, accounting, 0, 0, 0, intro_bus, g).
major_class(4001, business, accounting, 0, 0, 0, english_comp, g).
major_class(4001, business, accounting, 0, 0, 0, elem_math, g).
major_class(5000, computer_sci, business, 0, 0, 0, intro_bus, g).
major_class(5000, computer_sci, business, 0, 0, 0, english_comp, g).
major_class(5000, computer_sci, business, 0, 0, 0, intro_comp, g).
major_class(6000, economics, accounting, 0, 0, 0, intro_bus, g).
major_class(6000, economics, accounting, 0, 0, 0, english_comp, g).
major_class(6087, economics, computer_sci, 0, 0, 0, english_comp, g).
major_class(6087, economics, computer_sci, 0, 0, 0, intro_comp, g).
major_class(7001, accounting, economics, 0, 0, 0, intro_bus, g).
major_class(7001, accounting, economics, 0, 0, 0, english_comp, g).
major_class(7555, accounting, business, 0, 0, 0, intro_bus, g).
major_class(7555, accounting, business, 0, 0, 0, intro_comp, g).
major_class(7555, accounting, business, 0, 0, 0, elem_math, g).
major_class(8005, economics, accounting, 0, 0, 0, english_comp, g).
major_class(8005, economics, accounting, 0, 0, 0, elem_math, g).
```

Prolog has the capabilities of combining the SELECT, PROJECT, and JOIN operators in a single rule, so that a two- or three-step query in relational algebra could be expressed in a Prolog rule and query. For example, suppose we wanted to produce a mailing list for all business majors enrolled in a class. This would consist of finding student numbers for all the business majors, finding those student numbers in the **class** relation, and finding the addresses of those students whose student numbers are on both relations.

In relational algebra, the above task can be accomplished by the series of queries:

```
JOIN major with class over Snum giving major_class.
JOIN major_class with student over Snum giving
student_major_class
SELECT student_major_class where Major = business giving
student_business_class
```

```
PROJECT student__business__class over Lname, Fname,
Street, City, State.
```

or in Prolog, via the rule:

```
business__add__list(Lname, Fname, Street, City, State):-
      major(Snum, business, __, __, __, __, __),
      class(__, Snum, __, __, __),
      student(Snum, Lname, Fname, Street, City, State).
```

and the query:

```
?-business__add__list(Lname, Fname, Street, City, State).
```

The discussion above is intended to show that Prolog has the potential of developing into a very powerful query language. It is easy to see why the Fifth Generation Project is based on it. I do not mean to imply, however, that Prolog in its present form is suitable for use in an actual database environment. I find that Prolog is an excellent intuitive approach to database concepts in general, and to relational databases in particular. In this context, I use Prolog in my introductory database classes, along with a discussion of Prolog's shortcomings—Prolog is not a number cruncher, sorts can become very cumbersome, and often it is necessary to write procedural programs in order to use Prolog efficiently. These shortcomings, coupled with Prolog's search strategy of combing the database one entry at a time for each query, make it slow and inefficient to manage a database of any reasonable size.

Bibliography

Prolog and Logic Programming

Campbell, J. A., ed. *Implementations of Prolog.* New York: Halsted Press/John Wiley, 1984.

Clark, K. L., and Tarnlund, S.A. *Logic Programming.* New York: Academic Press, 1982.

______, and McCabe, F. G. *micro-PROLOG.* Englewood Cliffs, N.J.: Prentice-Hall, 1984.

Clocksin, W. F., and Mellish, C. S. *Programming in Prolog, 2nd Edition.* New York: Springer-Verlag, 1984.

Coelho, H.; Cotta, J. C.; and Pereira, L.M. *How To Solve It With Prolog.* Lisbon: Laboratoria Nacional de Engenharia Civil.

Ennals, Richard. *Beginning micro-PROLOG.* New York: Harper & Row, 1984.

______. *Artificial Intelligence: Applications to Logical Reasoning and Historical Research.* New York: Halsted Press/John Wiley, 1985.

Gray, Peter. *Logic, Algebra, and Databases.* New York: Halsted Press/John Wiley, 1984.

Hogger, C.J. *Introduction to Logic Programming.* New York: Academic Press, 1984.

Kowalski, Robert. *Logic for Problem Solving.* New York: North-Holland, 1979.

Li, Deyi. *A PROLOG Database System.* New York: John Wiley, 1984.

Wos, Larry; Overbeek, Ross; Lusk, Ewing; and Boyle, Jim. *Automated Reasoning.* Englewood Cliffs, N.J.: Prentice-Hall, 1984.

Artificial Intelligence and Expert Systems

Alty, J. L., and Coombs, M. J. *Expert Systems*. Manchester, England: National Computing Centre, 1984.

Bramer, M. A., ed. *Research and Development in Expert Systems.* New York: Cambridge University Press, 1985.

Bundy, Alan. *Computer Modelling of Mathematical Reasoning.* New York: Academic Press, 1983.

Charniak, E., and McDermott, D. *Introduction to Artificial Intelligence.* Reading, Mass.: Addison-Wesley, 1985.

Coombs, M. J. *Developments in Expert Systems.* New York: Academic Press, 1984.

Harmon, Paul, and King, David. *Expert Systems.* New York: John Wiley, 1985.

Hayes-Roth, F.; Waterman, D. A., and Lenat, D. B. *Building Expert Systems.* Reading, Mass.: Addison-Wesley, 1983.

Hayes, J. E., and Michie, D., eds. *Intelligent Systems.* New York: Halsted Press/John Wiley, 1983.

McCorduck, Pamela. *Machines Who Think.* San Francisco: W.H. Freeman, 1979.

Michie, D., ed. *Expert Systems in the Micro-electronic Age.* Edinburgh, Scotland: Edinburgh University Press, 1979.

__________. *Introductory Readings in Expert Systems.* New York: Gordon & Breach, 1982.

Naylor, Chris. *Build Your Own Expert System.* New York: John Wiley, 1985.

O'Shea, Tim, and Eisenstadt, Marc. *Artificial Intelligence: Tools, Techniques, and Applications.* New York: Harper & Row, 1984.

Reitman, Walter, ed. *Artificial Intelligence Applications for Business.* Norwood, N.J.: Ablex, 1984.

Rich, Elaine. *Artificial Intelligence*. New York: McGraw Hill, 1983.

Shirai, Y., and Tsuiji, J. *Artificial Intelligence*. New York: John Wiley, 1984.

Simons, G.L. *Towards Fifth Generation Computers*. Manchester, England: National Computing Centre, 1983.

________. *Introducing Artificial Intelligence.* Manchester, England: National Computing Centre, 1984.

Sowa, J.E. *Conceptual Structures.* Reading, Mass.: Addison-Wesley, 1984.

Waterman, Donald A. *A Guide to Expert Systems.* Reading, Mass: Addison-Wesley, 1986.

Winston, P.H. *Artificial Intelligence*. Reading, Mass.: Addison-Wesley, 1984.

________, and Prendergast, K. A., eds. *AI Business: Commercial Uses of Artificial Intelligence*. Cambridge, Mass.: MIT Press, 1984.

Solutions to Exercises

Chapter 1

1a) *Predicate* is the name of the relationship between various objects. In this example, the predicate is **income**.

b) The objects related by the predicate are the *arguments*. Here, we have two arguments, **john**, and **30**.

c) An *atom* is normally a sequence of characters starting with a lowercase letter: **john** is an atom.

While this is the normal way an atom is expressed, any sequence of characters enclosed in single quotation marks is an atom. We could have expressed the first argument as '**John**'. Because of the single quotes, Prolog would not attach any significance to the fact that the first letter is in uppercase.

Constants have a fixed value and are either atoms or numbers, so both the arguments here are constants.

Variables start with an uppercase letter; neither argument here is a variable.

Obviously, **30** is a number.

d) Yes, the predicate is an atom. In most versions of Prolog, the predicate must be an atom.

2) **Asserta** and **assertz** respectively add a new clause to the beginning or end of a database. **Retract** removes a clause from the database.

3) One could express the information as:

```
signed(declaration_of_independence, 1776).
```

or, as in the above answer regarding atoms:

```
signed('Declaration of Independence', 1776).
```

Notice that when you are using an atom without single quotes, blanks are not allowed, and you use the underline character to connect words. But when single quotes are used, Prolog takes the whole string of characters as an atom, including the blank spaces.

4a) You would ask the question in the form (you might use a different name for the variable):

```
?-capital_of(montana,WhatCity).
```

The points to keep in mind are that variables start with uppercase letters, and predicates with lowercase, and that Prolog matches the pattern of the question to the pattern of facts in the database. In carrying out this matching, it can match variables flexibly, but constants and predicates have to be matched exactly.

b) The question would be:

```
?-capital_of(WhichState,albany).
```

The comments on (4a) above apply here.

c) The question would be something like:

```
?-capital_of(WhichState,WhichCity).
```

The point to remember is that Prolog always starts its search at the top of the database, so the first answer will be based on the first **capital_of** fact in the database, i.e. **capital_of(michigan,lansing)**. As we saw, some implementations of Prolog will produce all possible answers, others will wait for us to indicate if we want a search for alternative answers.

5) I am sure you have thought of some good example. Mine is in question 7.

6a) One possibility is: **?- income(john,WhichGroup).**

b) This was meant to emphasize that if you use an atom starting with a lowercase letter, Prolog looks for an exact match. So, it will respond "no" to this question.

c) Here, Who and WhichGroup are both variables, so we will get the first response based on the first fact with predicate **income** in the database:

Who = john, WhichGroup = high.

and then if we ask for more solutions, Who = mary, WhichGroup = middle, . . . etc. Remember, the search for solutions is always in the order in which clauses with the required predicate are found in the database.

7) We want to match the second argument for first name of the author, but we want to suppress its display, so we use the anonymous variable(_) as the second argument in our question:

```
?- book(tom_sawyer, _ , Who).
```

and we would get the response Who = twain.

8) We say a variable is *instantiated* when the pattern-matching process matches a variable and a constant. So, when we get the first solution to

```
?-income(Who,WhichGroup)
```

by the matching of the question and the first fact, income(john,high), the variable Who is instantiated to the value john, and the variable WhichGroup is instantiated to the value high. *Resatisfaction* is when we ask for an alternative solution to the same goal. The things to remember are:

- ☐ The variables which have been instantiated become uninstantiated.
- ☐ The search proceeds further from the "marker" which indicates where the goal succeeded the previous time. Each time we ask for one more solution, the variables are uninstantiated, and the search goes "down the database."

Chapter 2

1a) We could ask the question as:

```
?-income(Who,high),age(Who,young).
```

We are using two arguments which are constants, high and young, and one variable, Who. Since our first goal is based on the income predicate, we know that searching from the top of the database, the first goal can be satisfied by using the clause income(john, high), thereby instantiating Who = john. We know this value will be passed on to the next goal, so that the second goal is age(john,high). This can be satisfied from the database, so the first solution displayed will be Who = john.

If we ask for a second solution, we know that a further search will be made, starting from where the second goal was satisfied, after uninstantiating any variables instantiated by the first success. But there were no variables which were instantiated by the success of the second goal, age(john,young). Prolog will run through the database and fail in its attempt to resatisfy the second goal. Now it will backtrack to the first goal, and uninstantiate Who, so that it is trying to resatisfy income(Who,high). Following the same line of analysis, we see that the next solution for the first goal instantiates **Who = anne**. The second goal is now **age(anne,young)**. Because this goal is being satisfied, not resatisfied, the search again starts at the top of the set of age clauses, and the second solution **Who = anne** is found.

Another backtrack will uninstantiate Who, and resatisfaction of the first goal will instantiate it to **jim**. But the second goal cannot be satisfied, nor is any more resatisfaction of the first goal possible. Thus, when the leftmost goal fails, that is it.

This question was meant to emphasize the concepts of instantiation, the difference between satisfying and resatisfying a goal, and backtracking.

b) We can see that if we reverse the goals, and frame the question in the form:

```
?- age(Who,young),income(Who,high).
```

the order in which the solutions are found will change. The first solution will be **Who = anne**, and the second will be **john**. Moreover, it cannot find any third solution to the first goal, and will fail at that stage; with the goals in the other order, it found a third solution to the first goal, but failed in trying to satisfy the second goal.

2a) We could ask:

```
?- lives_in(Where,Who), knows(Who,What).
```

We can see that with the goals in this order, the system will first find **Who = john** and successively tell us that John knows Russian and Chinese; then it will backtrack to find **Who = mary** and tell us Mary knows Spanish. Then it will backtrack to Anne, tell us she knows French, and then backtrack to Zach, and tell us he knows Latin, and French.

b) On the other hand, if we put the goals in the reverse order and ask:

```
?-knows(Who,What), lives_in(Who,Where).
```

we would be told that Zach knows Latin, Anne knows French . . ., i.e., in the order the names are found in the **knows** list—with of course the added information about the state where they live.

c) If we are interested in finding out name and state of persons who know French, it makes sense to check that as the first goal and then extract the information about their state:

```
?- knows(Who,french), lives_in(Who,Where).
```

If we change the order of the goals, we see that the goal

```
lives_in(Who,Where)
```

will be satisfied for every person in the **lives_in** set of clauses, and Prolog will then check for each whether they know French, which is clearly a bit of extra work.

d) Again, if we want to focus on people in Michigan, it makes sense to put the goal:

```
lives_in(Who,michigan)
```

first, and then check the languages they know by **knows(Who,What)**, rather than check for every person in the **knows** set of clauses, whether or not they live in Michigan.

e) We might want to ask something like:

```
?- knows(Who,What), used_in(Where,What).
```

This will start with our **knows** database, and follow the order of names in it. If we think of the answers as establishing a connection between persons and countries whose language they know, we will get Zach first, connected to the Vatican, then Anne connected to France, . . ., with the same person appearing again if his or her name is in the database more than once.

f) If we change the order of the goals, clearly we will first get Spain connected to Mary, then France connected to Anne and Zach, then Argentina connected to Mary, and so on.

g) This question was meant to emphasize that in using an anonymous variable we are saying, "Find some match, and I don't care what the value is." So the first goal, **knows(Who,_)**, will match with **knows(zach,latin)**, and instantiate **Who = zach**. Now the second goal is **used_in(Where,_)**. This will match with **used_in(spain,spanish)**, so the first solution we get is:

```
Who = zach, Where = spain.
```

which we can see is a wrong connection. The question was meant to emphasize that an anonymous variable is not like other variables, which "pass on" the values to which they have been instantiated. To put it another way, the anonymous variable in the first goal is *not* the same as the anonymous variable in the second goal; they both just mean "don't care."

3a) We could ask, for instance:

```
?- state(casper, Which), time_zone(State,Zone).
```

if we want to find the time zone for a particular city, Casper.

b) It may not be a good idea to reverse the order of the goals, because then the system will test, one by one for each state in the database, whether the city we want is in that state, and keep backtracking till it finds the correct state. It is obviously more efficient to find the state and then check the time zone.

Chapter 3

1) All we need to add is a suitable head goal:

```
is__yuppie(Person) :-
      income(Person,high),
      age(Person,young).
```

2) One rule could be:

```
knows__language(Person,State,Language) :-
        knows(Person,Language),
        lives__in(Person,State).
```

We should always remember that in Prolog there are different ways of using the same general rule. If we give a specific value for any of the variables when we ask the question, we are able to use this same rule for finding all persons who know a particular language, that is, by asking:

```
?- knows__language(Who,State,french).
```

or we can find all information about people in a particular state by asking:

```
?-knows__language(Who,michigan,What).
```

and so on.

Similarly, another rule we could design is:

```
can__fit__in(Person,Country):-
      knows(Person,Language),
      used__in(Country,Language).
```

Incidentally, notice though Language is a variable which is instantiated when the first goal in the body of the rule is satisfied, and whose value is passed on to the second goal, its value is not finally displayed because it is not a variable in the head goal. Thus, this rule will achieve the purpose we could not achieve by using anonymous variables in part (g) of question 3 in the last chapter, that is, suppressing the value of the variable Language.

3) We could add a head goal:

```
in__zone(City,Timezone):-
      state(City,State), time__zone(State,Timezone).
```

so that we could ask questions like :

```
?- in__zone(casper,Which).
```

Chapter 4

1) Here is one solution:

```
product(First,Second,Result) :-
    var(Result),
        Result is First * Second.
product(First,Second,Third) :-
    var(First),
        First is Result/Second.
product(First,Second,Third) :-
    var(Second),
        Second is Result/First.
```

You can see that the principle used is the same. We use var to check which one is the uninstantiated variable, and instantiate it using the values of the other two variables.

2b) We need to extract from the database the average income in the U.S.A., then the average income of each country in turn, and then compare them. The question we might ask would be:

```
?-average_income(u_s_a,USinc),average_income(Country,Cinc),
    Cinc > USinc.
```

c) To find countries whose average income is less than it is in the U.S.A., all we have to do is to change the third goal from Cinc > USinc to Cinc < USinc.

d) If we have a rule which compares the average income of two countries, we could use it either way by supplying suitable arguments when we ask the question. Let us consider the following rule:

```
higher(First,Second) :-
    average_income(First,Firstinc),
    average_income(Second,Secondinc),
    Firstinc > Secondinc.
```

We can see that if we ask:

```
?- higher(u_s_a,Country).
```

it would fetch us the names of countries with lower average income, and if we ask:

```
?- higher(Country,u_s_a).
```

it would fetch us the names of countries with lower income.

3a) If, for instance, we wanted to find out the winners in both the men's and women's tournaments, we would ask:

```
?-wimbledon(_,1981,Person,Country).
```

We could use an anonymous variable for Country, or a variable for the first argument if we want the information about the sex of the player to be printed out as well.

b) The question could be:

```
?-u__s__open(__,Year,austin,__).
```

if, for instance, we wanted information on when Austin won the U.S. Open.

c) The multiple-goal question could be:

```
?-wimbledon(__,Year,Person,__), u__s__open(__,Year,Person,__).
```

Note that when we want the instantiated values from the first goal to be passed on to the second goal, using the same variable name does what we want. (Contrast this with the two problems which follow.) To convert this into a rule, we add a suitable goal for the head of the rule:

```
both__titles(Year,Person,Country) :-
      wimbledon(__,Person,Year,Country),
      u__s__open(__,Person,Year,Country).
```

I am assuming we would want the information about the Country also to be displayed.

d) If we were asking a multiple-goal question, we could say:

```
?-u__s__open(__,Year,Person,Country), Country < > u__s__a.
```

if we wanted to list only winners other than from the U.S.A. However, in making a rule, we might want to make it flexible to provide for listing winners from any country other than whatever country we choose. We would need a suitable variable for this in the head of the rule:

```
others(Person,Year,Country,Otherthan):-
      u__s__open(__,Year,Person,Country),
      Country < > Otherthan.
```

e) We want to make sure the two years in which the person won are different, so we introduce a goal for this:

```
multiple__winner(Person,Year,Country):-
      u__s__open(__,Year,Person,Country),
      u__s__open(__,Year2,Person,Country),
      Year2 < > Year1.
```

f) To find three consecutive years, we need to use the "is" operator, to make sure Year2 is Year1 + 1 and Year3 is Year2 + 1, so we could have the rule:

```
triple__winner(Person,Year1,Year2,Year3) :-
      winner(Person,Year1), Year2 is Year1 + 1,
      winner(Person,Year2), Year3 is Year2 + 1,
      winner(Person,Year3).
```

4a) This question could be expressed as:

```
?- winner(1921,Who,ForWhat).
```

We need three arguments, two of them variables. Since there may be a number of winners in 1921 for different fields, the solutions will be produced in the order in which they were entered in the database.

b) This question could be expressed as:

```
?- winner(When,roosevelt,ForWhat).
```

c) The solution which first suggests itself is that we should have two goals:

```
?-winner(Year,Who,Forwhat), winner(Year2,Who,ForWhatElse).
```

But the problem here is that if we ask a two-goal question of this type, Prolog will give us the same name twice. It is instructive to see why this happens by tracing how Prolog backtracks. Prolog will first solve for the first goal and start from the beginning of the database and obtain the solution:

```
Year = 1901,Who=roentgen,and ForWhat = physics.
```

Now, it will start to solve for the second goal. The only variable in the second goal which has been instantiated is Who. This means that Prolog is trying to solve for the second goal as:

```
winner(Year2,roentgen,ForWhatElse).
```

Now, since this is the first time it is trying to solve the second goal, it will start the search once again at the top of the database, and succeed with the following instantiations:

```
Year2 = 1901,and ForWhatElse = physics.
```

This is not what we want! We have to give a third goal as well, to make sure that the value to which it instantiates ForWhat in the first goal is not the same as the value to which it instantiates ForWhatElse in the second goal. So we need to give it a third goal:

```
ForWhat < > ForWhatElse.
```

With this third goal, it will backtrack suitably until finally it can satisfy all three goals. (With the sample database given, it will find the solution as:

```
Who = pauling, ForWhat = chemistry, ForWhatElse = peace).
```

We see that though Prolog comes nearer human communication than other languages, we still have to be careful. Another human being would know from the very fact that we have named the variables as ForWhat and ForWhatelse, that they have got to be different. But we have to give some additional information to Prolog for it to register this fact that different fields should be found.

d) All we need to do is to add a suitable head goal to the multiple goals we already have for the body of the goal. We could express the rule as:

```
versatile(Person,Field1,Field2) :-
      winner(Person,Year1,Field1),
      winner(Person,Year2,Field2),
      Field1 < > Field2.
```

5a) We could ask the question in the form:

```
?-president(Who,john,Start,End).
```

Since we have given the second argument as a constant **john** and the other three as variables (starting with uppercase letters), the system will search through the database and give us successive solutions:

```
Who = adams, Start = 1797 , End = 1801
Who = tyler , Start = 1841 , End = 1845
```

b) We want to find two persons who have the same first name. We could set the two goals as:

```
?- president(Who,Firstname,Start1,End1),
      president(Whoelse,Firstname,Start2,End2).
```

Since Prolog always starts at the top of the database, it will find a solution for the first goal as:

```
Who = washington, Firstname = george, Start1 = 1789 , End1 = 1797.
```

It will now try the second goal. The only variable in the second goal which has been instantiated is Firstname. So Prolog will consider the second goal to be:

```
president(Whoelse,george,Start2,End2).
```

But because of Prolog's characteristic that searches start at the top of the database, when trying to satisfy a goal for the first time, it will find a solution for the second goal as:

```
Whoelse = washington, Start2 = 1789, End2 = 1797.
```

This is not what we want. This is similar to the situation we had in the previous problem. We need to give it a third goal to make sure that the two names are different. We can do this by expressing the third goal as **Who < > Whoelse**. Now the third goal will fail, and the system will backtrack to the second goal and try to find another solution for:

```
president(Whoelse,george,Start2,End2).
```

Remember, Firstname was instantiated to **george** by the first goal not the second one. So backtracking to the second goal will not uninstantiate this. It will go through the database and since, in the example given there is no other **george**, it will finally backtrack to the first goal. It will resume the search at where the first solution was found, and we can see that now it will find a second solution:

Who = adams, Firstname = john, Start1 = 1797 , End1 = 1801.

By following this process, we can see it will again find **adams** for the second goal, fail on the third goal, again backtrack to the second goal, . . . until finally it is able to satisfy all three goals with:

Who = adams, and Whoelse = tyler

in addition, of course, to the values for Firstname, Start1, End1, Start2, and End2.

c) Since a rule is really a combination of multiple goals in the body of the rule, we could formulate it as:

```
same_first_name(Who,Whoelse) :-
      president(Who,Firstname,Start1,End1),
      president(Whoelse,Firstname,Start2,End2),
      Who < > Whoelse.
```

A useful thing to keep in mind when designing rules is to ask yourself: How would I like to pose the question, and what values would I like displayed? In this case it seems natural to ask something like:

```
?-same_first_name(First,Second)
```

and that indicates what predicate and how many arguments we need for the head goal of the rule. Incidentally, it is a good idea when designing rules to write each goal on a separate line, as shown above. In designing the rule above, we have the head goal as

```
same_first_name(Who,Whoelse).
```

So, when we ask a question, we cannot control the search to restrict it to only some particular first name we might be interested in (John for example). If we want to have this option, we need to introduce one more variable into the head goal, and make it:

```
same_first_name(Firstname,Who,Whoelse):-
```

By expanding the head goal this way, we have the option to give a value to Firstname when asking the question:

```
?-same_first_name(First,Second,john).
```

or to leave it as a variable:

```
?-same_first_name(First,Second,Anyfirstname).
```

Chapter 6

1) When we extracted the first item of a list, we had the inherent distinction between the first item, the head, and the rest of the list. To find the last item, we still have to use this characteristic, but in a modified form. Thinking recursively, we can say that the last item of a list is also the last item of the tail of a list. As we keep recursing down the tail of the list, the boundary condition is reached when there is only one item left. We can express our Prolog clauses as:

```
last([Only], Only).
```

which covers the boundary condition, and

```
last( [First|Rest],Result) :-
    last(Rest,Result).
```

2) Looking at the problem, we can guess that the solution must be:

```
First = [a,b,c].
```

This problem illustrates the fundamental characteristic of Prolog: because the programs are declarative, the same program can be used in different ways. We can give two lists to the **append** program and get a combined list, or give it the combined list and part of the list and extract the other part.

However, the purpose of this question is to give some more practice in analyzing the process by which Prolog finds solutions. We start by considering whether the question can match the first clause in the database with the predicate **append**. We see that a match is not possible, since the first clause:

```
append([ ],Anylist,Anylist).
```

requires the second and third arguments to be the same—which they are not in our question:

```
append(First,[d,e],[a,b,c,d,e]).
```

We have to drop down to the next **append** clause:

```
append([Head|Tail],Seclist,[Head|Newtail]):-
    append(Tail,Seclist,Newtail).
```

When the question is matched with the head goal of this rule, the instantiations which take place are:

```
Head = a, Newtail = [b,c,d,e]
```

and

```
Seclist = [d,e].
```

In addition, it is important to note that the variables which share are **First** and **[a|Tail]**. The goal in the body of the rule now has the form:

```
append(Tail,[d,e],[b,c,d,e]).
```

We see that once again this will fail on the first **append** clause, go to the second

append clause, and again go to a new goal:

    append(Tail2,[d,e],[c,d,e]).

I have designated this as Tail2, because when this recursion is made the variables which share are the original **Tail**, and **[b¦Tail2]**. This will again lead to a new goal:

    append(Tail3,[d,e],[d,e]).

The variables which share are now **Tail2** and **[c¦Tail3]**. This goal will succeed with the first append clause by instantiating Tail3 to **[ ]**. Because of the way the variables share at the different stages of the recursion, we see our original variable First acquires the value **[a,b,c]**.

3) We have the two clauses for append with the recursive clause first:

```
append([Head¦Tail],Seclist,[Head¦Newtail]) :-
        append(Tail,Seclist,Newtail).
        append([ ],Anylist,Anylist).
```

a) Our question:

    ?-append([a,b],[c,d],What).

will be able to match the head of the first clause by instantiating Head to **a**, tail to **[b]**, Seclist to **[c,d]**, and making What share with **[a,¦Newtail]**. So it will "call" the goal in the body:

    append([b],[c,d],Newtail).

This will again start at the top of the database, match the head goal in the first clause, and call:

    ([ ],[c,d],Newtail2)

where we use Newtail2 to indicate it is a different variable in a different copy of the clause used in recursion. At this stage, **Newtail2** and **[b¦Newtail]** are variables which share. We see that this goal will fail on the first clause, which requires a list with at least one variable in it as the first argument, whereas here we have the empty list as the first argument. However, this goal can match the second clause, instantiating Anylist as well as Newtail2 to **[c,d]**. So, because of the way the variables share at each stage, we will get the response as:

    What = [a,b,c,d].

Thus, the order of the clauses makes no difference.

b) When we ask the question:

    ?-append(First,Second,[a,b,c,d]).

it matches the head of the first clause, instantiating Head to **a**, Newtail to **[b,c,d]**, and making **First** and **[Head¦Tail]**—i.e., **[a¦Tail]**—shared variables. Similarly, Second and Seclist are variables which share. Now the body goal is called as:

append(Tail,Seclist,[b,c,d]).

Prolog again tries to satisfy this goal starting from the top of the database, and in this recursive call, instantiates Head2 to **b**, Newtail2 to **[c,d]**, makes **Tail** and **[b¦Tail2]** shared variables, and also makes **Seclist** and **Seclist2** shared variables. We see the next call is:

append(Tail2,Seclist2,[c,d]).

This will lead to another recursive call:

append(Tail3,Seclist3,[d].

and again to:

append(Tail4,Seclist4,[ ]).

This one will fail on the first clause, because the head of that clause has the second argument as **[Head¦Newtail]**, which implies at least one element in the list, whereas we have only an empty list. Now this goal will succeed with the second clause:

append([ ],Anylist,Anylist).

Tail4, Seclist4 and Anylist are all instantiated to the value **[ ]**, the empty list. Because of the way values were shared at each recursion, we see that Seclist3, Seclist2 and Seclist, and Second all acquire the value **[ ]**, whereas Tail3 becomes **[d]**, **Tail2,[c,d]**, **Tail [b,c,d]**, and **First [a,b,c,d]**. We saw in the discussion in the chapter that if the clauses were in the other order, we would have gotten:

First = [ ]

and

Second = [a,b,c,d].

You would be able to guess that if we ask for further solutions, now we would get in succession:

First = [a], Second = [b,c,d]
First = [a,b], Second = [c,d]
First = [a,b,c], Second = [d]

and, finally,

First = [a,b,c,d], Second = [ ].

That is, the solutions are produced in the reverse order of what we got previously. However, I would request you to consider for a few moments the backtracking that takes place after the first solution, **First = [a,b,c,d]** and **Second = [ ]**, has been displayed. Which is the goal that is now tried? Where does it succeed?

The sequence of happenings is that the goal:

append(Tail4,Seclist4,[ ]).

succeeded on the second clause to produce the first solution. It cannot be resatisfied because there are no more clauses, so this goal will fail. This failed goal arose as the body goal of the head goal:

```
append(Tail3,Seclist3,[d]).
```

when it matched the head goal of the first clause. So the backtracking leads to this goal being now tried on the second clause:

```
append([ ],Anylist,Anylist).
```

It will now succeed, with Tail3 instantiated to **[ ]**, and Anylist and Seclist3 to **[d]**. So, we see that Tail2 will become **[c]**, **Tail [b,c]** and **First [a,b,c]**; Seclist2, Seclist, and Second will all become **[d]**. For the next solution, we now have to consider the backtracking caused by

```
append(Tail3,Seclist3,[d]).
```

as failing because there are no more clauses. The head goal which led to this,

```
append(Tail2,Seclist2,[c,d]).
```

will now try the second clause, making **Tail2 = [ ]**, and therefore **First = [a,b]**, and **Second = [c,d]**. We see the next time Tail1 will equal **[ ]**, and **First = [a]**, and finally **First = [ ]**.

You will see from this that sometimes even if the answer is intuitively clear, analyzing the backtracking steps at each stage can be a bit lengthy, but it is very helpful in getting a feel for how the mechanism works, especially when designing or analyzing recursive programs.

4) This is a good problem for getting more practice in thinking "backtrack." For the first solution, the question

```
?-member(a,X).
```

will be matched with the first member clause in the database:

```
member(Wanted,[Wanted|_]).
```

Wanted is instantiated to **a**, and X to **[Wanted|_]**, so we might expect the display to be **X = [a|_]**. However, typically Prolog systems do not display an anonymous variable in the same form you enter it (-). Instead, they use a number which has to do with the memory location where the anonymous variable was held, and would display something like **X= [a|_39]**. It is not important to know this number, or how it is obtained, only to remember that it is the typical way an anonymous variable is shown.

Now, if we ask for a second solution, the second clause for member will be tried, and Prolog will try to match the question:

```
?-member(a,X).
```

with the clause:

```
member(Wanted,[_|Rest] :- member(Wanted,Rest).
```

The matching of the head goal and the question produces the instantiation **Wanted = a**. Also, **X** and **[_|Rest]** are now variables which share. Now the goal in the body of the rule is tried, which is now of the form **member(a,Rest)**. This goal is being tried for the first time, so we know the solution would be something like:

Rest = [a|_37],

where 37 again is just an example of some anonymous variable. So, we see the second solution will be:

X = [_44,a,_33]

where 44 and 33 are really representations of anonymous variables; we could think of the solution as really being **[_,a,_]**.

So we see the pattern, the first solution is **[a,_]**, the second solution is based on the first solution to **member(a,Rest)**, with an anonymous variable attached before this solution which is **[a,_]**, giving us **[_,a,_]**. So we can see the third solution would be based on the second solution with another anonymous variable attached in front, and would be **[_,_,a,_]**. We can see that there would be an endless series of such solutions as we ask for further solutions. The **a** is successively the first, second, third, fourth, . . . , member in the successive solutions.

5) Let us see what happens if we enter the two clauses for member changing the order to:

   a) **member(Wanted,[_|Rest]) :- member(Wanted,Rest).**
   b) **member(Wanted,[Wanted|_]).**

When we ask the question:

?-member(What,[a,b,c]).

as always Prolog tries first the first clause in the database which has the same predicate as the question. When it tries to match the question with the parent or head goal of clause (a), **What** and **Wanted** become variables which share, and Rest is instantiated to **[b,c]**. Now the goal in the body of the rule has the form:

member(Wanted,[b,c]).

To solve this, once again Prolog starts from the top of the database, and we see it is led to the goal **member(Wanted,[c])**, and then to:

member(Wanted,[ ]).

Now, this goal will not match clause (a) because its second argument is an empty list, and the second argument of clause (a) has to be a list with at least one element, since it has the form **[_|Rest]**. So, having failed on clause (a), it will try clause (b).

But **member(Wanted,[ ])** cannot match clause (b) either, because clause (b) has a second argument which must have at least one element, since it has the form **[Wanted|_]**. Prolog will now backtrack. The goal **member(Wanted,[ ])** arose from the goal **member(Wanted,[c])** being tried on clause (a). The result of backtrack is that the goal **member(Wanted,[c])**, having failed on clause (a), will now try clause (b):

```
member(Wanted,[Wanted|_]).
```

We can see that it will succeed, by instantiating Wanted to **c**, which in turn means that the variable What (with which Wanted shares) will acquire this value, and we will get the response **What = c**.

What happens when we ask for one more solution? Since there is no other solution possible for **member(Wanted,[c])**, this goal will fail. This goal arose from trying **member(Wanted,[b,c])** on clause (a). So this goal will now try clause (b), and we can see that it will succeed with **What= b**, and one more backtrack will produce **What = a**. In other words, the members are now displayed in reverse order.

We see that changing the order of the clauses can produce different results, and this is sometimes regarded as one of the "unsatisfactory" features of Prolog; a declarative language ideally should not require us to be concerned with exactly how the execution of the program progresses. As this example shows, however, in Prolog we have to pay attention to this procedural aspect if we are to get the results we want. Different versions of Prolog which would remedy this "defect" are being developed, so Prolog as it exists today cannot be regarded as a definitively declarative logic programming language. Presumably, among the things which will emerge from the Fifth Generation Project will be languages which are free from the shortcomings of Prolog.

6) We can start by thinking of two possible situations. The element we want to delete might be the first element or head of the list, in which case all we have to do is to drop it and take the result to be the tail of the list:

```
a) delete(Unwanted,[Unwanted|Tail], Tail).
```

On the other hand, if the element we want to delete is not in the head of the list, but in its tail, we want to delete it from the tail of the list, but we want to keep the head. We could express this in Prolog as:

```
b) delete(Unwanted,[Head|Tail],[Head|Newtail]) :-
       delete(Unwanted,Tail,Newtail).
```

What if the element we want to delete is not in the list at all? We can see that in that case as the program recurses down the list using clause (b) it will ultimately empty the list. In that case, we do not want the program to fail, but attach back to an empty list all the elements it has passed over. To provide for this, we need a third clause:

```
delete(Anything,[ ],[ ]).
```

7) We can think in recursive terms that in order to find the total of all the numbers in a list, we should add the first number to the total of all the numbers in the tail of the list. We can say:

```
sum_of([Head|Tail],Total) :-
    sum_of(Tail,Tailtotal), Total is Head + Tailtotal.
```

As the recursion goes on, ultimately the Tail is reduced to the empty list. That becomes the starting point for our addition of the numbers, and we could use a boundary condition clause which says, in effect, to set the total to 0 for an empty list and then add the numbers:

```
sum_of([ ] , 0).
```

8) This operation of combining two lists which may have some common members so as to produce a combined list in which any element found in either list is included, but only once, is usually referred to as *forming the union* of the two sets. We will use that name for our predicate.

To start with, we can analyze the problem by saying there are two possibilities as we look in turn at each element of the first list.

- ☐ If it is already a member of the second list, we can forget about it, and form the union of the rest of the first list with the second list. We could express this in Prolog as:

```
union([[Head|Tail],Secondlist,Result) :
    member(Head,Secondlist), union(Tail,Secondlist,Result).
```

We can use the member predicate which we have seen already.

- ☐ On the other hand, if the element we are looking at is not already in the second list—that is, if our first clause fails—we know that we need to put it in the result list. We need a second clause to cover this case:

```
union([Head|Tail],Secondlist,[Head|Result]) :-
    union(Tail,Secondlist,Result).
```

Both of these are recursive operations, so we need to think of the boundary condition, when we have run through all the items in our first list:

```
union([ ],Anylist,Anylist).
```

This provides that when the first list is empty, forming the union with any other list simply leaves the other list unchanged.

9) The operation of picking out only the elements which are in both of two given sets is usually referred to as *forming the intersection* of the two sets, so let's use that name for our predicate. We can think in terms of checking the items in the first list, one by one, to see if they are members of the second list. If they are, we want to retain them; otherwise we want to drop that element and then carry out the same check with the rest of the list. We can express this in Prolog as:

```
2)  intersect([Head|Tail],SecList,[Head|Result]) :-
        member(Head,Seclist),
        intersect(Tail,SecList,Result).
```

3) **intersect([Head|Tail],SecList,Result) :-**
intersect(Tail,SecList,Result).

Ultimately, we would reach the boundary condition when the first list becomes empty. In that case, there are of course no common elements between an empty list and any list, so we can write the boundary condition rule as: 1) **intersect([ ],Anylist, [ ]).**

Index